Three-

Three-Pointer!

A 40-Year NBA History

Łukasz Muniowski

McFarland & Company, Inc., Publishers
Jefferson, North Carolina

All photographs are from Steve Lipofsky, Lipofskyphoto.com

ISBN (print) 978-1-4766-8295-2
ISBN (ebook) 978-1-4766-4121-8

Library of Congress and British Library
cataloguing data are available

Library of Congress Control Number 2020033198

Front cover image © 2020 Alphaspirit/Shutterstock

Printed in the United States of America

McFarland & Company, Inc., Publishers
Box 611, Jefferson, North Carolina 28640
www.mcfarlandpub.com

Table of Contents

Table of Contents

Acknowledgments

Every book is a joint effort and this one is no different. I owe thanks to a lot of people.

The most important person during this whole process was Albert Ambroziewicz, my first reader, who provided me with opinions and observations, evaluating my work just for the fun of it. His basketball knowledge is far greater than mine, but he is too busy to write his own book, I guess. Thanks also to the following:

The good people at McFarland who decided to give this project a shot, especially Gary Mitchem, who answered all of my questions and provided helpful advice whenever I needed it.

Steven Lipofsky, whose photographs you can see in this book—he has a vast archive of NBA photos available on his website.

All of my academic friends and mentors (in no particular order): Marek Paryż, Tomasz Jacheć, Anna Pochmara, Zbigniew Mazur, Dorota Mielcarek, Justyna Włodarczyk, Adrianna Grzegorzewska, Kamil Chrzczonowicz and Joanna Chojnowska. A special thank you goes to Aneta Dybska, without whose help the creation of this particular book would have been much harder than it turned out to be.

Wszechnica Polska University in Warsaw, for taking a chance on me.

I am forever indebted to my father for introducing me to basketball, although he probably should have taken more time in teaching me how to actually play the sport.

My mother, who kept me on the right path.

My wife, Natalia, for allowing me to write in relative peace.

My four dogs for being there for me whenever I needed them. Each page was produced with at least one of them sitting next to me.

Preface

I started (unknowingly) collecting materials for this book when I was about 11 years old. It was around that time that I bought my first NBA trading cards in a kiosk placed in the middle of my hometown. Inhabited by around 30,000 people, Płońsk was not exactly a town where such things were easy to come by, which made getting hold of them by a kid such as myself all the more unlikely. While I was enjoying NBA basketball earlier, watching games and regularly buying the two sole Polish magazines devoted to NBA basketball, the 1995–96 Fleer Basketball Trading Cards turned me into a fan. Thanks to them, my interests shifted toward the players whose pictures I could see on the cards. I have spent a small fortune on them, which made what happened later—the cards being sliced to pieces by rats and mice living in my basement—all the more heartbreaking.

While I was collecting materials for this book—although "conducting research" would be a more proper phrase now that I hold a Ph.D. degree—for more than 20 years, putting it together went rather quickly, as I started writing it in the summer of 2019 and submitted the manuscript to the publisher in the first week of the year 2020. I remember being just two weeks removed from defending my Ph.D. dissertation on narrating the careers of NBA players after the Michael Jordan era, when the idea for the book arose in my head. I was alone in my parents' home, as they went away on a week's vacation. Just me, three dogs, an enormous collection of basketball magazines which I still kept in my room, and a backyard hoop. With not much to do but read and shoot, I was able to regain my love for basketball, which had been buried under research papers and critical theory books during the last couple of years. This was pure, this was fun, this was what felt appropriate at the moment: I just had to write a book about basketball that was not complicated nor overtly sophisticated, yet would serve as an appreciation of the beautiful game. While it would still cover my two primary academic interests, sports and narratives, the approach to this project would have to be purely historical, its sources being either written down or recorded. I felt somewhat obliged to write a factual account of an important development in the history of the NBA.

Picking the topic was fairly easy, as today's game revolves around the three-point shot and no one had yet written a book covering its development. While some older, physical players criticize the direction in which the league is heading, the NBA has undoubtedly become a shooter's league. As a fan who worshiped long-distance bombers like John Starks, John Stockton, Tim Hardaway or Voshon Lenard, just to name a few—although my favorite player of all-time is Alonzo Mourning, a 6'10" center who made just 22 three-pointers during his NBA career—I wholeheartedly embrace that development. Conveniently, during the then-upcoming 2019-20 season, the league was about to celebrate 40 years since the line was first introduced, which gave me a good enough reason to further dwell on the topic and hope that such a book would actually get published.

The only thing remaining was choosing the right approach to the project. As a firm believer in the sport's storytelling potential, I felt it obligatory to tell the story through players who were either influenced by the shot or helped it gain importance. After all, the best stories are human-interest stories. Athletes mentioned in this work are true heroes, not only because they accomplished the incredible feat of actually joining the league, but also heroes in the narrative sense, whose adventures can be told through stats. However, I wanted to go beyond the data available on the best basketball-related website on the Internet, *Basketball Reference*, therefore I found myself often looking for links between former and present players, and coaching philosophies and career narratives, in order to put these achievements in a proper context.

While the selection of players analyzed in this project is explained in the Introduction, the approach requires further justification. The fact that I focus on particular games also stems from my interest in sports narratives. Every game or contest is a different episode, a different adventure in a series of 82+ available every season to the fans, but moreso to the players, allowing them to leave their mark on the league, as well as influence the trajectory and perception of their careers. With such a ridiculous number of games played year after year it is easy to forget how significant one contest can actually be.

The discussion of particular performances is, however, not always detailed, as they serve more as representations of particular developments or trends in the history of the league. For example, Chris Ford's first NBA three-pointer is used to show how league executives arrived at the decision to implement the three-point shot, while George McCloud's record-setting performance represents the impact of the NBA's shortened three-point line in 1994–97. The best game of Michael Adams' career demonstrates how the shot helped smaller players influence the game of basketball on a very large scale, while Dirk Nowitzki's triumph in the 3-Point Contest serves as proof how dominant a big man with a jumpshot can be. The present state of affairs would not have been possible without such athletes, and it is these special individuals that this book appreciates.

The need to appreciate NBA basketball became even more evident during the outbreak of the COVID-19 pandemic in early 2020, as every new development regarding the status of the suspended season brought on bittersweet emotions. The fan in me grew tired of reruns of old games and wanted to see something new, but, more importantly, human lives were at stake and player safety was more important than anything. As I write these words, I am still conflicted about the whole thing, and I cannot help but think about how spoiled we all were, being able to follow our favorite sport for such a long time with no significant interruptions. That is why it is important to appreciate what we have and truly consider how fragile even such an everyday occurrence as a regular season basketball game can actually be.

Introduction

Basketball, like no other sport, gives one an opportunity to score 50 percent more points during a single play, when a player takes a shot from a greater distance from the goal, than points gained from a regular shot taken closer to the goal. In soccer, you always get one goal, no matter if you score from eleven meters or from the middle of the field. The same goes for football, as a touchdown always counts for six points. It was baseball, the most American sport of them all, that was actually crucial in making the three-point shot a regular fixture at professional basketball games. George Mikan, the commissioner of the American Basketball Association (ABA)—a relatively short-lived basketball league that tried to compete with the National Basketball Association (NBA) in the '60s and '70s—said that the shot was inspired by the most exciting play in baseball, the home run, because it also brought fans out of their seats.

In both cases the ball soared through the air, but instead of going into the stands, in basketball it headed towards the hoop. Released from long distance, the ball gained a life of its own, was freed from all limitations for literally just a second, in consequence becoming the object of desire of the spectators. That extra moment of suspense—will it go in, will it bounce—is what made the long-distance shot worth the risk, at least from a fan's perspective.

When the ABA ceased to exist in 1976, the three-pointer somehow managed to find new life, although it took some time for it to be fully accepted by basketball purists. Three years later, despite strong opposition from some players and head coaches, the NBA finally introduced the three-point shot. The 1979–80 season would transform the league like few before or since. Because the NBA was dealing with image issues and criticism regarding on-court violence, introducing the three-point line offered to change the game, add more space on the court and limit the players' interactions under the boards. In *Sprawlball*, Kirk Goldsberry states that "with the exception of the forward pass in football, no rule change in American sports history has reshaped the aesthetic of its sport more than the three-point line has deformed the NBA."[1]

But what really is a three-point shot and why was it so influential on the shape of American sports? Three things are necessary to make the three-point shot: the hoop, the ball and the distance. Without the first there is nothing to aim at, without the second there is nothing to shoot with, and without the third the magnificence and complexity of that shot cannot be fully embraced. Twenty-two feet away from the hoop at the corners and 23.75 feet behind the top of the key make the three-pointer the most risky (when taken) and the most viable (when made) shot in basketball. However, without the shooter there is no shot. Somebody has to make the bold decision and courageously throw the ball from long distance, with the belief that it will land in the basket.

That is why this book looks at the development of the shot primarily through notable performances by selected shooters who changed the perception of the three-point shot from gimmick to mainstay of today's game. It salutes the heroes, who defied convention, years of coaching, and peer pressure, in order to make basketball a more inclusive, attractive sport. In a way, it is also a homage to human curiosity, as well as the willingness to try new things in the name of personal and group triumph. Made three-point shots brought joy to millions of basketball fans, misses resulted in tears, misery and broken dreams.

Each three-point play starts with a single individual, brave enough to put everything on the line and release a shot from long distance. A number of factors predispose an individual to become a three-point shooter. Dale Ellis—1989 3-Point Contest champion,[2] 1,719 career three-pointers made—in a 2011 interview with the *Boston Globe* described himself as the best shooter of all time: "I set the standard. I gave them something to shoot for. I was the first player in the history of the game to get 1,000 3-pointers. To be able to play on that level, you have to have that attitude about yourself."[3] Although calling himself the best shooter of all time may be a bit too much, the point that Ellis tries to make is evident: confidence is key when attempting a three-point shot. Without the belief that a shot will go in, there is no point in taking it.

Apart from confidence, there is the form, the way one shoots the ball, the exact amount of force necessary to make the ball go through the net, no matter if it is a clean shot or a bank shot, if it requires a lucky bounce or not. Without a certain pattern, a repetition included in the way one releases the ball, one cannot become a pure shooter—"a basketball player who consistently makes jump shots, mostly those from three-point range."[4] A good example of such a player is Kyle Korver, who became the first rookie to ever compete in the 3-Point Contest, despite averaging just 4.5 points per game. Reportedly, in one practice during the 2003–04 season Korver made 100 consecutive free throws. When he was in college, his jump shot was already described as one of the purest in the country.

This basically means that Korver's shot is impeccable, his body movement perfect, also a bit poetic, but a beautiful (or pure) form does not turn one into a great three-point shooter. Rather, it is the ability to repeat over and over again the same successful shooting motion, in spite of the changing circumstances: "despite the stress on technique, many coaches will concede that the most important factor in developing a dependable jump shot is not uniformity but consistency—essentially, faith in and allegiance to one's personal style."[5] Shawn Marion's or Kevin Martin's shooting forms were far from beautiful—Marion released the ball just as it was in front of his face, with both elbows bent; Martin kept both hands in front of his body, the left was holding the ball, the right pushed it out towards the basket—but they worked, which is why the players never changed them and finished their careers with 33 percent and 38 percent, respectively, of their three-point shot attempts made.

There are only a few players who have not made a single three-point shot during their careers and even less who did not try to make the shot at all. Michael Cage, Dale Davis, Tyson Chandler and Robert Parish were never known for their jump-shooting ability and never made a three-pointer during an NBA game despite attempting it a number of times. Almost all players, from the tallest in the history of the league, 7'7" Manute Bol (20 makes during the 1988–89 season alone) and Gheorghe Muresan (one attempt during his NBA career), to the smallest, 5'3" Tyrone "Muggsy" Bogues (106 of 381 from three during 14 seasons in the league), at least gave it a shot. Shaquille O'Neal made one three-pointer during his whole NBA career despite 22 attempts, David Robinson converted 25 of his 100 attempts, while Charles Oakley made 68 of 269 threes. Does the ability to make that shot allow us to consider these players as three-point shooters?

One would be inclined to think that way, since their shot attempts were preceded by the belief that they could make that particular shot from long distance, even when they had not attempted it during previous NBA games. That is why in that moment, when the ball went into the hoop, they were, in fact, three-point shooters. However, circumstances probably played a role in their decision making, which is not the case for typical three-point shooters—it was either a shot of desperation or the game was already out of reach. Shooters, like James Harden or Steph Curry, attempt a three-point shot whenever they are open, whereas these players needed to have a special occasion to do so.

Consider Game Four of the 2002 Western Conference Finals between the Kings and the Lakers. With seven seconds left, the Kings were leading 99 to 97. Kobe Bryant had the ball in his hands and was driving into the lane to tie the game. The Kings' defense was all over him, but he still somehow managed to shoot the ball. He missed, and during the fight for the rebound the ball was swiped by Kings' center, Vlade Divac, towards the top of the key, where it bounced and reached the three-point line. Robert Horry of the Lakers caught it and with 0.8 seconds left released the ball. He scored, the Lakers won that game 100 to 99, tied the series, and eventually headed to the NBA Finals for the third time in a row.

This was not the first time Horry rose to the occasion during a clutch moment, making an important shot when his team needed it. Since his rookie year, Horry was performing greatly in crucial games, earning the moniker "Big Shot Rob." However, he was not supposed to take that shot. Granted, he was behind the three-point line for a reason, but the original play was called for Kobe Bryant, it was supposed to be a two-point shot to tie the game. Why did the Lakers not run the play for Horry in the first place, even though in the previous round he scored an important corner three against the Blazers, winning a game for his team? Why was he not as trustworthy in Game Six of the Conference Finals? Well, the obvious answer is that a two-pointer was the safer option, plus the game was too important to risk a long-distance miss.

Also, while he undoubtedly was a clutch performer even then, Horry was a good, but not a great, career three-point shooter. Up to that moment, he converted a bit over one-third of his career three-point attempts during the regular season, which was the same as the Boston Celtics' Antoine Walker, who was largely criticized for his on-court egotism, predominantly his three-point shot attempts. With both of them having their three-point percentage around 33, why was it more desirable to hand the ball to Horry than, for example Walker, not only during a crucial moment of a game, but during its early stages as well? Why is Horry remembered so fondly as a shooter but not Walker?

This "historical injustice" may be somewhat explained through the number of three-point shot attempts by both men. Up to that point, after nine seasons in the league, Horry made 531 out of 1,543 three-pointers, while Walker made 724 out of 2,160 despite 2001–02 being just his sixth

season in the NBA. Horry was never the focal point of the offense on the Rockets, the Suns or the Lakers, teams he played on up until that time. The player himself said about his late-game shots: "If I hit it we win, if I miss y'all are going to blame the stars for losing the game anyway. There's no pressure on me."[6]

Walker, however, was the primary offensive option on the Boston Celtics, which meant he was supposed to score throughout the whole game. By 2001–02, he made 44 percent of his two-point shots, so it was more desirable from his teammates', coaches' and fans' perspective for him to take shots from short distance, but Walker had great

Antoine Walker doing his famous shimmy celebration, probably after making another ill-advised shot (2001).

confidence in his shot and the mindset of a true shooter. When asked why he took so many threes, he simply replied "because there are no fours."[7] Moreover, he led the league in three-point shot attempts for three straight seasons (2000–01 to 2002–03). In the first of these three seasons he also led the league in three-point field goals made, making 221 of his 603 attempts. In 2001–02, Walker attempted the shot 645 times. In the 2003–04 season, he attempted 582 shots from beyond the arc. He shot so much despite not being in the top 50 of three-point percentage shooters even once throughout the mentioned seasons.

The thing with shooters is that they are expected to shoot. If a player may improve his team's chances of winning a game by attempting a three-point shot, he should do it, just as a defender should attempt a steal or a rebounder should jump for a lose ball. Making an ill-conceived shot is obviously a sign of overconfidence and egotism, whereas attempting an open three is clearly a good decision that might benefit the team if the shot goes in. All of the NBA teams see it as such, which is reflected in the stat sheets.

When the three-point line was introduced, it was treated with skepticism, as teams attempted an average of only 2.8 three-point shots per game in the 1979–80 season. In the 1994–95 season, the league shortened the three-point line and the number of attempts per game rose to 15.3 from 9.9 the season before. After three years, the line was reversed to its former distance, as making the shot was then considered too easy. Following further rule changes which favored the offense, and the remarkable success of spacing, small-ball playing teams like the Phoenix Suns, the Miami Heat, the Golden State Warriors or the Houston Rockets, the league average in the 2018–19 season rose to 32 three-point shots attempts per game. Brian Taylor of the San Diego Clippers led the 1979–80 NBA in three-point shots made and attempted, taking 3.1 three-point shots per game. The 2018–19 season leader, James Harden, attempted ten more three-pointers a game (13.1) alone.

This was a gradual, almost natural development that would not have been possible without exceptional players whose ability to shoot the ball from long distance transformed the way modern basketball is played. The chapters in this book are devoted to memorable performances by leading three-point shooters. Not all of them were career-defining moments, yet each performance in a game or a contest represents a particular development in the 40-year history of three-point shooting in the NBA. The focus of each chapter is obviously not limited to particular games but also to the circumstances, which were crucial in making that transformation possible.

The three-point shot was first introduced in the NBA in the 1979–80 season, but as mentioned previously, it was born in the imagination of basketball pioneer, coach Howard Hobson, almost 40 years earlier, and officially tested for the first time on February 7, 1945. Before the game between Fordham and Columbia, the new rule was advertised as "an effort to make basketball a more interesting and wide-open game."[8] "Tested" is the proper word, as college players were primarily concerned with making the most of the opportunity to "drain the three"—Columbia made eleven three-pointers, whereas Fordham made nine.

The title of the first chapter, "October 12, 1979," refers to the season opener in Boston, during which Chris Ford scored the first three-pointer in NBA history in a game against the Rockets. The chapter is primarily concerned with retracing the history of the shot up to that moment, starting with coach Hobson, through Abe Saperstein's short-lived American Basketball League and the ABA, up to that important, first-made three-pointer. That date was also important because it marked the professional debut of Larry Bird, one of the greatest shooters in league history.

Bird is the subject of the second chapter, as his three consecutive wins during the 3-Point Contest—a competition during the All-Star Weekend which served primarily as a marketing tool for the still new and not yet fully accepted shot—played a vital role in earning the play the respect it undoubtedly deserved. Bird's third performance during the contest was especially dominant, as he proclaimed in the locker room that he would win and triumphed without even taking off his warm-up jacket. Part of the chapter is also devoted to Dale Ellis, who came in second during the contest on February 6, 1988, and later on became the first NBA player to make 1,000 three-point shots during his professional career.

While Bird and Ellis had one of the purest, eye-pleasing shooting forms in the NBA in the 1980s and early '90s, a rather forgotten player named Michael Adams made a name for himself by shooting almost one-handed, particularly ugly-looking three-point shots. On March 23, 1991, while playing for the Denver Nuggets, Adams scored a career-high

54 points (7 of 16 from three) against the Bucks. He ended his career with 949 three-pointers made. Short (by NBA standards) and quick, he was the type of player Hobson had in mind when he said he wanted to make basketball a more inclusive sport.

Another step in the rising importance of the three-point shot was made when it was embraced by one of the best players of all time, Michael Jordan. Jordan was primarily an athletic inside scorer when he entered the league, but as he got older, he started to move away from the basket and transformed into an all-time great shooter. In the 1989–90 season, the number of his three-point shot attempts per game rose from 1.2 to 3.0, and he even appeared in the 3-Point Contest, tying Detlef Schrempf's record of the lowest amount of points scored during the competition with five. Just two years later, on June 3, 1992, Michael Jordan made six three-pointers in the first half of Game One of the NBA Finals against the Blazers. He followed them with a gesture which after the game became known as "The Shrug," a title denoting one of Jordan's historical performances, like "The Shot" or "The Flu Game."

Bird and Jordan were great shooters, but Reggie Miller was the first NBA player to become synonymous with the three-point shot. He was the best player on one of the best teams to never win the NBA championship. With his ability to shoot from long distance, Miller turned the struggling Indiana Pacers into annual contenders. At the time of his retirement, he was the league leader in career three-pointers made (2,560). His most memorable shooting performance took place on May 7, 1995, when he scored eight points in nine seconds against the Knicks, the team whose fanbase loathed Miller more than any other.

The sixth chapter is devoted to a period of three seasons—1994 to 1997—when the three-point line was shortened to 22 feet. One of the beneficiaries of that change was Miller's teammate of four years, George McCloud, then of the Dallas Mavericks. The small forward was a role player who was once thought of as a draft bust, but turned his career around during his best season, 1995–96. On April 19, 1996, he set the single-season record of three-point shot attempts with 678. The record stood for 20 years and was only beaten by Stephen Curry in the 2015–16 season.

The next chapter is the only one devoted to two nights, February 8–9, 1997, as that year the All-Star Weekend featured two solid performances by two of the best three-point shooters of the 1990s: Steve Kerr and Glen

Steve Kerr made great use of the three-point shot both as a player and a coach (1994).

Rice. On All-Star Saturday they both participated in the 3-Point Contest, which was won by Kerr. On Sunday, Rice was named All-Star Game MVP after breaking the in-game record for points scored during one quarter and one half. Kerr is the NBA's all-time career leader in three-point shot percentage with 45.4, while Rice made 40 percent of his three-point shots during his NBA career.

On May 26, 2002, Robert Horry became immortalized after prolonging the chances of the Lakers making the NBA Finals with the last-second shot against the Kings in Game Four of the Western Conference Finals. A career 33 percent shooter, Horry's reputation does not tell the whole story of his career, as he was not as efficient from behind the three-point line as he is remembered to be. On the flipside, he won seven NBA championships, the most by an individual player since the 1970s. On his example, this chapter explores how the three-pointer can serve as a chance for regular players to make league history.

The 7'0" Dirk Nowitzki is the tallest player ever to win the NBA 3-Point Contest, which happened on February 18, 2006. Nowitzki ended his career with 1,982 three-pointers made. With his ability to both play under the basket and stretch the court, Nowitzki is representative of other big men of his time, like the 6'10" Rashard Lewis (1,787 career three-pointers made) or the 7'0" Andrea Bargnani (507 career three-pointers made), who purposely moved away from the basket. In the present-day NBA it is almost required of big men to shoot from long range, as proven by the shooting evolution of players like Brook Lopez (from 0.2 the season prior to 5.2 threes attempted per game in 2015–16) or Marc Gasol (from 0.1 the season before to 3.6 three-point shot attempts per game in 2016–17). In the past, players like Bill Laimbeer, Sam Perkins or Arvydas Sabonis where not allowed to fully utilize their three-point shooting skills.

Ray Allen is the only player who was able to make more three-point shots than Reggie Miller during his NBA career, and Allen is still the all-time leader in the category of three-point shots made. While Allen made 2,973 three-pointers in the regular season and 385 in the playoffs, it can be argued that none was more important than the corner three for the Heat in the final seconds of Game Six of the NBA Finals against the Spurs, on June 18, 2013. With yellow tape already stretched around the court, since the Spurs were leading the series and the game, Allen made the shot that tied the game. The Heat won in overtime and went on to win the NBA championship that year. In that series, the Spurs also set an NBA record for shots made by a team in a finals game with 16. The team's shooting guard, Danny Green, set another one with 27 three-point shots made by a single player during a finals series, beating the previous record by five. It was set by… Ray Allen during the 2008 NBA Finals.

The last chapter of this work is devoted to Steph Curry, the ultimate embodiment of the change in the attitude towards the three-pointer. Curry will probably retire as the all-time leader in three-pointers made, as there has never been a shooter like him in the NBA, one able to score from every spot on the court. One of the most significant shots of his career is the one made against the Clippers on March 8, 2015. Curry was surrounded by three defenders and the shot would earn him a lot of criticism if it were not for his exceptional status. Curry would not have been able to enjoy it, had it not been for the shooting performances by the many, many players who appear in this book. Shot after shot, they have shaped the modern NBA, and their contributions deserve proper appreciation.

October 12, 1979

Chris Ford Makes the First Three-Pointer in League History

George Mikan is probably the most influential person in the history of basketball, at least when it comes to the evolution of the rules of the game. When he was starting off as a player, the lane under the basket was just six feet wide, goaltending was still allowed, and there was no shot clock. Basketball was a game played very close to the rim, where one missed shot could spell the difference between winning and losing. Mikan was, in fact, so dominant that when his Minneapolis Lakers came to face the New York Knicks, the game was famously advertised on the marquee of Madison Square Garden as "Geo Mikan vs. Knicks." Long before the 1980s strategy of marketing stars, not teams, Mikan drew actual crowds to the biggest arenas in the country. Before that particular game, his teammates jokingly sent Mikan alone onto the court, while they remained in street clothes, stating that if it was just him playing the Knicks, then he should do as the advertisement says.[1]

These games received substantial publicity, which contributed to the growth of basketball fandom, and Mikan's outstanding play was part of the sport's appeal during its early years. The 6'10" center was the reason why to this day NBA teams are so fixated on athletic big men. Frank Layden, the coach of the Utah Jazz from 1981 to 1988, famously said: "you can't teach height,"[2] and the half-serious statement is still considered a universal truth, as evidenced by every NBA draft, where rather raw giants are selected in front of more talented, albeit smaller, players. For examples of such a trend, one must look no further than the 2009 NBA draft, where Hasheem Thabeet was selected in front of James Harden and Steph Curry, or the 2011 NBA draft, where Tristan Thompson and

Bismack Biyombo were picked in front of Klay Thompson and Kemba Walker.

Because of his imposing height, Mikan dominated primarily on the defensive end. His main tactic was what we now know as goaltending, standing near the basket—just outside the six-feet-wide painted area— and swatting the ball away or catching it just as it was heading downward. Mikan and his most famous NCAA rival, the 7'0" Bob Kurland, stood out so much among their peers—Kurland is one of the first-known dunkers in basketball history—that in order to level the field, the college organization banned their efficient defensive move in 1944. This made the game of basketball more open, but one man went even further in his crusade to make basketball quicker, more entertaining, and most of all, more inclusive.

Howard A. Hobson, head basketball coach at Yale University from 1947 to 1956, published his outstanding book, *Scientific Basketball*, which would introduce a new way of thinking about basketball. While the sport had already come a long way from the 1881 Springfield gym in which two nine-player teams tried to outscore one another by throwing a soccer ball into peach baskets, it was still a far cry from the sport as we are familiar with today. It was Yale University, the college team Hobson would later coach, that played the first game of five-on-five basketball against the University of Pennsylvania on March 20, 1897. Still, that was an exhibition game, as basketball would not become competitive until much later, with the aid of coach Forrest Allen, who succeeded the creator of the sport, James Naismith, as head coach at the University of Kansas. Allen was influential in bringing basketball to the 1936 Olympics and establishing the NCAA Tournament in 1939.[3] Hobson himself refers to Allen's 1937 book, *Better Basketball*, as "probably the most complete book on basketball,"[4] which is no small compliment coming from the author of such a visionary work.

Hobson was one of the first coaches who understood the importance of scouting and began collecting field-goal data. In *Scientific Basketball*, he notes that these "are of great value to the coach.... If an opponent is able to score only certain types of shots, this fact has valuable implications as to how to play against the opponent."[5] More importantly though, Hobson gathered the data from 460 college basketball games, and used his observations to revolutionize basketball by dividing the court into three scoring zones, dependent on shot probability. The first zone ended at 12 feet from the basket, the second ended at 24 feet, and the third stretched beyond that distance. Those zones, respectively, were devoted to the Short Shot, the Medium Shot and the Long Shot. When referring to the last one, Hobson noted that since the shooting average from this area did not compare favorably with the averages from other zones, it was becoming neglected, which was a shame because "no shot has more player and spectator appeal, or is more helpful to the entire offensive plan in any style of play."[6] According to Hobson, efficient long-distance shooters could lure big men away from the basket, making the game of basketball more eye-pleasing and free-flowing. He urged coaches to teach the two-handed shot because of the ways it could influence the game. In that time, most players depended on close one-handed shots instead.

A decade later, his ideas were put into action; however, the opinions on this development were… well, divided. In *Rise and Fire*, Shawn Fury quotes the complaints of journalists Jimmy Breslin and Harry Grayson as examples of the negative perception of the two-handed shot. They both hated the idea of players pulling up and scoring jump shots, only to have the other team do the same. This supposedly turned games into high-scoring festivals by players who valued individual records above team play.[7] While these arguments sound preposterous from today's perspective, there was indeed a large opposition to the jump shot in the '50s. However, the wheels were already set into motion and with the shot came the invention of gunners, "players whose shooting skills made them stand out on the court."[8] Three-point shooters would appear much, much later, as the line was still a subject of discussion and experimentation, even by Hobson himself.

The idea for the three-point shot was inspired by the home run, which Hobson called "the most spectacular play in baseball."[9] Years later, when reminiscing about why the ABA introduced the three-pointer, George Mikan, who, in addition to his playing career mentioned earlier, also later became the first commissioner of the league, used the same comparison: "we called it the home run, because the 3-pointer was exactly that. It brought the fans out of their seats."[10] Mikan mentions Abe Saperstein as his inspiration for the idea, but before him, there was Hobson, who introduced the "area-method of scoring,"[11] in order to encourage players to attempt more long-distance shots, since they were more difficult to make.

That type of basketball was supposed to be more attractive for the casual viewer by increasing the possibility of celebrating basketball's equivalent of a home run.

Hobson also planned for Short Shots, those made within the radius of 12 feet from the basket, to be scored at one point each, but he settled on the three-point line and a widened foul lane (12 feet instead of 6) during the historical, first incarnation of the three-point line, in a game between Columbia and Fordham, on February 7, 1945. As noted in the Introduction, both teams made the most of the opportunity to fire away from long distance, and the fans, as anticipated by Hobson, reacted with excitement. In a survey conducted after the game, they voted 60–40 in favor of the introduction of the three-point line, and 70–30 for widening the lane.[12]

Saperstein was the founder of the Harlem Globetrotters, an all-black team that would travel around the country and dominate professional, semi-professional and amateur (mostly white) teams. On February 19, 1948, they defeated the best team in the country, George Mikan's Minneapolis Lakers of the National Basketball League (established in 1937, in 1949 it merged with the Basketball Association of America to form the NBA). In *The Chosen Game*, Charley Rosen presents Saperstein as being far from the advocate for African American rights, though, as the owner would decry players from big cities as potential troublemakers, underpay his stars and give them just one uniform each for the duration of the whole tour.[13] With time Saperstein's ambitions grew and he wanted to establish his own NBA team in Los Angeles.

Feeling betrayed after the league vetoed his idea and simply moved the Lakers from Minnesota to California, he reacted by founding his own league, the American Basketball League, in 1961. One of the things that were supposed to help the ABL in competing with the NBA was the introduction of the three-point line for the first time in professional basketball. The advice to use it came from former Celtics' player, Bill Sharman, who years later used a familiar analogy when describing his and Saperstein's feelings towards the long-distance shot: "I thought it was great because I was an outside shooter.… He thought it was going to be as popular as the home run."[14]

The ABL, which featured eight teams, disbanded after one and a half seasons, yet "the new rules, particularly the three-point shot, proved to be very popular with fans, despite the fact that 'traditionalists' said that there was no room in the game for such 'gimmicks.'"[15] Apart from Saperstein, no man was more influential when it came to the whole shape of the short-lived league than Sharman, four-time NBA champion, eight-time All-Star, whose jersey was ultimately retired by the Boston Celtics. Sharman spent ten seasons with the Celtics and, with Bob Cousy, formed one of the best backcourts in early basketball history. Cousy was not very appreciative of the jump shot himself, calling it in 1963 "the worst thing that happened to basketball in ten years,"[16] while Sharman is considered one of the best shooters in the time before the introduction of the three-point line. During his 11 years in the league—before being traded to the Celtics, he spent one season on the Washington Capitols—he averaged 17.8 points per game, making 42.6 percent of his shots.

Bill Sharman was also responsible for setting the distance of the three-point line to where it is today in the NBA. Saperstein wanted the line to be placed 25 feet from the front of the rim, Sharman urged him to set the distance from the back of it, which was exactly 23 feet, 9 inches up front and 22 feet at the corners.[17] The first three-point shots of professional basketball were made in the first game of the season, which took place on October 27, 1961, between the San Francisco Saints and the Los Angeles Jets, albeit there is no record of who made the first one, George Yardley or Mike Farmer.[18]

Sharman's impact on the league did not end there, as he was named head coach of said Los Angeles Jets team and won the first (and only) ABL championship, although with a different team. After the Jets folded and the coach of the Cleveland Pipers—John McLendon, who was the first African American head coach in the history of professional basketball—stepped down, Sharman took his place, leading the team to the title. The league completed the 1961–62 season, but disbanded on the final day of the season.

As head coach, Sharman is best known for inventing the morning shoot-around. When he was a player, he started going to the gym in the mornings to calm his nerves before games, and began to implement that strategy as he was coaching in Cleveland, Utah, and Los Angeles. The workouts proved successful, as the Cleveland Pipers won the ABL title, the Utah Stars won the ABA championship in 1970, and the Los Angeles Lakers won the NBA championship in 1972. He would win five more titles on the Lakers as the general manager and team president. The shoot-around itself revolutionized coaching in the NBA, because after the Lakers won in 1972, every other team in the league adopted the idea. It was dropped by some teams only around 2009 due to new developments in sleep science.[19]

The ABL may have died too quickly, but the three-pointer was far from gone—it was adapted by the newly created American Basketball Association in 1967. Dennis Murphy, the founder of the league, said that the three-pointer was supposed to be a part of it from the very beginning: "Everybody involved in putting together the ABA liked the idea because it was good for the little man—it had to be exciting."[20] This group included basketball great George Mikan, then retired. The ABA's creators wanted Mikan to become league commissioner so much that they decided to move their headquarters to Minneapolis just to accommodate him.

As a player, Mikan was so good that he inspired three rule changes,— goaltending, the 24-second shot clock, and the so-called "Mikan Rule"— implemented in order to allow other players and teams to keep up with him. The Mikan Rule contributed to the widening of the key from 6 to 12 feet, and with the three-seconds rule already in action,[21] tall players' scoring ability near the basket was severely limited. The key would be widened to 16 feet after the success enjoyed by Wilt Chamberlain.[22] Mikan was the one who made life even harder for future big men, further limiting their impact on the game by introducing the three-point line. Even though his tenure as commissioner lasted only for two seasons, he legitimized the upstart league and its supposedly gimmicky rules.

Thanks to the line, the ABA could offer a different product than the NBA—it was largely the same game, but with a twist. The three-point line allowed shorter players, who were excluded from the NBA due to their height, to play professional basketball and impact the game like never before. Some coaches, like Hubie Brown, remained skeptical, because they had to completely change their playbooks and coaching strategies, but most players embraced the idea. Charlie Williams, who was a guard in the ABA for six seasons, said: "the 3-point shot helped make our league special, but you had to be careful, because it could be addicting. It was like we all had found a new toy."[23]

No player from the ABA was more synonymous with the long-shot than Louie Dampier. Dampier had been with the league since its inception and remained there up until the end, from 1967 to 1976, playing for the same team, the Kentucky Colonels. The 6'0" point guard played the most games (728), had the most assists (4,044) and scored the most points (13,726) in league history. He also drained the most threes, 794—almost 300 more than the second all-time career ABA three-point shooter, Billy Keller (506). Dampier would later play for three seasons in the NBA, but without the three-point line, he failed to make a significant impact on the San Antonio Spurs, despite playing under Doug Moe, the ultimate players' coach. Dampier could not succeed in the league, because apart from not being tall enough to be seriously considered by an NBA team, he was also not especially fast. And yet, no other player could shoot from 25 to 30 feet quite like him or his backcourt partner for five years, Darel Carrier. They both attempted three three-pointers per game in their ABA careers. Hubie Brown, who coached Dampier and Carrier for two seasons, said of the former:

> [He] was a good player who used the 3-pointer to make himself great. He was one of those guys who would be a Mark Price type today, the smart 6-foot guard who could beat you with the shot or the pass. It was just too bad that he spent his whole career in the ABA, because very few people now appreciate him for what he accomplished.[24]

The new league was exciting; it made the NBA look "prudish and conservative,"[25] but it was the latter that emerged victorious from the rivalry between the two. Three years after the 1976 merger—which was synonymous with the bigger league (the NBA) absorbing the smaller one (the ABA)—the three-point shot also became an element of the NBA landscape, following a lot of resistance from prominent league figures. There was obviously some logic to that thinking. The NBA had just beat out its most serious rival to date and was the biggest professional basketball league not only in the United States, but in the world as well. Why should it succumb to the ABA's rules, when, apart from the players and coaches who jumped ship from the ABA to the NBA, nobody knew how to play basketball with the three-point line in place? This applied not only to shooting from long distance but also to spacing and pace of the game.

The executives thought differently, as the league was dealing with some serious image issues that were threatening its existence. One of the main problems was drug use among players. Bernard King, who would become a genuine star in later years, was arrested for marijuana possession during his rookie season, 1977. Just one year later, he earned another arrest, this time for cocaine possession. John Lucas II was banned from the NBA twice for drug and alcohol use. Spencer Haywood, the Lakers' reserve center, got so addicted to crack that he would fall asleep during workouts. In consequence, the team suspended him during the 1980 Finals, to which Haywood reacted by plotting to kill the team's head coach.[26] While the league's drug-related problems would continue into the '80s, hurting the careers of David Thompson and Michael Ray Richardson, and culminating with the death of Len Bias—the second pick in the 1986 NBA draft, his death caused by a cocaine overdose—the commotion caused by the three-point shot allowed the NBA to partially redirect the attention to the on-court product.

Before the start of the 1979–80 season, the product needed fixing as well. Attendance was down drastically in the previous season, especially in the big market cities—in New York and Los Angeles by 11 percent, in Philadelphia by 19 percent and in Chicago by 31 percent—than the year before. This was very alarming, considering how, thanks to the success of the New York Knicks and the Los Angeles Lakers in the early '70s, professional basketball was hailed as the sport of the decade due to huge numbers of fans watching and attending games. Television ratings were down by 26 percent in comparison to the previous season,[27] and the reason for such retreat was associated with the league becoming... too black:

> Athletes in all team sports are finding themselves more accountable to fans today, because their salaries are routinely reported along with their batting averages and rushing yardages. Add the fact that almost 75% of the players in the NBA are black—while more than 75% of the fans are white—and the issue of race as a contributing factor to the league's troubles cannot be simply dismissed with whispers and off-the-record comments.[28]

To avoid accusations of racism, some simply said that the league was too undisciplined, which implied basically the same thing, without stating it directly. When Kermit Washington, a black player, punched Rudy Tomjanovich, a white one, during a 1977 game and almost killed him, this furthered the notion that the NBA was in need of some disciplinary action. The incident was so infamous that even years later, before the 1994 NBA Finals, Tomjanovich, then employed as coach of the Rockets, had to answer questions regarding the punch. "To Tomjanovich, every mention of the punch was another piece of evidence that, no matter how much he accomplished, up to and including coaching an NBA championship team, he could not escape the shadow of that night."[29] Washington, who was regarded as a good teammate before the incident, could never fully restore his reputation, despite earning an appearance in the 1980 All-Star Game. In 2018, he was sentenced to six years in prison for charity fraud.

Howard Hobson encouraged league commissioner Larry O'Brien to introduce the line, as "making the three-point basket a permanent part of the game will help eliminate the violence he and basketball fans are concerned about in the NBA."[30] The line would create more space between players, who would often just crowd under baskets waiting for a pass or a rebound, which made physical contact inevitable and supposedly led to violence. However, the aggressive plays were not the only reason why fans were turning away from the league. NBA players made more money than ever before, which was also problematic, as they were now perceived as overpaid and lazy. Due to the constantly rising overall field-goal percentage numbers, basketball seemed almost too easy. With 82-game schedules, it should be obvious that, if anything, the players were overworked. Hiring public relations agencies and marketing big superstars was not enough; the NBA needed to also add something to the game itself, to show that it was constantly developing and looking for new ways to please spectators. Enter the three-point shot, heavily criticized before even being tested in an NBA game.

Coach Dick Motta said that the three would definitely make the league interesting, even though for him it was still a "gimmick," and a player should shoot with at least 33 percent accuracy to even attempt it in a game.[31] Actually, his Washington Bullets never worked on that shot during training and only Kevin Grevey, the best shooter on the team, was allowed to fire away at will from long distance. He made a three-pointer in the first game of the 1979–80 season, against the Sixers, and it is still a subject of some debate whether it was Grevey or Chris Ford that made the first three-pointer in NBA history, as there is no play-by-play available from both games. Grevey himself does not dwell on the fact of being officially considered the second three-point shooter: "It made no difference to me.... At that moment I wasn't thinking history. I was thinking Dick would bench me."[32]

The player officially credited with making that historical shot is Chris Ford of the Boston Celtics, which is kind of ironic, considering that team president, Red Auerbach, became the face of the resistance against the shot. The Celtics were at the time the most successful franchise in league history and Auerbach would become a part of their every single title run up until 1986, winning nine championships as head coach and seven as team executive. His opinion mattered in the league, and it was not favorable towards the shot:

> We don't need it. I say leave our game alone. Putting in the 3-point play reminds me of a team that trades four, five and six players every year. Everybody starts panicking. TV panicked over the bad ratings. You'll see a dramatic uprise in the league next year when Bill Walton, Larry Bird and Magic Johnson come in. These players have charisma. There is no way you can measure it. Charisma starts before you can play the game.[33]

And in a way he was right, because Bird and Johnson transformed the NBA, at least from a marketing standpoint. However, the three-pointer is part of Larry Bird's legacy, it is what turned him into one of the best scorers, clutch players and entertainers in league history. He legitimized the shot in its NBA infancy, but the shot helped immortalize Bird in more ways than one.

Auerbach was obviously not alone in the resentment he felt toward the shot. Jack Ramsey, who would later coach such esteemed three-point shooters like Chuck Person and Reggie Miller, also dismissed the shot as a gimmick, proposing instead to make big-market teams more successful—an idea that did not have much to do with fair play or parity. On the other side of the fence were Gene Shue, head coach of the Clippers, and Pat Williams, general manager of the Sixers. Williams believed that the shot would make the scores closer and keep the teams on their toes up until the last seconds of games.[34] Red Holzman, who coached the New York Knicks to their only NBA championships in 1970 and 1973, said that after the introduction of the line, "the defense will have to be honest now. It will definitely open things down low for the big man."[35]

With such divisions within the league, it was evident that the three-point line would create some controversy, but the shot was never particularly encouraged by league coaches. In its first season in the NBA, the three-point shot was attempted by each team 2.8 times per game, with a 29 percent completion rate (0.8 makes per game). Fred Brown of the Seattle SuperSonics led the league in three-point field goal percentage with 44.3. Behind him were the Celtics' Chris Ford (42.7 percent) and Larry Bird (40.6 percent), both brought to Boston by Auerbach, who so eagerly fought back against the shot.

Ford was 31 years old at the time, playing his first full season for the Celtics after the Detroit Pistons traded him away in 1978. After he turned himself into a reliable long-distance shooter, Ford said, "My success with the shot became my little revenge against Dick Vitale who traded me from Detroit to Boston because I couldn't shoot."[36] Vitale was the coach for the Pistons for a bit over one season, going 34–60 during his tenure before being fired. It was the last coaching gig in Vitale's career, and he would go on to become a recognizable broadcaster for the ESPN.

Ford was traded to Boston for Earl Tatum, nicknamed "The Black Jerry West" by his college coach at Marquette. Tatum was supposed to become a star in the NBA, and was recruited by 390 colleges. He even played with number 43, which was not-so-coincidentally close to West's 44 Lakers' jersey. He was even drafted by the Lakers, but would never enjoy the same success as in college, let alone as the man whose shape is used in the logo of the NBA. After just three games into the 1978–79 season, the Celtics traded Tatum to the Pistons for Ford. The next season would turn out to be Tatum's last in the league.

In Ford, the team got a solid player who immediately became a starter and, following his best shooting year, as he was attempting 14.2 shots and averaging 15.6 points per game for the Celtics, gave away half of his attempts a season later to an amazing rookie out of Indiana State, Larry Joe Bird. Apart from Ford, Bird and center Dave Cowens were the only other Celtics who attempted the three-point shot in the first game of the 1979–80 season, but they both missed. The Rockets, against whom the Celtics were facing off that night, attempted ten three-pointers, but made only one. The author of that make was Rick Barry, who attempted the shot a total of three times during the game. Thirty-five at the time, Barry was, for the first time in his career, playing less than 30 minutes and, for the second time, averaging less than 20 points per game. It would be the last season of Barry's stellar career, involving 12 All-Star selections, an NBA championship, and career averages of 24.8 points, 6.7 rebounds and 4.9 assists per game.

The fact that it was Ford, a role player, who made that shot and not a future superstar like Bird, or a former MVP and scoring champion like Barry, was great for the league because it showed how the shot allowed lesser players to make an impact in ways thus far unthought of. Hobson's intention of opening up the game by moving the big men away from the basket was gradually realized, despite early reluctance from coaches and players to do so. It would take a new generation of players to truly understand and embrace the possibilities provided by the three-point line.

Once the NCAA introduced the line in the 1986–87 season and, after fighting off initial skepticism—Duke's Mike Krzyzewski implied scoring from long distance was lazy, Dayton's Don Donoher qualified the three-point line as the symptom of declining American morality, while La Salle's Speedy Morris called those in favor of the three-point shot simply "idiots"[37]—coaches began to make use of it, while players who learned how to operate with it in college arenas took that knowledge with them to the professional leagues. With the three-pointer a part of their game now, they made basketball more exciting, one shot at a time. And it all began with a single make by a role player who is now associated not with winning an NBA title as a player for the Celtics, nor with coaching the Celtics, the Bucks, the Clippers or the Sixers, but with that one important moment that changed professional sports forever.

February 6, 1988

Larry Bird Reclaims the Title of the Three-Point King

Calling Larry Bird an exceptional player is clearly an understatement. It is almost impossible to think of another athlete who has been as dominant in the sport despite being as physically limited. Dominance does not only characterize his shooting, which during the 1980s became part of the appeal of NBA games. Magic Johnson, Bird's biggest on-court rival, wrote in the Foreword to Bird's autobiography, *Drive*, that "the reason [he] love[s] to watch Larry play is that he can dominate a game without even taking a shot."[1] Shawn Fury shares that opinion, stating that "simply calling [Bird] a pure shooter might erase the way he controlled the game with his passing, rebounding, tenacity, team defense, and floor game."[2] These observations are backed up by Bird's career averages, as he was able to score 24.3 points per game and still average 10 rebounds, 6.3 assists, 1.7 steals and almost one block in the 13 seasons he played for the Boston Celtics. He was the ultimate all-around player, a fact which is somewhat forgotten due to his amazing shooting ability.

His numbers look even more impressive when taking into consideration the beatings Bird took on the court, playing close to 40 minutes per game (38.4) throughout his career, jumping for loose balls, drawing fouls and occasionally engaging in fights—like the one with ABA and NBA basketball legend, Julius Erving, in an early game of the 1984–85 season. His more famous brawl came during the 1987 playoffs against the Pistons. After being knocked down by Dennis Rodman and Bill Laimbeer as he was driving towards the basket, Bird hit Laimbeer twice on the head when both men were laying on the court. The Pistons won that game, but the Celtics won the series 4–3 on their way to their last NBA Finals in the 20th century.

Three-Pointer!

Bird truly hated Laimbeer, even though the Piston was just as competitive as the Celtics legend. Unlike Bird, Laimbeer was primarily a dirty player, always the first to instigate a fight or intimidate the opposing team. He was behind the infamous handshake snub in the 1991 NBA playoffs, when the Pistons' stars declined to shake hands with Michael Jordan and other Chicago players after the Bulls eliminated them in the Eastern Conference Finals. Instead of congratulating their opponents, as is customary, they walked by their bench before the game was even over. More importantly, at least for this book, Laimbeer was an efficient long-distance shooter, at least when given the chance. The 6'11" center joined the Detroit Pistons through a mid-season trade with the Cavaliers on February 16, 1982, and was the heart and soul of that team for 11 seasons. Isiah Thomas was their best player, but Laimbeer was the source of the team's whatever-it-takes-to-win mentality.

In his 30s, Laimbeer started to move away from the basket and rely more on his three-point shooting. During the Pistons' two championship seasons (1989–90) he averaged 1.5 long-distance shots per game, making 35.7 percent of his attempts. In Game Two of the 1990 NBA Finals he tied the finals single-game record with six three-pointers—set by Michael Cooper of the Los Angeles Lakers in 1985—making five in the fourth quarter, and taking the game to overtime. The Pistons would lose to the Blazers 105 to 106, but they ended up winning the series 4–1. Throughout his career Laimbeer made 202 threes on 32.6 percent accuracy. He was much more than an enforcer, yet is remembered mostly as one of the biggest villains in the league, especially by Celtics' and Bulls' fans.

Even though he used different means to reach the same end, Bird shared a similar devotion to winning:

> My thoughts were always that that night was the most important game in the world. Everybody in the world was watching that one game. And I had to be the best player on the court and win that game that night. That was my mentality, and it stuck with me all the way through my career. But knowing that, I knew that I was going to pay for it in a hard way. That's probably why, when I retired, after the press conference, I probably felt relief.[3]

The results of that relentless style of play were numerous injuries, which Bird had to play through in order to make an impact on the court.

During a friendly softball game in college he dislocated the index finger in his right hand, which caused him some difficulty when shooting throughout his professional career. The finger would not bend, and Bird was right-handed. Still, in 1985 he claimed that it was "not a major injury … if I can walk and talk, it's not a major injury."[4] Jimmy Rodgers, an assistant and later head coach on the Celtics, thought that Bird was so efficient because he shot with his wrist, "just a little flick of the wrist and he had his shot."[5] Bird himself described wrist training while 10–12 years old as crucial for elevating his shooting form. He never complained about his finger; rather, as was the case throughout his career, he found a way of working around his bodily limitations in order to remain efficient.

Something that Bird would characterize as a major injury occurred three years later, when during the sixth game of the 1988–89 season against the Miami Heat, Bird had to leave the court. That turned out to be the final game of his season, as he had to have bone-spur surgery on both heels and was able to return to action after 11 months. That injury was a result of Bird's back problems, which started in the summer of 1985, at one point forcing him to spend two weeks in bed. The back was a serious issue for him throughout the whole season, which makes his 1986 MVP trophy and that year's championship run all the more praiseworthy. At some point during that season, Bird was actually contemplating retirement, but he was more concerned with winning a championship, notwithstanding the bad back. He was driven to outperform himself, and the 1985 MVP award did not give him any joy because his team failed to win the title.[6] At the beginning of the 1986–87 season, he was forced to take a year-long break from professional basketball.

Years of playing with a bad back caused Bird to alter his running style, and he did a lot of running, before and after games, on the second level of Boston Garden, often when the other team was practicing. This had an effect on his heels, which eventually had to be operated on. Bird was not strong nor fast, he could not jump very high, but he overpowered more athletic players with his mental toughness. Kevin McHale, Bird's teammate, once reminisced about Bird's first encounter with Anthony Mason, a muscular forward playing for the Knicks. Mason was so big and intimidating that he actually used to serve as a bouncer during barbecues organized in Queens by rapper LL Cool J.[7] After complementing the rookie on his physique and calling him "muscles," Bird said that those muscles were still not enough to stop him from scoring on Mason.[8]

While Bird claimed he never practiced three-point shots during his playing days,[9] he is considered the first great three-point shooter in NBA history. Actually, Bird's NBA debut also coincided with the debut of the three-point line, where his teammate Chris Ford made the first credited three-pointer in league history, so the connection between the player and the play was somewhat already established. Bird also attempted his first three-point shot in an official game on that night, but he missed. In his next four games he noted just two total attempts, both misses, before making two out of three three-point shots during the October 23 loss to the Spurs. He ended his rookie season with 1.7 attempts and 0.7 makes per game, shooting 40.6 percent from three. Bird was third in shooting percentage behind Ford and league leader Fred Brown, who made 44.3 percent of his shots from long distance. During that season, only two players attempted more than 200 three-pointers, Rick Barry (221) and Brian Taylor (239). Taylor also made the most threes (90), Barry was second (73), and Bird was fifth with 53 makes. It was only during the 1983–84 season that another player broke Taylor's record of three-point shot makes—Darrell Griffith made 91 threes as a member of the Utah Jazz. The player behind Griffith in makes during that season, Michael Cooper, nailed just 38 shots from behind the three-point line.

Throughout his career, Bird never made more than 100 three-point shots during the regular season and only twice attempted more than 200. His percentage was over 40 in 6 of his 13 seasons in the league. His approach to the three-point shot evolved as the Celtics switched coaches from Bill Fitch to K.C. Jones. Fitch was a disciplinarian, concerned with tactics and approaching the game in a certain way—basketball was supposed to be played near the basket. K.C. Jones gave his players more offensive freedom: "The game was opened up for me. If I came down on a break and was open, I could throw up a three. I started drifting toward the corner and shooting them. We made it a much bigger weapon."[10] When Bird became a coach, he borrowed from both men, taking his devotion to tactics from Fitch and approaching his players just like Jones did.[11] He had great success as the coach of the Indiana Pacers, leading the team to the NBA Finals in his third and final season on the job.

Bird not only made the first three-point shot in the history of the All-Star Game, but he also made the three-pointer a vital element of his game during clutch moments. It was Larry Bird who single-handedly validated the three-point shot in its early NBA years. Before we get to that, it is first important to acknowledge how special Bird was as a player, since a lesser athlete would not have made such an impact on the perception of the shot. Replays of Bird making the three-point shot in television highlights were a strong, inescapable image. He was selected the league's Most Valuable Player for three years in a row (1984–86), as one of only three players in league history to achieve that honor, Bill Russell and Wilt Chamberlain being the other two. Bird actually pretended to be either Russell or Chamberlain during one-on-one games with his cousin, even though he never actually saw them play.[12]

Bird became an icon of white basketball, as he was perceived as silent, blue-collar and inconspicuous, which was in sync with typically (white) American values of humility, hard work and dedication. Bird was also very appreciative of his occupation, saying about himself and fellow basketball players: "We practice for two hours. We play a game. That's our job. Other people get up at the crack of dawn and work all day."[13] His main rival, Magic Johnson, was seen as his exact opposite—cocky, flashy and flamboyant. At least that was the narrative throughout their careers, because, as proven by retellings of various stories by former NBA players and coaches, Johnson was extremely competitive—one time hitting his close friend, Isiah Thomas, with an elbow to the face in their first game against each other in the finals—while Bird was a world-class trash talker. He was so confident in his craft that he would often talk to his opponent about what he was going to do either during a particular play or the game.

Bird was especially offended when the opposing coach delegated a white player to guard him:

> The one thing that always bothered me when I played in the NBA was I really got irritated when they put a white guy on me…. I still don't understand why. A white guy would come out (and) I would always ask him: "What, do you have a problem with your coach? Did your coach do this to you?" And he'd go, "No," and I'd say, "Come on, you got a white guy coming out here to guard me; you got no chance." … For some reason, that always bothered me when I was playing against a white guy.[14]

Since the members of the media—who since the 1979–80 season were given the task of selecting the best player in the league—were (and still are) predominantly white, it was suggested that Bird won the trophy because of being a dominant white player in a black man's sport. These concerns were voiced by Dennis Rodman, who claimed that Bird was overrated after the Celtics eliminated the Pistons from the already mentioned series in the 1987 playoffs. Rodman was backed up by teammate Isiah Thomas, who said that if the Celtics' player was black, he "would be just another good guy."[15]

Bird scored 37 points, grabbed nine rebounds and had nine assists in the elimination game after which the interviews were conducted. In a conversation two days later, Thomas elaborated on his point: "When Bird makes a great play, it's due to his thinking, and his work habits. It's all planned out by him. It's not the case for blacks. All we do is run and jump. We never practice or give a thought to how we play. It's like I came dribbling out of my mother's womb."[16] Indeed, Bird was often presented as a white savior. The problem with that narrative was that Bird *and* Johnson both saved the league, neither of them did it on his own. Thomas apologized following the public backlash he received, and the league flew him to Los Angeles so that he and Bird could have a joint press conference, even though Bird himself, always weary of the media attention, was unmoved by the comments. He was in the middle of the finals series against the Lakers and would much rather concentrate on that than discuss something he did not care much about in the first place.[17]

Bird's approach to the sport was simple: he just wanted to play basketball, make important shots and go home. Bill Walton, one of the most innovative centers in the history of the league, and Bird's teammate on the 1986 championship team, said that Bird was only happy three times in his life—after winning each of his three NBA championships.[18] Bird dedicated his first title to Indiana State University in Terra Haute, his college team which lost to Magic Johnson and Michigan State in the NCAA 1979 championship game, sparking a rivalry that would last for over a decade. Even though they played different positions and were very different as players, Johnson and Bird saved the NBA by keeping their teams competitive through the '80s. The Celtics and Lakers rivalry already had some history, dating back to the 1959 NBA Finals. Before their arrival to the NBA, their teams met in the finals seven times, with the Celtics emerging as winners in all of those confrontations. Because Bird and Johnson were so different—not only from each other, but also from all the players that came before them—and because they led teams from opposite coasts, they were vital cogs in the league's marketing machine.

Unlike Johnson, Bird did not celebrate much during games, as if the sport did not bring him joy. He occasionally blew kisses or pumped his fist, but that was as expressive as he got. However, he took great pride in his game, constantly adding new elements to his repertoire every offseason. Back home in Indiana, Bird trained on his own, free from all distractions—and for him almost everything not connected to basketball was a distraction. He practiced so much that he became extremely confident in his abilities, and started to make guarantees and challenges for himself, as if only to see if he was going to meet them.

When it comes to Bird's trash talking, it is worthy of a book of its own, so here I highlight only three examples of his boastful statements, one now and two later in the book, while discussing his performances in the 3-Point Contest. In a special episode of the NBA.tv talk-show *Open Court*, in which NBA legends discuss various issues concerning basketball, Kevin McHale talked about one particular game in Phoenix (February 26, 1983), during which Bird had a terrible fourth quarter, yet still demanded the last shot of the game. Instead of taking the game to overtime with a rather safe play for team center, Robert Parrish, with one second left on the shot clock, Bird decided to take a three-pointer. Before the play, Bird walked by the Suns' bench and said to the reserves that he was going to make a three-point shot so that everybody could just go home. As Cedric Maxwell inbounded the ball, Bird was able to shake off his defender, catch the ball near the sideline with his back to the basket, turn around on one leg and release it before the buzzer. After the ball went through the net, Bird raised his hands in the air, then pointed at the Suns' players sitting on the bench and said: "I told you so."[19]

Another memorable long-distance shot made by Bird was the three-pointer in the "300 Point Game," as it is now remembered, played on March 15, 1992, against the Blazers. The 35-year-old Bird had 49 points, 14 assists and 12 rebounds in the Celtics' double overtime win. He took the game to overtime with an improbable three-point shot, closely guarded by Clyde Drexler, scoring with a spin move behind the three-point line. The Blazers protested that Bird was over the line, but he made the off-balance shot count and the Celtics ultimately won the game, 152–148.

The most incredible three-point clutch performance of his career came in a road game against the Bullets on November 7, 1987. First, with four seconds left on the shot clock, Bird forced overtime with the score tied at 119. With two seconds left in the first overtime, he missed a three and the game was still tied. In the second overtime, with 24 seconds remaining, he once again shot for three, made the shot, but before the ball was inbounded coach K.C. Jones had called for a timeout so the shot did not count. The same situation occurred during the final play, with one second left, as Bird took a turnaround three near the sideline, only this time nobody called the timeout, the shot went in and the Celtics won, 140–139. "I'm glad [Bird] didn't hear me"—Jones said after the game, revealing that he actually wanted to call another timeout.[20] Later during the same season, on February 12, 1988, in a game against the Mavericks, with his team down 102–104, Bird hit a running three, leaving four seconds left on the clock. The home team failed to score and the Celtics won.

The most memorable shooting performance of Bird's career came three years earlier, on March 12, 1985, against the Atlanta Hawks. The game was played in New Orleans due to a deal the Hawks' owner had with a local promoter. Various players said that they considered that game an exhibition, with the crowd consisting mostly of people who came to see the Celtics rather than the Hawks. Bird scored just one of four three-point shots, but was 21 of 32 for two, with a 61.1 shooting percentage for the game. Bird scored 60 points that night, but he does not remember the game too fondly. In his autobiography he wrote: "I wouldn't consider it one of my great games. It was just a freaky fun thing."[21] Nine days earlier, Kevin McHale scored 56 points against the Detroit Pistons but left the game early, which infuriated Bird, who said: "He should have stayed in there. Should have got 60."[22] McHale beat the Celtics' all-time scoring record of 53 points scored in one game set by Bird during the 1983–84 season. After the game, Bird jokingly proclaimed that he would quickly beat it. At halftime Bird had 23 points, but he instructed his teammates to just give him the ball because the Hawks were not guarding him properly. As he was draining shot after shot even the players from Atlanta eventually started laughing, celebrating and falling off the bench.

The first three 3-Point Contests (1986–1988) organized by the NBA played a great part in cementing Bird's legacy as a shooter. He provides a very detailed retelling of his success in the competitions in *Drive*. Bird describes them with great seriousness, stressing how important it was for him to win even though other former players, for example Walt Frazier, point to the first slam dunk and 3-Point Contests as the beginning of the end of hard-fought All-Star Games, which would eventually turn into scoring exhibitions with very little defense.[23] Bird was the biggest name in the first contest, which also featured Dale Ellis, Craig Hodges and

Larry Bird won the first three Three-Point Contests and was the first NBA player to make the three-pointer relevant (1987).

Leon Wood. It was Wood, an NBA journeyman who played for six teams during his six seasons in the league, that Bird considered to be his biggest rival that night.

Bird got into some mind games in the locker room before the contest, first talking about the slickness of the colorful moneyballs—the red, white and blue ABA-style balls worth two points—eventually posing the now famous question: "who's going to get second place today?"[24] He repeated the line before the third contest and was so confident about emerging victorious that he participated in it without taking off his warm-up jacket. During the second competition his elbow was hurting so he avoided any boastful statements, yet he still won. That contest was decided by two points, with Detlef Schrempf (the first non-American player to participate in the contest), Bird's opponent in the final round, missing the last moneyball which could have tied the score.

What is forgotten and what somewhat tarnishes Bird's legacy is that he gave the contest one more try, in 1990. He scored just 12 points in the first round, outscored by his opponent on the other side of the court, Craig Ehlo, by two points. Ehlo is universally associated with one play—being on the wrong side of "The Shot," an iconic move by Michael Jordan, who scored over Ehlo in the last play of an elimination game against the Cavaliers in the first round of the 1989 playoffs. Ehlo tried to block Jordan and, after failing, fell to the floor in defeat. Known as "Mr. Everything," Ehlo was a lockdown defender and a competent three-point shooter on the Cleveland team that also featured Mark Price, one of the best pure shooters in league history, and Steve Kerr, who would join the Cavs in the 1989 offseason. Ehlo was actually the reason that particular game against the Bulls was so close in the first place, since he not only led his team with 24 points, but also scored a layup that set the score at 100 to 99 with three seconds left. The best game of his career was spoiled by one mistake. Instead of being remembered as the man who beat Larry Bird at his game, it is his failure to stop Jordan's shot that comes to mind upon hearing Ehlo's name.

The winner of the 1990 contest was Jordan's teammate, Craig Hodges, who would go on to appear in all of the first eight contests, getting an invitation to the last one despite being out of the league. Hodges' career has greatly suffered due to his political views. He was a follower of Muslim minister Louis Farrakhan and was traded by his second NBA team, the

Milwaukee Bucks, to the Suns, after attending his rally. Before the 1991 3-Point Contest, some league officials voiced their concerns about inviting Hodges to participate—as is customary of the winner of the previous contest—because he might have said something "unpatriotic" regarding the Persian Gulf War. Sam Smith adds that "there was talk of asking Hodges not to mention Allah in any postgame speech if he won."[25] Before that year's NBA Finals, Hodges urged Jordan and Magic Johnson to sit out the opening game of the series to point to racism and inequality, which moved to the forefront of social issues in the country at the time. Both players declined.[26] Hodges, however, did not allow his politics to influence his behavior as a teammate. The Bulls' coach Phil Jackson appreciated him as a locker room presence and a "glue guy" so much that he employed Hodges as an assistant on his first two Los Angeles Lakers championship teams.

In the season he played on the Bucks and the Suns (1987–88), Hodges averaged a career-high 49.1 percent from three, which was a league record at the time. That record was beaten just a season later by Jon Sundvold of the Miami Heat, who made 48 of his 92 attempts, which gave him a 52.1 percent efficiency. Sundvold participated in the 3-Point Contest twice and ended his career shooting 39.2 percent from long distance. He was out of the league in 1991, while Hodges was gone a season later, released by the Bulls in June 1992, a few days after criticizing Jordan for not taking the stand against the racial injustice which led to the L.A. Riots. During the same post-game interview, Hodges criticized the NBA for not employing enough African American head coaches, as only two of them were black at that time.[27] Despite being only 31 years old, Hodges could not find another team willing to sign him, and in 1996 he filed a lawsuit against the league, accusing it of blackballing him because of his political views.

Hodges won the 3-Point Contests in 1990, 1991 and 1992, while Bird's last triumph came in 1988. The 1989 contest was won by Dale Ellis, another exceptional three-point shooter, the only player next to Hodges who has participated in all contests up to that point, and appeared in seven overall throughout his 17 seasons in the NBA. The man who Bird called "the new 'The Three-point King'" after he won the contest while Bird was injured and unable to participate.[28] Ellis not only became the first player other than Larry Legend to win the competition, but, more importantly, he was the first to make 1,000 career three-point shots. He was the league career leader in three-pointers made since April 17, 1989, when he made his 456th shot to pass Larry Bird for the top spot. In the 1997–98 season, Reggie Miller and Ellis were at one point tied at 1,561, but the Pacer eventually surpassed Ellis and was the three-point shot leader in makes up until the 2010–11 season.

During his first three years in the league, however, Ellis did not see much playing time, as he was behind either Mark Aguirre or Rolando Blackman in the Mavericks' rotation. Aguirre and Blackman were the starting small forward and shooting guard, respectively, on the Dallas team that drafted Ellis with the ninth pick in 1983. Both men were great scorers who rarely depended on the three-point shot, and Ellis was forced to play the same way. Even though he shot well from behind the three-point line, he was expected to stay in the post and battle with much taller and stronger players. While on the Mavericks, Ellis made just 117 threes in three seasons, a number he would eclipse in seven single seasons. Here it is worth pointing out that since the NCAA did not implement the three-point line until 1986, Ellis, like most of the players from that era (apart from those playing in the ABA), had to learn to shoot from long distance as a pro. During the four years Ellis spent at the University of Tennessee, he was mostly an inside scorer.

In his first season on the Sonics, Ellis attempted league-leading 240 three-pointers, just 61 less than his total from the three years in Dallas. His scoring average almost quadrupled—from 7.1 to 24.9 points per game—and he was voted Most Improved Player for the 1986–87 season. Seattle was supposed to be one of the worst teams in the league, yet it made the playoffs. Ellis owed his transformation to Sonics' head coach Bernie Bickerstaff, who recognized his player's strengths and moved him to the backcourt. With the Sonics frontcourt occupied by forwards Xavier McDaniel and Tom Chambers, Ellis was allowed to play as a shooting guard, which meant he was allowed to stay behind the three-point line and shoot. Not much of a dribbler, Ellis would rely on his teammates to find him whenever he was open. He averaged at least 23.5 points per game for four seasons in a row on the Sonics.

A foot injury forced Ellis to miss the first 17 games of the 1990–91 season. That and a coaching change contributed to Ellis being unable to regain his position in Seattle. The team was moving in a different direction, as signified by the arrival of the very talented but also very raw point guard-power forward duo of Gary Payton and Shawn Kemp. Ellis' point average dipped to 15 and he took around five shots per game less than the previous season. He was traded mid-season to the Milwaukee Bucks for Ricky Pierce. In his first season as a Sonic, Ellis was able to take his new team to the Western Conference Finals. In the first round of the play-offs, the team eliminated the second-seeded Mavericks in four games, and then the Houston Rockets in six. Seattle was not able to find much playoff success in the following years and, after failing to make the postseason in 1990, Bickerstaff was replaced by K.C. Jones. While playing for the Sonics, Ellis made the Third All-NBA Team in 1988–89 and appeared in his only All-Star Game in 1989, during which he scored 27 points.

More importantly, in 1989 he won his only 3-Point Contest. During that season, Ellis set his career highs in points scored in a single game with 53 and three-point percentage with 47.8. He was the league leader in three-point percentage only once, nine years later, as a 37-year-old reserve for the Sonics (1997–98). The year 1998 was also the last time he participated in the 3-Point Contest. After his first stint with the Sonics, Ellis played for the Bucks, the Spurs and the Nuggets. He made history on March 19, 1994, by becoming the first player ever to make 1,000 three-point shots in his career. The arena in San Antonio erupted, as this was quite an achievement, especially for a former post-up player, who learned how to play basketball before the three-point line was even introduced. He retired at age 39, with a total of 1,719 threes made on 40.3 percent accuracy.

By February 6, 1988, Ellis had already found his form when it came to shooting from long distance. Up until that point of the season, he was making 42.6 percent of his three-point attempts, averaging 3.3 shots from long distance per game. His biggest rival, Bird, was making 38.1 percent of his attempts, yet it was the Celtic who was better than Ellis in the first round, although by just one point. With 17 and 16 respectively, the players were placed in the middle of the four best opening scorers, as Detlef Schrempf barely made the second round with 15, edging out Mark Price and Bird's teammate Danny Ainge by just one point.

During that season, Danny Ainge set the league record with 15 games in a row with at least one three-pointer made. Ainge was Bird's teammate, drafted by the Celtics in the second round of the 1981 NBA draft. He worked his way up to the starting lineup and won two championships alongside Bird as the starting shooting guard. Despite making the All-Star team in 1987, two years later Ainge was shipped to Sacramento alongside Brad Lohaus, in exchange for Joe Kleine and Ed Pinckney. It was a move intended to rejuvenate the Celtics second unit, as the starting frontcourt of Robert Parrish and McHale was getting older, and in need of relief. Ainge played for the Kings, the Blazers and the Suns, ending his career shooting 37.8 percent from three.

The winner of the first round was Byron Scott of the Lakers with 19 points. This was the second (and last) appearance by Scott in the contest and by far his best—he managed to score just nine points a year before. In a way Scott was Ainge's counterpart, as he was the starting shooting guard on the Lakers and the team's leading three-point specialist. Selected with the fourth pick in the 1983 draft by the Clippers, Scott joined the Lakers via draft day trade and immediately became a member of the starting lineup. Scott won three NBA championships but no individual accolades apart from making the All-Rookie First Team. Throughout his career he made 37 percent of his three-point shots. Whereas Ainge would enjoy great success as the general manager of the Celtics, leading the team to its only championship in the 21st century, as well as keeping it competitive for numerous seasons, Scott became the worst coach in Lakers history, finishing his tenure with 38 wins over the course of two full seasons, including a franchise-worst 17–65 record in 2015–16.

In the second round of the 1988 contest, Bird exploded with 23 points while Ellis beat out Scott 12 to 11. Scott had nine points and ten shots left, but made only two. In the final round, Ellis went first and made 15. When it was Bird's turn to shoot, he started really slow, missing his first two shots. With 25 seconds to go and just seven points, it seemed unlikely that Bird would catch fire like he did, especially after making just one shot from the third rack. As all of the five balls from the fourth rack were finding their target, Ainge was counting each make down with excitement. Bird would then miss two first shots from the last rack, which left him with just three balls—exactly enough to win. After releasing the moneyball after the two makes, Bird raised his hand, index finger pointing triumphantly into the air, even before it went through the net. With that performance and that reaction, he created what would become another memorable moment in the career of one of the greatest shooters in league history.

March 23, 1991

Michael Adams Scores 54 Points with Particularly Ugly Shots

Michael Adams was never supposed to make it to the NBA, let alone become an All-Star, due to his height, as he was deemed too small to become a professional basketball player. The 5'8" high school player—who would eventually grow to be 5'10"—flew under the radar while playing at Hartford Public High and was recruited by only one school, Boston College. Playing college basketball before the three-point line was even implemented in the NCAA, he was able to average 13.9 points and four assists a game in a highly competitive Big East Conference. The school eventually retired his number. His coach, Gary Williams, said of Adams: "Michael has taught me a lot. In recruiting, I don't label players as too small or too slow anymore. I try to be more objective. It's hard to measure a player's heart when he's being recruited."[1] Most NBA coaches did not think that way, as the trend was still to draft height over talent, and Adams was selected in the third round of the 1985 draft, with the 66th overall pick by the Kings, who were about to play their first year in Sacramento. The previous season the team missed the playoffs, one of three teams in the West to post a 31–51 record. They had a solid backcourt in Reggie Theus and Larry Drew, which limited Adams' prospects of playing a considerable role on the roster. He appeared in just 18 games and played a total of 139 minutes.

Sixteen years later, the Kings were in a similar situation—they had a bad team and a 5'9" point guard selected very low in the draft, only this one actually got a chance to play, and in a couple of years, on a different team, blossomed into one of the best players in the league, at least for a while. Isaiah Thomas, just like Adams, would go on to play for the Kings, the Bullets/Wizards and the Nuggets (among others), but he would enjoy his best years while playing for the Boston Celtics. The Kings selected Thomas with the last pick of the 2011 draft, yet by the end of the season he was able to become a starter over the player who was actually supposed to be the team's point guard of the future.

The Kings already had their playmaker in Tyreke Evans, who would play as a shooting guard/small forward and bring the ball upcourt. Evans was one year removed from being selected the 2010 Rookie of the Year. He was not a long-distance scorer though, and the team was in desperate need of one, as the league was already becoming more shooter friendly. The Kings thought that they had solved that problem by acquiring the tenth pick in the 2011 draft, Jimmer Fredette, from the Milwaukee Bucks on draft night.

During his senior year at BYU, Fredette led the NCAA in scoring with 28.9 points per game (39.4 percent from three) and was selected national college player of the year. The fact that Fredette fell to the tenth spot in the draft was already a sign that the teams were not sold on "Jimmer Mania"—a belief that he was "the best scorer in the world," as expressed in a tweet by Kevin Durant during Fredette's last season at BYU. The problem with Fredette's game after he turned pro was that he could not get off as many good shots against much tougher and quicker defenders, and his style did not translate well onto the courts of the NBA, as it was just too one-dimensional. The player was struggling, averaging just 7.6 points per game, but he still managed to make a respectable 36.1 percent of his three-pointers. Two seasons later he made 49.3 percent of his threes, but because he was not showing any signs of progress, the Kings bought out his contract. From then on, Fredette has been somewhat stuck in basketball purgatory, performing greatly in inferior leagues, like the D–League and the Chinese Basketball Association (at one point scoring 75 points in a single game) but failing to make an impact in the NBA, despite several attempts.

Thomas, on the other hand, truly blossomed, in no small part due to his three-point shooting. The 2016–17 season was by far the best by any player of Thomas' height (5'9"). With 28.9 points per game and a 37.9 three-point percentage, Thomas made the All-NBA Second Team as a member of the Boston Celtics. He set the franchise record for most consecutive games with at least one three-pointer made with fifty games.

More importantly, despite a bad hip, which would eventually eliminate him from playoff contention, and fighting through personal problems— as his sister passed away in a car crash when his team was facing the Bulls in the first round of the playoffs—Thomas turned up his scoring, and largely due to his individual heroics, the Celtics reached the Eastern Conference Finals. Because of his ability to score in crunch time he earned the nickname "King in the Fourth," a nod to the "King in the North" from the *Game of Thrones* television series. That magical playoff run remains the high point of Thomas' career.

Before Thomas, Adams was the second-best player officially listed below 6'0" to ever play in the NBA, others in the top five being Terrell Brandon, Damon Stoudamire, and Calvin Murphy. Stoudamire was the first player ever selected by the Toronto Raptors in the NBA draft and earned Rookie of the Year honors in the 1995–96 season, setting a single-season record for three-pointers made by a first-year player with 133. Later on, he was the point guard of a stacked Trail Blazers team with Rasheed Wallace, Arvydas Sabonis, Scottie Pippen and Detlef Schrempf, that almost eliminated the Los Angeles Lakers from the 2000 Western Conference Finals, before collapsing during the final quarter.

Brandon made two All-Star teams as a member of the Cleveland Cavaliers and one time appeared on the cover of *Sports Illustrated* with the tagline: "The Best Point Guard in the NBA," even though in the story, Richard Hoffer focused mostly on how good of a teammate and person Brandon was.[2] The player was not able to realize his full potential due to injuries but was a positive influence, when healthy, on the Cavs, the Bucks and the Timberwolves. His development was the reason why the Cavaliers moved on from franchise point guard Mark Price, and for the three seasons he was the starter in Cleveland, Brandon averaged 17.5 points and 6.1 assists per game.

The number one spot among players below 6'0" belongs to Calvin Murphy of the Houston Rockets, who began his career when the team still played in San Diego. Active from 1970 to 1983, Murphy ended his career with averages of 17.9 points and 4.4 assists, making 89.2 percent of his free throws. He played with the three-point line for only four seasons and only twice managed to average over 20 percent from long distance. Throughout his career Murphy earned only one All-Star nod, which should position him lower than Thomas or Adams, but due to longevity and the fact that he was able to contribute so greatly despite not having the same free-dom of movement as the players that came after him, Murphy is still the best short player in NBA history. He is the only one of the group who is a member of the Hall of Fame and has his number retired by an NBA team.

Murphy did not need the three-point line to enjoy a productive NBA career, while Adams was exactly the player the three-point line was created for. He really blossomed on a team which gave him the freedom to just shoot from long range. Adams set an NBA record by making a three-pointer in 79 consecutive games (January 28, 1988–January 23, 1989) as a member of the Denver Nuggets. During the last game of his impressive streak he attempted seven long-distance shots, made none and finished with just eight points, whereas during this improbable series he went 193 of 530 from three. After the game he said: "I had a number of shots at continuing the streak, but it just wasn't there tonight. It had to end some time. I'm just glad I was able to enjoy something like this."[3]

His record was beaten by another player under 6'0", the 5'11" Dana Barros, who made at least one three-pointer in 89 consecutive games (December 23, 1994–January 10, 1996). Barros was also a one time All-Star, in 1995, which turned out to be the best season of his career. His performance also earned him the title of the NBA's Most Improved Player. As a member of the Sixers, he exploded for one season, noting career highs in points (20.6), assists (7.5), steals (1.8) and rebounds (3.3). He never again came close to those averages and ended his career with 41.1 percent from three. Interestingly, just like Adams, Barros attended Boston College and the university also retired his number. Unlike Adams though, Barros was selected in the first round of the draft and immediately became a part of the rotation of the Seattle SuperSonics, whereas Adams was waived by his first NBA team and signed with the Washington Bullets.

On the Bullets, Adams had a solid season as a reserve, having com-parable numbers to the starter, Ennis Whatley, while playing just four minutes less. Still, he was traded during the summer with Jay Vincent for Darrell Walker and Mark Alarie. When he returned to the Bullets after four seasons in Denver, in 1991, he said: "That sort of thing stays in the back of your mind. All I've had to do my first three or four years in the league is prove people wrong again and again, just to try to prove to peo-ple that I can play. I think that after this year people realized that I can play."[4]

That was actually a humble assessment of his performance during the 1990–91 season. He ended his last season on the Nuggets averaging 26.5 points, 10.5 assists, 3.9 rebounds and 2.2 steals a game, and did not even make the All-NBA team. He was sixth overall in points, third overall in assists and seventh overall in steals per game, yet Magic Johnson, Kevin Johnson and John Stockton were selected over him. His omission had partially to do with pure name recognition—all three point guards were legitimate NBA superstars at the time. Statistically only KJ had a similar season to Adams, but all three players led their teams to the playoffs, while the Nuggets were dead last in the league with just 20 wins. The fact of the matter was that the team from Colorado had a really bad roster after it lost three of its crucial figures: small forward Alex English, shooting guard Fat Lever and coach Doug Moe.

Moe left the team after ten seasons at the helm, fired by Bernie Bickerstaff just two months after he took office as general manager. Under Moe the Nuggets made the playoffs in all seasons but his first, which was a remarkable streak in itself. He was the man responsible for releasing the offensive potential of English and Lever, and turning them into legitimate All-Stars during his tenure. Adams played some part in their development as well, as it was his acquisition and introduction to the starting lineup that allowed Lever to play as a shooting guard. Before, he was struggling as a point guard—a role that did not particularly fit his abilities.

Moe's Nuggets played a quick brand of basketball, which was based on motion and separation. The players were supposed to run around as much as possible and pass the ball a lot, tiring individual defenders, as zone defense was illegal back then. Their style was chaotic and completely unorganized, which made it impossible to decipher. It was all about understanding your teammates, knowing their strengths and providing them with the best chance possible at scoring. Moe's team led the NBA in scoring for six out of the ten seasons he was in charge in Denver.

Moe was always a players' coach, one that catered to their strengths and completely trusted them on offense. A North Carolina alum, Moe played for coach Dean Smith, who was synonymous with organized, team-first basketball. His teammate on that Tar Heels team was Larry Brown, another future NBA coach, who also grew up with Moe in Brooklyn. The two would go on to play together in the ABA as well. Bob Bass, an ABA coach, said: "the ABA was made for Doug and Larry. It was a wide-open league, a league that ran the fast break and didn't have a lot of big men clogging the middle."[5] Brown was considered too small for the NBA, being 5'9", while the 6'5" Moe was banned by the league due to his alleged connection to a 1961 point-shaving scandal. They formed a great on-court partnership, even though their basketball philosophies were very different even as players—Brown was a tactician, Moe just wanted to play basketball.

Moe got his first head coaching job in San Antonio in 1976, as he was named the team's first NBA coach after the NBA-ABA merger. Since the beginning, his plays were impossible to crack by the opposition: "Nobody knew what the hell we were doing. Other coaches were diagramming our plays on the blackboard, and we weren't running any."[6] Moe was rarely given respect by his peers, especially those obsessed with tactics. He was known for being frank and honest, once proclaiming before a series against the Lakers that his team stood no chance against Pat Riley's team.[7] Other coaches also did not appreciate that he got such great results by presumably not working that hard. His team reached the Western Conference Finals in 1985 and he was selected the 1988 Coach of the Year. His system was called simply "the passing game" and that was the best way to characterize it. His practices were all about setting screens, distributing the ball and cutting toward the basket. The system worked with the right players—quick, athletic shooters and/or passers, such as Adams, English or Lever.

The last two struck a great understanding during their time in Denver. In 1987, English even petitioned the league to give Lever his place on the All-Star team. After falling out with Moe during the 1989–90 season, the 36-year-old English was signed by the Mavericks on August 15, 1990, Lever had been traded there two months earlier. Dallas was not a good fit for both players, as Lever played in just four games that season, whereas English averaged less than ten points for the first time in 13 years. However, it was still better than staying in Denver, which deteriorated into chaos under new ownership, changing managers three times during the span of two months, and completely squandering the teams' chances to improve the roster at the trade deadline. Despite the turmoil, Moe wanted to stay, but was fired, leaving the team along with its best players. Adams thought management broke up the team too soon and considered the off-season moves unfair to the players.[8] On November 7, 2002, the Nuggets honored the coach by retiring the number 432—the amount of games he won in Denver.

English played for the Nuggets for ten and a half seasons, averaging 25.9 points per game. It was only during his last season there that his average dropped below 21 points. In the 1983–84 season, English led the league in scoring with 28.4 points per game, shooting primarily from mid-range and making only two three-point shots throughout the whole season. Moe described English as a player who "couldn't dribble, couldn't pass, couldn't do a lot of things, yet was terrific."[9] One thing English knew how to do was shoot. He was the first player in league history to score over 2,000 points for eight straight seasons. He had a peculiar shooting motion, stretching out his whole body, as if it were a board, taking his time, and when it seemed that he was holding the ball for too long, he would release it. While it was not the most eye-pleasing of shooting techniques, it was still rather conventional when compared to the way Michael Adams used to score, mostly because Adams was smaller than English, yet shot from a longer distance, so needed more strength to score.

David Astramskas very vividly and accurately describes Adams' shooting technique as "the ugliest golden shot ever" and the "herky-jerky push shot."[10] When pulling up from long distance, Adams would lift the ball up with both hands until it was in front of his face, and then he would push it out with his right, the left already falling back, since it was no longer necessary. He would also often make the shot on the run, as he found it hard to get open during set plays: "when I'm crossing half court, I'll look up for it, but not after that. Seven out of 10 times, I'll be within half a foot of the line just on feel."[11] Adams' name comes up whenever the ugliest or weirdest shooting techniques are discussed, alongside those of Shawn Marion or Kevin Martin, among others. As different as the three players were, they are all remembered mostly due to their uncommon shooting motions, which would not have even been worth remembering if they were not so efficient in the first place.

Shawn Marion was one of the players who ushered in the small-ball era in the 21st century, while playing for the Phoenix Suns next to Steve Nash. Marion was just 6'7" yet capable of playing both forward positions. He grabbed nine rebounds per game in eight consecutive seasons, and finished his career with averages of 15.2 points and 8.7 rebounds. He also made 33.1 percent of his three-point shots, releasing the ball as it was in front of his face, with both arms bent. Far from textbook perfect, the form was very quick, therefore hard to defend whenever Marion found himself one step in front of his defender. He won the 2011 NBA championship as a member of the Dallas Mavericks.

Kevin Martin, on the other hand, was a pure scorer, averaging at least 20 points a game in 5 of his 12 seasons in the league. At one point in his career, he successfully replaced future MVP, James Harden, on the Oklahoma City Thunder, after being traded for him from the Rockets. The three-pointer was a vital part of his game—Martin ended his career with a 38.4 percentage from deep and 1,141 three-pointers made. Whenever shooting from outside the paint, Martin would bend his elbows and keep the ball in front of his face, then strengthen his arms and push it out with a flick of the wrist.

Another player whose shooting form was surprisingly efficient despite looking rather curious was Matt Bonner. He would shoot the ball almost solely with his right hand, the left was there just for the first phase of the shooting motion, adjusting the ball in a similar way that Adams' left did. The Red Rocket, as Bonner was affectionately called by the Spurs' fans due to his red hair, spent ten years in San Antonio as a stretch four, after playing for two years for the Raptors. Bonner's college team had made great use of his long-distance shooting—in his senior year at Florida he made 47.4 percent of his three-point shots. He ended his NBA career with two NBA championships (2007 and 2014), 797 three-pointers made on 41.4 percent efficiency and an undeniable reputation as the league's utmost sandwich hunter, running a blog about his visits to sandwich shops all over the United States.

While all the unorthodox shooters mentioned so far used to put the ball in front of their face before shooting, Michael Redd would catapult it into the air from behind his head. Redd lifted the ball over his head, bent his elbows and then released it as he was straightening them. He placed the ball in the middle of his head, which, by principle, a shooter should not do—the ball should be next to the head. That unofficial rule of jump shooting was taken to the extreme by Derek Fisher, who used to put the ball as much as possible to the left side of his head and push it out, with the right hand holding the ball from behind. His shot was unusually high arcing, but it worked for the 6'1" point guard, which was all that mattered, as was the case with all the other players mentioned in this chapter. Redd

Shawn Marion possessed a rather curious shooting technique, yet made about one-third of his three-point shot attempts during his career (2000).

ended his career with 1,045 three-pointers made, a 38-percentile shot from deep and a 2008 Olympic Gold Medal. Fisher won five NBA championships with the Lakers, while making 37.4 percent of his threes, and earning a reputation as a clutch shooter. The most important shot of his career was the two-pointer taken with 0.4 seconds left in Game Five of the 2004 Western Conference Semifinals against the Spurs. Tim Duncan had put the Spurs up 73–72, but with less than half a second left on the clock, Fisher was able to score a turnaround jumper over Manu Ginobili, and the Lakers took a 3–1 lead in the series, eliminating the reigning champions in the next game.

Regardless of their shooting form, all of the players mentioned above—as well as others, whose shooting techniques and careers were not analyzed here, like Tayshaun Prince or Josh Childress—profited extraordinarily from the possibilities provided by the introduction of the three-point line. Danny Ainge, then playing for the Suns, gave Adams as an example of the way the three-pointer allowed smaller players to dominate during a game: "Take Michael Adams in Denver. You can't give him the 3, but when you get up in his face, he goes by you like you're standing still."[12] Thanks to the three-point line, Adams became a much better player not only because of his shooting—the change in spacing allowed him to dominate other aspects of the game, and transform into one of the best passers in the league as well.

For 13 years, Adams was the shortest player in league history to record a triple-double, until Isaiah Thomas, then of the Sacramento Kings, recorded his on March 18, 2014. Thomas had 24 points, 11 rebounds and 10 assists in an overtime win against the Wizards. Adams' achievement was more impressive, as he not only ended the game with 45 points, 11 rebounds and 12 assists, leading his team to a victory over the New Jersey Nets on January 31, 1991, but he also did it all in regular time. Afterwards Adams said: "The triple-double is really something. I never even thought I'd get one. I really never thought I'd get one with rebounds."[13] The game was the sixth in an impressive streak of seven games during which Adams scored 27, 24, 31, 37, 41, 45 and 31 points, respectively. The streak ended one game before the All-Star Break, with the player not invited to Charlotte to participate in either the All-Star Game or the 3-Point Contest. He was snubbed during the selection of the team representing the Western Conference in favor of bigger names like Magic, KJ and Stockton, as well as Tim Hardaway of the Golden State Warriors and Terry Porter of the Portland Trail Blazers.

The 1990–91 season was the best of Adams' career and, interestingly, it was his first as a Nugget under a different coach than Moe. While it was obvious that, with the team in a transitional mode, he would be tasked with being its on-court leader now that English and Lever were gone, the Nuggets' style of play became a lot less efficient. Partially it was due to the lack of good players, but more so it was simply easier to prepare for their offensive schemes after the team appointed Paul Westhead as the next head coach. The creator of the "seven seconds or less" mantra urged his players to sprint into their designated spots and just shoot whenever given the opportunity. To Westhead it was all very simple: "The idea is to play ultrafast on offense and ultrafast on defense, so it becomes a double hit. And when it works, it's not like one and one is two. It's like one and one is seven."[14]

The flaw of the system was that it did not work on defense, the team just did not have the players able to physically keep up the same intensity on both ends of the floor. In consequence, the Nuggets ended the season with an NBA record of 130.7 allowed opponent points per game. The previous record was also held by the Nuggets, who under Moe allowed 125.95 points per game during the 1981–82 season, while also averaging 126.5 points per game, which was (and still is) an NBA record as well. Westhead's 1990–91 Nuggets led the league in points per game, with 119.9. They managed to win 20 games that season and improved their overall record during the next one by just four wins.

This slow progress marked the end of Westhead's tenure as head coach, but not the end of the fast-pace basketball philosophy being implemented in Denver—they were the first NBA team to take a chance on Mike D'Antoni, who would enjoy great success coaching the "run and gun era" Phoenix Suns with Marion, Steve Nash and Amar'e Stoudemire, as well as the ultimate three-point shooting team, the James Harden–led Houston Rockets. His stay in Denver was rather short though, as D'Antoni was fired after going 14–36 during the lockout-shortened 1999 NBA season. His failure pushed him to go against the grain—when working for the Nuggets he was still relying on post-up plays and slower pace.[15] Interestingly, these Nuggets would probably flourish playing the same way as D'Antoni's future teams, as on their roster they had solid shooters in

Nick Van Exel, Bryant Stith, and Chauncey Billups, as well as the athletic forward Antonio McDyess, who was capable of playing as center in a small-ball lineup.

Westhead, partially due to the lack of possibilities, put the ball in Adams' hands and organized the offense around the fast-paced point guard. Since one of the objectives of the system was to minimize passing, Adams' passes were usually the first and only ones used during a given play, which somewhat explains why he never came close to repeating his career-high in assists (10.5) after his sole season under Westhead. In the summer, Adams, undoubtedly the team's best player, was traded back to the Washington Bullets along with the 19th pick in the 1991 draft for the eighth pick. The Bullets owner, Abe Pollin, called trading away Adams one of the biggest mistakes of his career and expressed great enthusiasm after getting him back.[16]

The Nuggets parted ways with Adams because they had a younger, presumably better point guard in Chris Jackson, the third pick in the 1990 NBA draft. Jackson was paid twice as much as Adams despite coming off the bench, which was the reason why Adams demanded more money in free agency. His demands made sense, since he was the one carrying the 1990–91 Nuggets on his back, albeit with poor results. Bickerstaff, however, decided to trade him and keep Jackson. The GM's belief in Jackson was so high that, despite the player never performing a dunk in an actual NBA game, he participated in the 1993 Dunk Contest based on his performance on a tape which Bickerstaff had sent to league officials. Jackson finished sixth out of seven contestants.

At age 17, Jackson was diagnosed with Tourette syndrome and in college appeared in public service announcements for the Tourette Syndrome Association. At 21, he converted to Islam and two years later, in 1993, legally changed his name to Mahmoud Abdul-Rauf. At times, because of religious fasting, his playing weight fell to 140 pounds, yet he continued to play, which shows enormous strength of character. He was an important element of the Denver Nuggets team that eliminated the Sonics in the first round of the 1994 NBA Playoffs. The Nuggets were the first eight seed in playoff history to eliminate the team with the best record in the conference.

The Nuggets traded Abdul-Rauf in the summer of 1996 for Sarunas Marčiulionis and a second-round pick to the Kings—a modest return for the team leader in points (19.2) and assists (6.8) per game, but somewhat justified when taking into consideration Abdul-Rauf's rather unjustified reputation as a troublemaker. A couple of months earlier, before a game that took place in March of 1996, Abdul-Rauf refused to stand during the national anthem. He would eventually work out a compromise with the league, even though such should not have been necessary, as there was no code of conduct regarding the player's stance during the national anthem. Instead of sitting down, Abdul-Rauf would stand with his hands open and pray. He played for two seasons in Sacramento and, after a while, returned to the NBA from Europe for a brief stint on the Grizzlies, but was out of the league by the age of 32.

Adams retired when he was one year older than Abdul-Rauf, after appearing in just 50 games over the course of two seasons for the Charlotte Hornets. He was traded there by the Bullets in the 1994 offseason for two second-round picks, even though he was the team's starting point guard for three years. While Adams never managed to dominate statistically in Washington like he did in Denver, he was voted to his first and only All-Star Game in his first season after his return there. He scored nine points and had four steals in the game. While the selection was well deserved, it seems that the snub the year before motivated Adams to elevate his game even more.

For years, Adams had to hear accusations of being too small and too out of control. He was the last one selected during local pickup games. The scholarship from Boston College only came his way because Patrick Ewing decided on Georgetown and the school had an extra spot on the roster.[17] During the 1990–91 season, he was supposed to sit on the Nuggets' bench behind Jackson, yet despite all of the adversities he was not only a starter, but had one of the best individual seasons by a point guard in the modern-day NBA. During the March 23, 1991, home game against the Bucks, Adams scored a career-high 54 points, which would also turn out to be the most by any player during that season.

At the start of the game, the Nuggets were on a losing streak, unable to win for the past five games in a row. Adams, already renowned for his long-distance shooting, was the holder of the then–league record 15 three-point attempts in a single game. He beat that record that night, attempting 16 threes and converting seven of them. On the other side of the court was Dale Ellis, another great shooter, who joined the Bucks

55

in a mid-season trade from the Sonics. Ellis played for 37 minutes and scored a team-high 25 points, but only six of those came from threes. His whole team went 9 for 15 from three, while the Nuggets made 10 of their 22 long-distance shots. Adams had an incredible second half, making four threes in a row, but that was not enough to win the game, as Jay Humphries, a career 29.7 percent shooter from long distance, made a three-pointer to take the game to overtime with 0.4 seconds left. The Nuggets failed to convey a shot and lost in overtime, 136–140.

The way Adams made use of the three-point line, both as an occasion to shoot from long range and to lure out defenders to get past them with a quick dribble, serves as proof that players considered small by NBA standards were able to face off against much taller opponents, precisely because of the introduction of the line. Not only by shooting from behind it, but more so by stretching the court, baiting rebounders away from the basket, and being able to grab longer rebounds themselves, as these are more about quickness, positioning and agility than just height. Seeing the way such players were able to impact games, coaches had no choice but to adjust their playbooks and use their basketball skills to their team's advantage, no matter how unorthodox their shooting techniques were. If the shots went in and the team won, that was enough for them to earn their place in the league.

June 3, 1992

Michael Jordan Shrugs His Way
to Another Memorable Performance

Michael Jordan was selected with the third pick in the 1984 NBA draft, behind Akeem Olajuwon,[1] and Sam Bowie. The first selection in that draft was understandable, as Olajuwon, picked by the Houston Rockets, was a college superstar at the University of Houston, taking the Cougars to the NCAA championship game for two years in a row. Apart from being a homestate hero, he was also a center, a position which was in high demand since the beginnings of basketball. In the second year, the Nigerian was the lone superstar on his college team, as Clyde Drexler, the Cougars' shooting guard, entered the NBA draft in 1983 and was selected with the 14th pick by the Portland Trail Blazers. The Rockets had the first selection in that year's draft as well and they picked Ralph Sampson, who, like Olajuwon, was a center. On the 1984 draft day, the Rockets were actually approached by the Blazers about a trade that would send Drexler and the 1984 second pick to Houston in exchange for Sampson, who was the reigning Rookie of the Year, averaging 21 points, 11.1 rebounds and 2.4 blocks during his first year in the NBA. Drexler, by comparison, was mostly a bench player, starting just 3 games out of 82 and averaging a measly (by his future standards) 7.7 points per game.

The Blazers thought that the Rockets would agree to the deal because Olajuwon and Drexler together had headlined "Phi Slama Jama," a nickname for the Houston Cougars in the early 1980s due to the team's explosive and athletic style of play, filled with dunks and fast breaks. As promising as that reunion might have been, Drexler was not a legitimate NBA star yet, while Sampson was considered a once-in-a-generation talent. With the selection of Olajuwon, the Rockets strongly believed that they were building a team for the future, one able to start two centers at the same time, hence dominating the most important element of the court—the paint. In a way, their strategy shows how basketball was played in those days—inside the painted area—despite the three-point line already being present in the NBA for four seasons. The general manager of the team, Ray Patterson, was right in calling them "a new phenomenon,"[2] and they inspired other successful big man duos, like Tim Duncan and David Robinson, and Pau Gasol and Andrew Bynum.

While Wilt Chamberlain and Nate Thurmond were the first NBA duo of centers playing alongside each other, Olajuwon and Sampson were the first tandem to be referred to as "the Twin Towers." Coached by Bill Fitch, who won his first NBA title with the Celtics in 1981 and left the team on May 27, 1983, only to sign with the Rockets four days later, the Rockets made it to the NBA Finals in 1986, but fell to Fitch's former team, the Celtics. In the next season, Sampson injured his left knee and rushed his rehab, which pretty much destroyed his career. He would never be the same player again, while the Rockets would have to wait eight years for their next title shot.

The team's decision to not trade Sampson for Drexler and the second pick seemed savvy at the time, but in the long run the Rockets could have landed three NBA Hall of Famers—Sampson made the Hall of Fame for his illustrious college career—on their roster, as Michael Jordan, Charles Barkley and John Stockton were still available for selection, and one of them would probably join Olajuwon and Drexler. Drexler's success in the NBA seemed unlikely at first, but in his second season he became a regular starter for the Blazers. The fact that the team from Oregon did not pick Jordan, but settled on Sam Bowie from Kentucky did not have much to do with Drexler, but everything to do with Bowie still being available. Jordan was regarded "a certainty to become a superstar," yet the Blazers were still expected to pick Bowie.[3]

Even though the Portland physical staff thoroughly examined Bowie, who had missed his whole college junior year due to a leg injury, it turned out that the player lied about being completely healthy and able to compete on the highest professional level.[4] During his senior year, Bowie averaged 10.2 points and 9.2 rebounds per game, which were pretty solid numbers, but it was Jordan who was named the 1984 college Player of the Year. Blazers' power forward Mychal Thompson also said publicly that the team needed to draft Jordan and pair him up with Drexler. Team management chastised him for speaking up, saying that their primary need was at center.[5] Even though Bowie repeated his NCAA senior year numbers in his rookie year, during the next three seasons he would only appear in a total of 63 games due to recurring injuries. The Blazers traded him to the Nets in 1989, a year after Jordan won his first MVP trophy.

Rod Thorn, the Bulls general manager at the time, justified his decision to select Jordan to the press as follows: "There just wasn't a center available.... What can you do? ... We've taken a step in the right direction. Jordan isn't going to turn this franchise around. I wouldn't ask him to. I wouldn't put that kind of pressure on him."[6] While Thorn was right in his decision to pick Jordan, his assumptions were quickly proven to be terribly wrong. As a rookie, Jordan started all 82 games, playing 38.3 minutes per game, averaging 6.5 rebounds, 5.8 assists, and 28.2 points, making 51.5 percent of his shots (but only 17.3 percent from three, 9 of 52). He never hit a rookie slump, nor showed any signs of slowing down.

Apart from having extraordinary talent, part of the reason Jordan achieved so much during his rookie year was that the Bulls were a really bad team. Only Jordan and Orlando Woolridge averaged more than 20 points per game. Woolridge was a great teammate, universally loved for his sense of humor, but because his style did not mesh well with Jordan's, the team decided to allow him to sign with the New Jersey Nets in exchange for the first-round pick in the 1987 NBA draft, and two second-round picks in 1988 and 1990.

Thanks to that 1987 pick, the Bulls were able to construct their frontcourt of the future—Scottie Pippen (fifth pick) and Horace Grant (tenth pick) were both selected in that draft. It was actually the Sonics who selected Pippen, while the Bulls went with center Olden Polynice at the eighth pick. The draft day trade involved three other picks, the most important of which would be point guard B.J. Armstrong. Originally a Bulls' pick, he was selected by the Sonics, but traded on 1989 draft night to the Bulls in exchange for Brad Sellers. The Bulls would win three NBA championships with Pippen, Grant and Armstrong, while Woolridge admitted to having a cocaine problem during his second season on the Nets, for which he was fined by the team and suspended without pay. Despite his issues, he would still enjoy some success in the league, as well as in Europe.

Three-Pointer!

Up until Pippen and Grant turned into the players they were eventually supposed to become, Woolridge was the best teammate Jordan ever had on the Bulls. When Jordan got injured during his second NBA season, it was Woolridge who picked up the slack and carried the team to the playoffs for the second year in a row. Jordan came back just in time for the playoffs and noted one of the most memorable games of his career, scoring 63 points in a Game Two loss to the Celtics. He did that without firing a single three-point shot. Despite Jordan's heroics, the Celtics swept the Bulls, Woolridge was gone in the summer, and Doug Collins was hired as head coach. Jordan responded with his best season yet. In 1986–87, he averaged 40 minutes and 37.1 points per game, the most in his career. That did not amount to much though, as his team was once again swept by the Celtics in the first round of the playoffs.

It was the first full season in which Jordan was sharing backcourt duties with John Paxson, brought in from the San Antonio Spurs. That partnership would bring three championship titles to the Bulls. Paxson was a rare type of point guard at the time, one who did not create many shots, but would rather wait for the ball to shoot from long distance. He was the younger brother of Jim, who played for eight and a half seasons for the Blazers, and even appeared in two All-Star Games. While his individual statistics pale in comparison to Jim's, the younger Paxson could do one thing better than his older brother—shoot the three.

Since Jordan was the *de facto* point guard for the Bulls, bringing the ball upcourt and calling the plays, he could not function with a regular playmaker. Steve Colter, a pure point guard, lasted for just half of the 1986–87 season on the team before being traded to the Sixers. Paxson, on the other hand, became a useful role player on three championship teams. One of the reasons for Colter's failure in Chicago was his inability to stand up to Jordan. Paxson himself said, "You've got to get Michael's respect to do well on the Bulls,"[7] and he earned it by shooting extraordinarily well from long distance. Jordan fondly remembered one shot in particular, made by the point guard during a college all-star tour in Europe that they had both been on. "In one game in a tiny gym in Yugoslavia, Paxson had hit a long jump shot at the buzzer to win. Jordan seemed to remember that shot, and he was never as hard on Paxson as he was on most of his teammates."[8] Paxson retired as a 35.5 percent three-point shooter, making 36.3 percent as a member of the Bulls for nine seasons. In Game Five of the 1991 NBA Finals, Paxson scored 10 of the last 14 points made by the Bulls, his last shot coming from just inside the three-point line after a pass from Jordan. Paxson was named player of the game and his play clinched the first title in Bulls history.

The most important shot of Paxson's career came in Game Six of the 1993 NBA Finals. With 14.4 seconds left, the Suns were leading 98–96 and about to tie the series, 3–3. So far the Bulls had scored nine points in the fourth quarter to the Suns' 12, all made by Jordan. They brought the ball upcourt, in what would turn out to be the second-to-last possession of the game. Jordan passed the ball to Pippen, who passed to Horace Grant, surrounded by defenders under the basket. The only open Bulls player was Paxson, standing behind the arc. Grant kicked the ball out to him and Paxson drained the three-point shot, making the score 99–98 for the Bulls. The Suns called a timeout and with 3.9 seconds left had a chance to win the game, but Kevin Johnson's running shot was blocked by Grant. Thanks to Grant and Paxson, the Bulls were able to complete the three-peat.

Led by Charles Barkley, the Suns also had great shooters in Dan Majerle and Danny Ainge, but Paxson turned out to be way more important for his team in the series. Called "Thunder Dan," Majerle was a shooting guard/small forward mostly known for his three-point shooting, even though his nickname came from his dunking ability. In the season the Suns went to the finals, Majerle attempted 5.3 threes per game—so almost twice as much as the season before (2.8)—and drained them with almost the same efficiency (38.2 percent in 1991–92 and 38.1 percent in 1992–93). Majerle made 1,360 threes during his NBA career, playing for the Suns, the Cavaliers and the Heat. Apart from being a great shooter, he was also a lockdown defender, selected to the NBA All-Defensive Second Team twice.

Ainge, who had just joined the Suns in the summer of 1992, had lost the previous finals to Jordan as well, although as a member of the Blazers. Sam Smith wrote that some people suggested in 1990 that the Bulls should bring in Ainge once he was made available by the Kings after just one season on the team,[9] but Ainge was traded to his homestate team, the Blazers, instead. He was really appreciated for his championship experience (two titles with the Celtics), tenacity and shooting ability (37.8 percent from three). The move made sense for Ainge as well, since he joined the team who just went to the 1990 NBA Finals and had a strong chance of staying competitive for years to come.

Apart from Drexler, who was now a legitimate superstar, the Trail Blazers had Jerome Kersey, Terry Porter and Kevin Duckworth on their roster. Porter was a solid three-point shooter, and participated in three 3-Point Contests during his 17 seasons in the NBA. He made 38.6 percent of his three-point shots while playing for the Blazers, the Timberwolves, the Heat and the Spurs. On the bench, the team had a young Clifford Robinson, who could play both forward positions, and in a couple of seasons would also turn into a three-point threat. Robinson was a player ahead of his time, a finesse 6'10" shooter, who retired with 1,253 threes made with 35.6 percent efficiency. In a 1993 *Sports Illustrated* feature on Robinson, Drexler said of his versatile teammate: "He's our best defensive big man off the ball and on the ball. Offensively, his potential is unlimited. He's a '90s-type player."[10]

However, it was Drexler who was undoubtedly the best player on the team, and some even considered him to be second-best in the league. Drexler actually came in second in the 1992 MVP voting, behind Jordan. Even though the vote was not really that close, for some Drexler was considered to be on the same level as Jordan. "Those who argued for Drexler pointed out that he was certainly a better rebounder, he might be a better passer, and he was a better three-point shooter. That year, for example, he had taken more than three times as many three-point shots as Jordan, and his percentage of accuracy was significantly higher."[11] While both men were known for their dunking in their earlier years—Jordan was referred to as "His Airness" and Drexler was called "The Glide"—they had worked hard on their jump shots and had elevated their games thanks to their developing shooting abilities. Drexler was not a big three-point shooter when he joined the league, attempting a total of zero long-distance shots in his rookie year. However, by the 1991–92 season, he was making 33.7 percent of his three-point shots with 4.4 attempts per game. For Jordan, the three-pointer remained one of the biggest flaws of his game, and the reason behind one of the bigger embarrassments of his career.

While Jordan holds many NBA records, one of the most shameful concerns the lowest amount of points scored in the 3-Point Contest with … five, along with Detlef Schrempf. As competitive as Jordan was, it was somewhat understandable why he decided to participate in the 1990

3-Point Contest in the first place. He had already won two Slam Dunk Contests, was named MVP, All-Star Game MVP and Defensive Player of the Year, all in the late 1980s. The only individual triumph left for him to achieve—Most Improved Player and Sixth Man of the Year awards were obviously out of the question—was the title of the best three-point shooter in the league. He had every reason to expect success, because apart from having the ability to rise to the occasion at almost any given moment, he was having his best season to date when it came to three-point shooting. Jordan was attempting three threes per game, over two times more than the season before (1.2) and shooting them with incredible—by his standards—efficiency (39 percent). He ended the season making 37.6 percent of his three-point attempts. However, in the contest, he was outscored in the first round by his teammate, Craig Hodges, who was shooting on the other side of the court. Hodges made 20 three-pointers on the way to his first 3-Point Contest trophy.

Jordan made only five three-pointers, one less than during one of his most memorable performances, which would later become known as "The Shrug." Similar to his other historical games, such as "The Shot,"[12] or "The Flu Game," it bore a short and snappy title, which was fitting for a superstar who was primarily known simply as "Mike." While Jordan was indeed a celebrity brand or a branded celebrity,[13] no player worked on his game more than Jordan, constantly adding new plays to his arsenal in order to remain efficient, with his athleticism slowly but steadily diminishing. He came a long way from the fast-food eating, skinny athlete he was when entering the NBA, and would eventually become one of the best basketball players of all time.

Some of his teammates, while praising his conditioning, competitiveness and natural gifts, questioned his basketball IQ. In his first seasons in the league, he would often ignore open players, as if he wanted to do everything on his own. It was only after Jordan put on some muscle and learned how to trust his teammates that he finally reached the NBA Finals. He did that by getting through the Detroit Pistons, whose infamous "Jordan Rules" also played their part in turning Jordan into an outside shooter. The rules were a defensive tactic constructed in order to stop Jordan from driving to the basket and earning easy points. The Pistons executed it by brutally fouling him every time he attempted a dunk or a layup.

Three-Pointer!

Jordan's development into a team player was a joint effort by coach Phil Jackson and the Bulls' players he constantly challenged in training. The triangle offense, which Jackson implemented in spite of Jordan's early resistance, allowed the ball to circulate between players, getting all of them involved in creating the best possible shot. Whether he wanted to or not, Jordan had to trust his teammates in order to be successful. And he trusted no other player more than Scottie Pippen. In the small forward from Central Arkansas Jordan found a perfect running mate, even though in earlier seasons he was frustrated with Pippen's play. Just two years earlier, during the biggest game of his career so far—Game Seven of the 1990 Eastern Conference Finals against the Pistons—Pippen went 1 for 10 from the floor in 42 minutes of playing time and, due to a migraine, was a non-factor in another painful playoff exit for the Bulls.

In the next seasons, though, Pippen proved to be more than reliable, and even carried the Bulls during the time Jordan spent away from professional basketball. It was in the first season without Jordan that Pippen doubled his three-point shooting input—2.7 to 1.1 attempts the year before—and became a more accurate shooter, finally establishing himself as an offensive threat. For one and a half seasons, the Bulls became his team. Pippen was so concerned with his role that when, during Game Three of the 1994 Conference Semifinals against the Knicks, with the game tied 102–102 and 1.8 seconds left on the clock, Coach Jackson decided that it would be Toni Kukoc and not Pippen taking the final shot, the small forward would not even leave the bench and enter the court. This was not the first instance of Pippen's egotism, who in the past would play selfishly in order to get a new deal.[14] Not always concerned with team chemistry, Pippen demanded to be traded by the Bulls several times, coming close to being exchanged for Shawn Kemp of the Sonics or Tracy McGrady of the Raptors. Following just one season as a member of the Rockets, in the summer of 1999 Pippen was shipped to the Blazers, heavily conflicted with teammate Charles Barkley.

Coming back to Jordan, the fact that he was moving away from the basket, while still being able to perform highlight-worthy plays almost on demand, made him a complete player, undeniably the best of his generation. Yet due to the aforementioned comparisons to Drexler, he still felt he needed to prove his doubters wrong. And their doubts were somewhat justified: the Bulls had won only one NBA championship at the time, the

Dream Team was yet to dominate globally in the next month or so and thereby popularize NBA basketball to unprecedented levels, and Jordan was yet to lead his team to five more titles, including the 72-win 1995–96 season, which for 20 years would remain the winningest in league history.

Even Michael Jordan had to eventually incorporate the three-point shot into his repertoire (1997).

Three-Pointer!

Two years after the 1992 NBA Finals, with Jordan officially retired from basketball, Jack McCallum captured the essence of the Jordan craze, that by the time had swept the whole world: "He crossed all lines—gender, race, age—as smoothly as he crossed over his dribble. He had no hidden agenda, no dark side, and so his appeal was uncomplicated and thoroughly wonderful. He played, he dunked, he stuck out his tongue, he smiled. We swooned."[15] It was thanks to his incredible performances that he was able to do no wrong in the eyes of popular opinion. Commercial aspects of the brand myth that he created aside, Jordan's on-court achievements were the golden standard to follow for the players that came after him.

In June of 1992, the shooting guard was still setting the standard for other players to follow. This time it was the Blazers who stood in his way on the quest for glory. Playing against the team from Oregon always gave Jordan an extra incentive to play well, as the company that he is still sponsored by, Nike, has its headquarters there. That, along with being passed over for Sam Bowie, and hearing/reading unfavorable comparisons to Drexler, gave Jordan enough motivation to stage the show he put on during the first half of Game One of the 1992 NBA Finals, setting a league record with the most three-pointers made and points scored in one half of the finals game.

The first shot came while Jordan got the ball behind the three-point line and Drexler was too far from him to block it. The Blazers' shooting guard decided to give Jordan some space, since he did not shoot for three that often, and the Bulls' player made the most of the opportunity. The second three came from the left corner, as Scottie Pippen was driving toward the basket and kicked the ball out to the best player in basketball, the reigning MVP, who was once again standing alone, uncovered. The third three was somewhat similar—as the Bulls were running with the ball, Pippen once again got inside the arc and passed to Jordan, who stayed behind the three-point line, alone. The Blazers were now tightly guarding Jordan and so he was able to trick them with shot fakes and do damage from the inside.

After a few plays, the Blazers once again gave Jordan some space and he responded by making a clean three-point shot. Another one came as he was over a step behind the three-point line, showing great range with the shot. He was now 5 out of 7 from three in the first half of the game, 12 for 18 overall and had 30 points so far. The sixth three came from a pass from

Paxson, with Clifford Robinson getting his hand up too late. The crowd erupted and Jordan responded with a shrug directed towards Magic Johnson, recently retired and commentating the game for NBC. "My threes felt like free throws," Jordan said after the game.[16]

On the whole, Jordan went 6 for 10 from three, ending the game with 39 points, 35 of those coming in the first half, good for an NBA record. He played only for 34 minutes during that game, the smallest amount in all of the 1992 playoffs, but he did not need to play more—thanks to his early outburst, the Bulls won easily, 122–89. They won the series 4–2, encountering some problems, but not in the same way as in the next season's finals, where they needed a decisive three-point play and defensive stoppage to clinch the title. Of the six finals the Bulls played in, apart from their first appearance in the last series of the season—against the Lakers, which they won 4–1—they would always lose just two games. Jordan won Finals MVP in all six NBA Finals he participated in.

The shrug was obviously far from a simple and humble gesture, considering the circumstances and the person who made it. Rather, Jordan performed it with typical boastfulness, which was always a part of his game. While this vice was not considered as such when it came to Jordan, due to his ability to charm audiences with his smile and wholesome public persona, it was no locker room secret how competitive Jordan was. Thanks to that willingness to win, as noted by his personal trainer Tim Grover, "Michael was the only player ... who was completely in the Zone every time he played."[17] Grover defines the Zone as complete focus on and utter devotion to a given goal. For Jordan, this meant emerging triumphant in every competition he participated in, regardless of if it was a game of basketball, ping-pong or Pac-Man. Not so much beating as embarrassing the player who was supposed to be better than Jordan at his own element was an opportunity Jordan simply could not pass up.

The fact that Jordan used the three-point shot to do so spoke volumes of his potential, as it was the part of his game he was not particularly known or respected for. However, due to the fact that he was able to use it to such an extent as to not only humiliate his opponent but also set an NBA record, showed that he was yet to reach his ceiling as a basketball player. His three-point shooting ability is not something Jordan is remembered for, after all, he made a name for himself by performing close to the basket, yet "The Shrug" is one of the most significant parts of his legacy.

Even though he made just 581 regular season three-point shots through-out his career, he was still a rather accurate shooter by the standards of his era, making 32.7 percent of his attempts from long distance.

By making six threes in one half and capping them off with a mem-orable gesture, he not only made good on one of the biggest disappoint-ments of his career, but more so further contributed to the growing importance of the three-pointer. While the shrug gesture was supposed to mean that making those shots was not that big of a deal, it actually was. After noticing Jordan making the shots, when the kids all over the world wanted to be "like Mike," that meant that they also wanted to shoot from long distance just like he did. The same applied for everything Jor-dan did, whether it was eating McDonald's burgers, drinking Gatorade or performing incredible feats on the court.

May 7, 1995

Reggie Miller Scores Eight Points in Nine Seconds Against the Knicks

Reggie Miller is associated with two NBA teams, even though he spent his whole career on only one of them. Miller was selected with the 11th pick in the 1987 draft by the Indiana Pacers. He was picked instead of another shooting guard, Steve Alford, for whom the city was deeply rooting to join the Pacers. The selection came as a surprise to Miller himself, since he barely talked with the Pacers before being picked.[1] In retrospect, it seems somewhat surprising that the fans in Indiana thought so highly of Alford and booed Miller on draft night, considering that not many teams saw potential in the Hoosier and he was ultimately picked 26th overall by the Dallas Mavericks.

The whole appeal of Alford is best summarized by a simple question from a *Sports Illustrated* article from the 1985–86 season: "has anyone ever looked more the part of the all-American boy than Steve Alford?"[2] White and athletic, Alford was a homestate product, born in Chrysler, Indiana. He played only for in-state teams, both in high school and in college. In 1983 he was named Indiana Mr. Basketball for averaging 37.7 points per game during his senior year at New Castle Chrysler High School, where he was coached by his father. Becoming so successful on a team from a town inhabited by about 18,000 people gave Alford the ultimate small-town feel and contributed to his statewide appeal.

When Bobby Knight, the old-school and short-tempered coach of Indiana University, recruited Alford, the local adoration for the player grew even stronger. Knight was very hard on his players, he shouted, used expletives, even physically abused them. In Sam Smith's *The Jordan Rules*, Bulls assistant coach Johnny Bach recounts a visit to Knight's home when

Knight got angry at his wife because she did not serve Bach coffee, as she was bathing their children.[3] While everybody turned a blind eye to this approach in the first two decades of Knight's coaching career, in the '90s more and more players started complaining about it and the university had no choice but to fire Knight in the year 2000. He won three NCAA championships as a coach for the Hoosiers and would even go on to coach the U.S. basketball team to the gold medal in the 1984 Los Angeles Olympics—a title which forever comes with an asterisk, as the USSR National Team did not participate in that tournament. The team featured three future Hall of Famers in Michael Jordan, Patrick Ewing and Michael Jordan, as well as eventually successful professional basketball players like Alvin Robertson and Sam Perkins. The youngest player on that team was 19-year-old Alford.

From a young age, Alford was basketball-oriented, sacrificing his social life in order to practice on his game. He worked on his shooting by throwing ping-pong balls into a Pringles can.[4] He even proposed to his girlfriend on the basketball court.[5] And, what is most important for this book, Alford was a very good three-point shooter in college. During his senior year, Alford attempted almost six three-point shots per game—5.9 to be exact—and made 53 percent of them. In the final game of the season, the 1987 NCAA Championship game against the Syracuse Orange team that featured future NBA stalwarts Derrick Coleman, Sherman Douglas and Rony Seikaly, the Hoosier's shooting guard made seven out of ten three-point shots and led his team to victory. It was a close game, which Indiana won, 74–73. None of the players on that Hoosiers team would go on to have even what can be characterized as decent NBA careers, which may stand as proof that it was Knight's system that allowed the players to be successful.

Knight purposely limited his players' individuality in order to achieve group success. However, he also favored certain players over others, and he handpicked who would fit his system the best, which is fairly understandable. The numbers speak for themselves (662 wins as the Hoosiers coach), but from today's perspective his approach may be seen as racist. R. Scott Carey writes that

> in placing restrictions and impositions on each player's individuality (on and off the court), and coaching wildly disproportionate White teams, Knight became a symbol of White supremacy and patriarchy who was read through a rearticula-

tion of Hoosier Whiteness. While he continued to preach the values of "Indiana basketball," he also symbolized a colonialist force on what was perceived as a threatening "Black Style" that emphasized competing values of individualism, flash and innovation in need of control.[6]

And Indiana basketball was, in fact, "white" basketball. When Bobby Knight came in to recruit Isiah Thomas, the player's mother was actually afraid for her son's life, because of the efforts of the local society to resurrect the popularity of the Ku Klux Klan. She asked the coach if her son would be protected, to which Knight responded: "If we're winning, they'll protect him."[7]

The whiteness of Indiana basketball was further emphasized by the movie *Hoosiers* (1986), where the all-white team triumphs over a predominantly African American—which here signifies more athletic, individualistic and less organized—high school powerhouse. It is a state championship game, which pretty much means that both teams are from Indiana, but only one *represents* Indiana basketball. The movie was based on the real-life success of the 1954 Milan High School Indians' (a highly problematic mascot) men's basketball team. The team is painted as an underdog, even though, as pointed out by Shawn Fury, "Milan put a powerhouse team on the court in 1954—and had the added experience of making it to the Final Four the previous season. Milan had Mr. Basketball."[8] Because of the movie's popularity, the myth of Hoosier basketball lives on. In Knightstown, Indiana, there is actually the Hoosier Gym, in which the fictional Hickory team played its home games. It can be rented for 30 dollars an hour as a basketball venue or a wedding location.[9]

In the Pacers' ABA days, an example was set by another inbred superstar, Rick Mount, a scorer who resisted the temptation to join the NBA in order to stay in his home state as a pro. This was very important for the locals, because, as noted by former Pacer Bob Netolicky, "in Indiana basketball almost comes before church and family. You see more rims and basketball goals hanging up in some towns than there are people."[10] This should partially explain the appeal of Steve Alford, the all–American boy, who led the team representing the state to a national championship. Alford was a hometown hero because of his looks and his work ethic; however, he was also a talented basketball player. The Hoosiers wanted to have one of their own on their pro team.

Even though in the 1984–85 season, Knight characterized Alford as unable to "lead a whore into bed,"[11] it was under the shooting guard's leadership that Knight won his last NCAA championship. The coach was one of the loudest critics of the three-point shot, openly calling it "horseshit."[12] He claimed that the line made the game unfair for teams that did not have shooters on their rosters, which was a very controversial statement, as if shooters were different than big men, passers or defenders. Although to be fair, Knight was not particularly fond of the three-point shot even at the press conference following the 1985 championship—won mostly thanks to Alford's three-point shooting—saying that the thing that he still liked "the least of all in basketball is the three-point shot."[13]

Alford was a two-time All-American, but more importantly, he was theirs. He was a Hoosier, and that meant more than anything else to in-state fans. However, the team's general manager, Donnie Walsh, had disappointed them a season before when he picked small forward Chuck Person over Scott Skiles, a point guard born in La Porte, Indiana. Skiles, the Michigan Spartans standout, was arrested before the draft for drunk driving and marijuana possession—which did not really fit well into the ethos of Indiana basketball—but in the eyes of the Indiana faithful he was still the right pick. Instead, Skiles would go on to play just 13 games in his rookie year for the Bucks, while Person immediately established himself as one of the best young shooters in the NBA, and was voted 1986 Rookie of the Year. While an injury limited his playing time in his first year, in his second pro season Skiles would don the uniform of his homestate team. Skiles' agent described the situation as ideal for the player and the Pacers as the only team that he wanted to play for in the first place.[14]

That enthusiasm eventually faded, as Skiles failed to make an impact on the unsuccessful Pacers team and even quit the NBA altogether in December of 1988. He had to be talked out of early retirement by Walsh.[15] Skiles joined the Orlando Magic in the summer of 1989, as the Pacers left him unprotected in the expansion draft. On December 30, 1990, Skiles set a single-game NBA record by dishing out 30 assists against the high-pace, all-offense Denver Nuggets. The move to bring in Skiles may have been seen as Walsh's attempt to appease the fans in Indiana, who were not really enthusiastic about the general manager's picking Miller over Alford a year after he passed on Skiles in the draft.

As observed on draft day by *Indianapolis Star* reporter David Benner: "the Pacers, with the 11th pick overall in the draft, got the player they wanted … but not the player the fans wanted."[16] The selection of UCLA shooting guard Reggie Miller was "welcomed" by 5,000 unanimous boos by the fans gathered at the Market Square Arena. Fans wanted Alford and they reacted the same way as the year before, when Person was picked instead of Skiles. The ESPN movie *Winning Time: Reggie Miller vs. The New York Knicks* shows the disappointment not only in the Alford household, but in the stands and on the streets as well.[17] People were really angry at Walsh, for once again going against general opinion. Miller himself was somewhat surprised with the selection, as other teams like the Golden State Warriors and the Los Angeles Clippers were much more interested in him than the Pacers, who began talking to him just a week and a half before the draft.[18] Himself a California native, Miller's selection by a local California team would have made for a similar narrative as the Pacer fans were hoping for with Alford—that of an inner-state product joining the professional team from his home state.

On draft day, a frustrated Alford called Miller "a good player and a good person, but where he fits in with the Pacers, I don't know. He can't play guard and he isn't going to play in front of Chuck (Person)."[19] Person himself was enthusiastic about playing with Miller, who was much taller than Alford (6'6" to 6'1"), as well as a better defender: "Steve is a good guard but he can't fit in with the rest of the team."[20] The fact that the team wanted to organize a trade for Alford around the 20th pick did not influence his or the fans' opinion in any way, even though he was picked pretty late, 26th by the Mavericks.

The first-round pick in next year's draft, which the teams interested in trading with Indiana wanted for Alford, proved to be too high of a price, and in retrospect the move would have looked really bad. Not only did the Pacers get to select second in 1988, using that pick on franchise center Rik Smits, but Alford himself could not translate his college success to professional basketball. He started just three games during his four years in the NBA. He played for the Dallas Mavericks and the Golden State Warriors, averaging less than ten minutes and one three-point shot attempt per game.

Meanwhile, Miller spent 18 seasons with the Pacers, following in a long tradition of shooters starting with the Pacers' ABA days with Roger Brown. Brown scored seven three-pointers during the last game of the 1970 Finals, sealing the team's first championship. Apart from his rookie season in which he started just one game (only because the starter, John Long, got hurt) and came from the bench for the other 81, as well as four games as a reserve in his second year, Miller was always a starter whenever fit to play. He finished his UCLA career as the second-best scorer in school history only behind Lew Alcidor (who would later change his name to Kareem Abdul-Jabbar) and after some adjustments, he turned into one of the most lethal shooters in the NBA. He ended his professional career with 2,560 three-point shots made and 6,485 attempts. A 39.5 percent career three-point shooter, these numbers may be just as much attributed to his longevity, as they are to his scoring ability. After all, Miller attempted more than six three-point shots a game only once during his professional career.

Part of Miller's appeal as a marksman was due to his ability to perform in the clutch during the last minutes of important games, which earned him a lot of enemies among opposing fans. Indeed, "in the final nine seasons of his career (regular season and playoffs), Miller made 142 three-pointers in crunch time, 54 more than the next closest player in that time period."[21] However, his reputation may actually be a bit overblown, as just one look at Indiana's playoff appearances shows that Miller lost more decisive games (six)—understood here as games numbered five (back then, the team that was the first to win three first-round playoff games was moving on to the next round) or seven—than he won (three). Still, the games he won were enough to earn him the hatred of numerous franchises and fanbases.

Miller's autobiography bears the title *I Love Being the Enemy*, which already speaks volumes about his willingness to be loathed by other teams and their fans. He presents himself as self-confident and boastful on the court, separating his private persona from who he is as a player. The book contains passages about fans of opposing teams such as "they're concentrating so much on me, screaming at me, rooting against me, and I love it. I love the attention. I love playing on the road,"[22] which prove that Miller evidently played off the crowd, but also loved to engage in rivalries against players from other teams. He reacted to being called a "bitch" with outrage, but did not refrain from calling other players that. One of the first sentences in *I Love Being the Enemy* goes: "I hate the Knicks. Absolutely hate those kids."[23]

Likewise, nobody hated Miller more than the New York Knicks' fans,

Reggie Miller was one of the most hated players of the '90s due to his ability to hit clutch three-pointers (2001).

as he faced off against their team six times in the postseason. The '90s Knicks were engaged in another rivalry, with the Miami Heat, but they usually emerged victorious against the team from Florida in the postseason, losing just one of their four confrontations. Allen Iverson's 76ers also considered Miller and his teammates as gatekeepers, as they eliminated the team from Philadelphia in 1999 and 2000 playoffs. In 2001, the Sixers beat the Pacers 3–1 in the first round of the playoffs and would go on to win the Eastern Conference Finals, and advance to the NBA Finals.

Earlier, in the previous decade, Miller positioned himself as the rival of the Chicago Bulls, as during a January 1994 regular season game he scored a deep two to make the game 95–93 with 0.8 seconds left, and bowed to the crowd in the middle of the Chicago Stadium. The Bulls won that game, however, thanks to a three-pointer scored by rookie Toni Kukoc. During the next game against the Pacers, which was played the next day in Indianapolis, it was the Bulls' small forward, Scottie Pippen, who bowed to the home crowd as his Bulls dominated the Pacers. Michael Jordan was absent during both games, as he had retired before the start of said season.

Surprisingly though, Miller met with with the Bulls in the playoffs only once, in the 1998 Eastern Conference Finals. The Bulls team was somewhat on its last legs, as the arguments between the team and the management were about to put an end to the best basketball team of the '90s and one of the best in league history. After a summer of uncertainty, as Jordan was rumored to join the New York Knicks in free agency,[24] Scottie Pippen was close to being traded for Raptors' rookie Tracy McGrady,[25] and Phil Jackson would have probably coached the Sixers, had Jordan not re-signed with the Bulls.[26] It was indeed going to be "the Last Dance" for that team, as that playoff run would later come to be known. Chicago made easy work of the New Jersey Nets and the Charlotte Hornets, but then came the series against the Pacers, playing in their third NBA Finals in five years.

In their previous appearance at that stage, in 1995, they were barely beaten by the young Orlando Magic. Shaquille O'Neal and Penny Hardaway's team would go on to be swept by the experienced Houston Rockets in the finals. Even though in the last game the Magic beat the Pacers rather easily, 105–81, they needed seven games to hold off Miller, Smits, and company. That was the second time in a row that the Pacers came very close to facing off against the Rockets. In the final game of the series, Miller was held to just 12 points, whereas he scored 36 in the previous one, won by the Pacers, 123–96. After the game he said, "I take the burden for this loss. I feel bad for the guys because I didn't play particularly well. They should have nothing to put their heads down about.

This was definitely Reggie Miller blowing it for them."[27] Still, they would not have gotten there without Miller's heroics in the previous round of the playoffs against the Knicks.

Coming back—or moving forward—to the 1998 series, the Bulls won the final game just 88–83 and Jordan scored 28 points, making 9 of 25 shots from the field. Miller scored 22 points in the first three quarters but only one in the fourth. The game was decided by rebounds, as the Bulls dominated the offensive glass, out rebounding the Pacers in that regard 22 to 3. Pippen, who grabbed 12 of his team's overall 50 boards said afterwards that "this was probably the toughest playoff series of my career."[28]

Throughout the series Miller played with a sprained ankle, but overcame the injury, leading his team to victories in Games Three and Four with crunch-time heroics. Thanks to those his team won both by a very close marking of two points. Following a decisive Game Five win by the Bulls, Pacers won Game Six by three points, once again thanks to Miller. The Bulls would go on to win the series and their last championship title under Jackson, whereas the Pacers would make the Conference Finals for three seasons in a row under their new coach, Indiana native Larry Bird. The third time would turn out to be the charm, as they would make the 2000 NBA Finals in Bird's last season as head coach—he announced his decision to quit before the team reached the ultimate series of the season.

There they would once again face O'Neal and Jackson, this time both leading the Lakers, the first on, the second off the court. In his second book, *Shaq Talks Back*, Shaquille O'Neal described the series as "Hoosiers against Hollywood,"[29] which is in opposition to the way Miller was perceived in the NBA. Marty Burns of *Sports Illustrated* described the shooting guard as "a Hollywood guy" with an affinity for movies going well beyond regular fandom.[30] He played himself in short roles in such movies as *Forget Paris* (1995) or *He Got Game* (1998), but he also had an affinity for the dramatic, which was emphasized by his clutch performances. O'Neal said of Miller that "of all the players in the league with the game on the line I think I still fear the dude the most."[31]

The bar was, however, as high as never before for Miller and his teammates, after all it was for the first time in team history that the Pacers had made the NBA Finals. The Lakers were by far the best team in the league, winning 12 more games than the second-placed Pacers, they also had the best player in the league, the reigning MVP Shaquille O'Neal. Kobe Bryant made the All-NBA Second Team and All-Defensive First Team. Phil Jackson lost the award for Coach of the Year to Doc Rivers, who almost made the playoffs with a gutted Orlando Magic team. With a starting five consisting of four undrafted players and one lottery pick in Tariq Abdul-Wahad, the Magic went 41–41. Rivers beat Jackson 60–53 in the voting for the award.

O'Neal was truly unique, the most dominant player in the NBA and yet he was mocked for his inability to win an NBA title. The player himself would joke about winning "at every level except college and pro,"[32] but there was nothing funny about the criticism he was receiving. This series was about O'Neal proving his haters wrong, not about Miller winning his first championship. The Pacers just could not find an answer for Shaq, who played 45.5 minutes per game, averaging 38 points, 16.7 rebounds and blocking 2.7 shots against them. Miller finished the series averaging 24.3 points per game, but he struggled to find his rhythm, going 8 for 32 in the first two games and making 37.5 percent of his three-point attempts. The Lakers won the series 4–2.

After that finals' series, the Pacers changed direction and tried to rejuvenate the roster. For the next three seasons the team played under Isiah Thomas, with Marc Aguirre as his assistant coach. The team immediately drew comparisons to the '80s Detroit Pistons, due to the fact that both coaches were former members of the infamous Bad Boys. The Pacers were accumulating flagrant fouls and were called "dirty" by other coaches. On that team, Miller was no longer the top scorer, taking the backseat to power forward Jermaine O'Neal, small forward Ron Artest, and/or center Brad Miller. The Pacers' center, as any other player on the team, still held Miller in high regard: "Reggie can go 0 for 12, and if I'm coaching the other team, I'm still saying, Don't leave him, It's not like you want to give him a wide-open three."[33] However, it was evident that the Pacers were no longer Miller's team. His production was steadily declining. In the 2001–02 season, for the first time since his rookie year, he attempted less than ten field goals per game. After three first-round exits, the team rehired Bird, this time as President of Basketball Operations and his first decision was to fire Thomas. The 2003–04 Pacers once again made the Eastern Conference Finals, only to lose to the Detroit Pistons, 2–4.

The next season proved to be the last of Miller's career. On November 19, 2004, the Pacers played the Pistons in Detroit and with the game already decided, both teams engaged in a brawl which is now known as the Malice at the Palace. The Pacers clashed with the Pistons, as well as with their fans. One of them threw a drink at Ron Artest, who ran into the stands, followed by teammate Stephen Jackson. Both punched fans. Artest was suspended for 73 games, Stephen Jackson for 30 and Jermaine O'Neal for 15. Miller was suspended for one game after trying to separate his teammates from the fans, even though he was injured and not dressed for the game. In February 2005, Miller announced that he was going to retire at the end of the season: "There's no ideal situation that I'm going to leave on. Last year would have been great, at least getting to the Eastern Conference Finals with a chance to get to the Finals. There's no ideal. I think what happened in Detroit ... gave me more motivation to work harder because I knew we were going to be short-handed for such a long period of time."[34] In his last season, Miller increased his production and despite being 39 years old, played 31.9 minutes, attempted almost 11 shots and averaged 14.8 points per game.

On April 5, 2005, Miller played his last game in Madison Square Garden. During his introduction, he was booed by the New York crowd, but the boos eventually turned to cheers just as Miller ran towards his teammates. This was an unexpected gesture, as Miller was almost universally loathed by Knicks fans. Through the years *SLAM*, a basketball magazine operating from New York, mocked and made fun of Miller because of his ongoing rivalry with the Knicks. Reggie Miller was "the anti-establishment poster boy ... all that was missing was the black cape and a taunting catchphrase."[35] After his last game in the Garden, Miller said, "I love being booed. Maybe it goes back to my childhood."[36] In an interview with *SLAM*'s Tony Gervino, conducted five years after Miller retired from professional basketball, the player admitted that "if there is one thing [he does] miss, it's playing in the Garden. And having the fans yell and scream and chant."[37] Like during Game Five of the 1994 Eastern Conference Finals, when the Knicks fans started chanting "Che-ryl! Che-ryl!" after Miller's slow start to the game.

The fans were referring to Reggie's sister, one of the best female basketball players ever. She was enshrined into the Naismith Memorial Basketball Hall of Fame in 1995, seven years before her younger brother. In high school, Cheryl scored 105 points in a single game, and in college, at

USC, she won two NCAA championships and an Olympic gold medal. She was one of the few women basketball players drafted by a men's team, joining the Warriors' 13th round 1969 pick Denise Long (111 points in a single high school game, averaged 62.8 points per game) and New Orleans Jazz' 1977 7th round pick, Lusia Harris. The Warriors' pick was voided so Harris became the only player to be officially drafted, as well as to actually try out for an NBA franchise. Cheryl Miller was selected by the Staten Island Stallions of the United States Basketball League. However, knee injuries cut her basketball career short. She became a coach and an analyst for *TNT*. Miller describes Cheryl as one of the reasons why he practiced outside shooting—whenever they faced off during pick up games she would block his drives to the lane.[38]

The Pacers entered the fourth quarter of Game Five of the 1994 Eastern Conference Finals trailing 58–70. The series was tied 2–2. With a win, the Knicks would have two elimination games at their disposal and a duel between two of the best centers in the league, Hakeem Olajuwon and Patrick Ewing, would decide which team was the best in the post-Jordan league. Considering how great defensively the Knicks were, the game against the Pacers seemed already decided. The team from New York was one game away from reaching the finals for the first time in 21 years, fulfilling the expectations associated with the 1985 NBA draft, when the Knicks' fortunes turned as they won the first pick and with it the right to draft Georgetown center Patrick Ewing.

Ewing's college team had already beat Olajuwon's once in the most important game of the season—the 1984 NCAA Championship game. Both players would go on to be selected with the first picks in consecutive drafts (1984 and 1985), but it was Olajuwon this time who had the upper hand. Not only has he enjoyed more team success as a pro (he made the NBA Finals in his second year in the league) but he was also voted the 1994 Most Valuable Player. Ewing and his Knicks, on the other hand, had never made it past the Conference Semifinals, losing to the Bulls in either the first or the second round of the playoffs in four out of the six times they made it to the postseason. This time, they seemed to have exorcised their demons, as they finally eliminated the Jordan-less Bulls, even though they needed seven games to do so.

Until that 1994 series, the Knicks had not considered Pacers as a serious threat. The team from Indianapolis made it somewhat of a habit to exit the playoffs early, and since the 1990 playoffs, they had fallen in the first round for four straight years: to the Pistons, twice to the Celtics and the last time to the Knicks. After three early exits in a row, Donnie Walsh fired coach Bob Hill and hired Larry Brown, who has just led the Los Angeles Clippers to the playoffs for the first time since 1976, when the team was still known as the Buffalo Braves. In just one and a half seasons—Brown joined the Clippers in the middle of the 1991–92 season, the team's third coach during that season—he made a significant impact on the Clippers, who were a perennial punchline for basketball fans.[39] Brown quit the team in the summer of 1993 to explore other options and the Pacers were immediately interested in acquiring his services.[40]

Brown was a coach obsessed with playing "the Right Way," a basketball philosophy he internalized while playing and coaching under Dean Smith at North Carolina. Brown's coaching tree actually validated his claims for knowing what he was preaching, as Smith played under Hank Iba of Kansas, who played for James Naismith himself. His roots were, therefore, reaching the beginnings of basketball, which earned him the right to claim he knew the purest form of basketball. Brown relied on defense, rebounding, passing and setting screens. Larry Platt points out just how conservative Brown's approach was, when even after the success he enjoyed thanks to Miller's long-distance shots he still "hated the three-point shot because it rewarded bad shot selection. The purpose of Dr. Naismith's game, after all, was to take the highest-possible percentage shot. The three-pointer was a low-percentage shot, yet the NBA now provided incentive to take it. Consequently, he was one of the last holdouts against the three-point specialist."[41] Still, Brown found the most success when having a three-point shooter on his roster, like Miller in Indiana, Aaron McKie (35 percent from three throughout his career) in Philadelphia or Tayshaun Prince (36.7 percent) in Detroit.

Coach Smith was often described as "the only man capable of holding Michael Jordan under 20 points,"[42] due to his authority as a coach and a mentor. All players playing under Smith had to adapt to the same style of play, which valued hard work, defense and unselfishness. The Pacers' general manager Donnie Walsh had a special connection with Brown as he had also played and coached under Smith. Tar Heels liked to stick together and it was a notion instilled in them by Smith, who claimed that a basketball team—not only the players, but the staff as well—should

81

be more like a family, a belief Brown tried to introduce to professional basketball players: "at least once the season began, this family would not desert you, leaving you to fend to yourself and those who relied on your guidance."[43]

While this was easier to achieve when dealing with college kids, Brown never abandoned his philosophy, and it eventually earned him his only NBA championship with the team-first, defensively oriented Detroit Pistons in 2004. Before that, he made the finals only once, in 2001 with the Philadelphia 76ers. While on defense the team played as a unit, on offense it was a one man show, with the spotlight on Allen Iverson. His tenure with the Pacers, during which Brown became known as someone who is "only happy when he is unhappy," did not prepare the coach for the arguments he would have on a regular basis with his sole star player.[44] Still, in Indianapolis he also had to sacrifice his team-first philosophy, at least on some nights.

On June 1, 1994, with 12 minutes to go, and trailing by 12 points, Reggie Miller started his own one man show by shooting from long distance. Teased by the crowd and Knicks superfan, movie director Spike Lee, he got to work. Every time Miller went to the line during the game, Lee shouted: "Reggie! Reggie!" to distract him. He was laughing and clapping whenever the Pacers missed or his team scored. That was enough for Miller to get going. The Pacers outscored the Knicks in the fourth quarter 35–16 and won the game 93–86. Despite a slow start, Miller finished the game with 39 points, 25 of those scored in the fourth quarter, with 6 of 11 shooting from three. After each shot made in that quarter. Miller stared at Lee, who got quieter and quieter. At one point, Miller grabbed himself by the throat with one hand, with the other holding his crotch, still staring at Lee, who was sitting next to his wife. After the game the director was asking: "Why me?"[45] Even though he claimed that he had no influence on the outcome of the series, Lee guaranteed that the Knicks would win the next game in Market Square Arena, and he would be there sitting courtside wearing a John Starks jersey.

He kept his word and the Knicks won that game thanks to a great shooting night by John Starks. Starks was a career 34 percent shooter from three and he did not make more than 36 percent of his threes during a single season. He was a streaky, somewhat erratic player, who would interlace great games and terrible ones. In Game Three of the 1993 first round series, Starks was ejected for head-butting Miller, who reacted the-atrically by throwing his hands into the air so that everyone could see that something out of the norm happened to him. Patrick Ewing and Charles Oakley started shouting at Starks because he allowed the trash-talking

John Starks went from undrafted to the second scoring option on the New York Knicks (1997).

Miller to get into his head. A year later, in Game Six, came his chance for redemption. Starks carried his team to victory, scoring 26 points and making five of six three-point shots. The Knicks won the next game and they went on to face Houston in the finals.

Game Seven of the NBA Finals would turn out to be the worst of John Starks' career and one of the worst individual performances in finals' history as well. In Game Five, Starks scored 11 points in the fourth quarter. In Game Six, the guard went 5 for 9 from three and scored 26 points, 16 in the fourth quarter. However, in what can now be seen as a sign of things to come, Starks was blocked during the last play of the game by Olajuwon and the Rockets won by two points, preventing the Knicks from taking home the trophy.

In Game Seven, Starks would score just eight points in 42 minutes of play, going 2 of 19 from the field and missing all 11 of his three-point shot attempts. The Knicks lost that game and would reappear in the finals five years later, with only Ewing remaining from the 1993–94 roster. The center did not play in a single game of the series due to injury and was traded to the Sonics in the summer. Starks left the team a couple of months earlier, as a part of the package sent to Golden State in exchange for Latrell Sprewell. He would go on to play for the Warriors, the Bulls and the Jazz before retiring in 2002.

Starks was always playing with a chip on his shoulder, as he made his way to the NBA not through the draft but by playing in the lesser-known World Basketball League and the CBA. When he joined the Knicks, he was making the league minimum and was at the bottom of the rotation. He was just a practice player when, in a preseason game, he attempted a dunk on Patrick Ewing. Starks failed and fell so hard on the court that he injured his knee. According to the NBA rules, the team was forced to sign him and put him on the reserve list. His first game as a Knick—but not his first NBA game, as he suited up for the Golden State Warriors for 36 games in the 1988–89 season—came against the Chicago Bulls on December 7, 1990. Starks claimed that his rocky road to the league was actually an advantage as "coming up the way I did is that you have to struggle, and that makes you appreciate what you have."[46]

Even though Miller was a much more coveted player than Starks, he shared the same ferociousness and hunger as the Knick. The Pacers' management was aware of how special Miller was, and following the 1994 playoff exit, it improved the roster, teaming Miller up in the backcourt with one of the greatest passers of all time, Mark Jackson. Born in Brooklyn, Jackson was picked 18th in the 1987 NBA draft by the Knicks and would go on to win the Rookie of the Year award. In his first year in the league, he averaged 10.6 assists per game, the most by any rookie in NBA history. He also averaged 2.5 steals, proving his versatility on both ends of the floor. Jackson, however, was not a great shooter, as he averaged ten points or more in just 6 of the 17 seasons he spent in the NBA. The player was especially reluctant to work with shooting coaches. He described himself as "not really a guy that believes in 'em. I never had to work with one. To me it's repetition, putting the time in."[47] He said that as the former coach of the Golden State Warriors, which may explain why Steph Curry blossomed into the best shooter in NBA history after he left, under the guidance of head coach Steve Kerr and player development consultant Steve Nash, both extraordinary long-distance scorers.

New York eventually traded Jackson after five productive seasons to the Los Angeles Clippers for three players, with the team's general manager Ernie Grunfeld saying that he needed quantity over quality. One of those players was Charles Smith, who infamously missed four layups in a row during one decisive play of Game Five of the 1993 Eastern Conference Finals against the Bulls. The Bulls began the series with two losses and the Knicks had homecourt advantage, but the Knicks still lost, 2–4. To this day, the game serves as representation of the team's inability to overcome Michael Jordan.

Apart from his passing ability, Jackson was an integral part of the Indiana Pacers for his ability to fire up Miller. In *Winning Time*, Jackson compares himself to Boudini Brown, the famous cornerman of Muhammad Ali. Apart from his regular functions of assisting "The Greatest," Brown wrote poems and speeches for the fighter, and was hyping him up before, as well as during, fights. Jackson used to read articles about Miller to Miller, and instead of serving as a censor, he picked out the most dismissive and offensive passages to feed the shooting guard's passion. Miller characterized Jackson as the only player who hated the Knicks more than him, because of the way he was treated by the organization.[48]

Jackson's contributions on and off the court turned out to be not enough for him to remain on the team. He was traded to the Denver Nuggets for Jalen Rose before the 1996–97 season, only to rejoin the Pacers at the 1997 trade deadline. When playing for the Nuggets, the player enjoyed the best passing season of his career, averaging 12 assists per game, while the Pacers fell to the tenth place in the Eastern Conference, and failed to make the playoffs despite improving significantly after Jackson's return. He remained a starter for the Pacers up to their sole NBA Finals appearance in the year 2000.

When the Knicks and the Pacers met again in the 1995 playoffs, this time in the Conference Semifinals, it was obvious that Miller was hungry for a rematch. Game One, played on May 7, 1995, at Madison Square Garden, set the tone for the series. Four out of the eventual seven games were decided by two points or less. The most dominant player in the first game surprisingly turned out to be Rik Smits. Known as the "Dunking Dutchman," the 7'4" Smits was usually the second scoring option on the Pacers during their most successful seasons. During the previous year's series against the Knicks, he averaged 16.3 points per game, but this time he needed to step his game up even more in order for the Pacers to avoid elimination. In Game One, he scored 34 points in 35 minutes of playing time before fouling out. More importantly though, he held Ewing (with no small help of Antonio and Dale Davis) to just 11 points and 26.7 percent from the floor. Smits finished the series with averages of 22.6 points and 6.4 rebounds per game.

Miller, in the meantime, was having a rather poor shooting night—he made 5 of his 16 shots, 1 out of 5 three-point shots. But at the end of the game, with Smits on the bench, he took it upon himself to lead his team to victory. With 18.7 seconds left, the Knicks were leading 105–99. Donnie Walsh went to his smoking room, thinking the game was over. After a timeout, the Pacers made a quick inbound pass and Miller made a quick three. There were 16.4 seconds left in the game. Anthony Mason was inbounding the ball to point guard Greg Anthony when Miller appeared from behind and caught it (visibly pushing Anthony to the floor, but the referees did not call a foul during the play). With the ball in his hands, Miller ran back to the three-point line and made the shot immediately after turning back. He commented on his decision: "when you're on the road, you go for the jugular. You don't go for the quick two and then try to foul; you go for the win."[49]

With 13.2 seconds left on the clock, the game was tied. The Pacers quickly fouled Starks, who missed two free throws. Patrick Ewing caught the rebound, but missed the shot as he was heavily guarded by Dale Davis and Miller. The latter grabbed the miss and was fouled. Miller drained two free throws to cap off one of the greatest achievements of his career—scoring eight points in nine seconds. With 7.5 seconds still left, Greg Anthony ran up the court but failed to find an open teammate and fell to the floor. The ball barely made it to Patrick Ewing, whose shot was blocked by Dale Davis. The Pacers won in Madison Square Garden and would go on to win the series in another thriller, which perfectly summed up this evenly fought series.

The Pacers led the series 3–1 but the Knicks managed to tie it and forced a decisive Game Seven. In that game, they were able to erase a 15-point third quarter deficit, leaving the whole series to be decided during the final play. With five seconds left, Patrick Ewing got the ball in his hands, however, due to problems with his knees, he was not able to jump as high as usual to make the deciding dunk. Instead, he settled for a layup and after he released the ball, it hit the back of the rim and fell out. The Pacers were heading to the 1995 Eastern Conference Finals.

Miller would face off against the Knicks two more times in the Eastern Conference Finals. Both series ended 4–2, but the Knicks won in 1999, whereas the Pacers triumphed in 2000. Both times, the rivals were unable to beat the best teams in the West—the Spurs in 1999 and the Lakers in 2000. Miller and Ewing both retired without championship rings. Both were enshrined in the Basketball Hall of Fame.

April 19, 1996

George McCloud Goes from Draft Bust to NBA Record Holder

George McCloud was considered a bust throughout the early years of his basketball career and still remains one of the worst draft picks in the history of the Indiana Pacers. During his four seasons at Florida State, the home-state product developed into a prolific scorer, improving from the pedestrian 4.3 points per game in his freshman year to 22.8 as a senior. No small part of that evolution had to do with McCloud working on his three-point shot. While he did not record a single attempt during his first year on the team, in his sophomore season he made good on 72 of his 159 attempts from long distance, whereas a year later he attempted 262 shots and made 115 of them. He was seventh in the country in threes attempted and sixth in makes. McCloud was always a streaky shooter, who could go 4 of 26 from three during the span of two games and then turn things around the next week with a 10 for 17 performance, like he did in February of 1989. This inability to stay consistent would not change during his professional career.

During his third year in college, McCloud switched positions from small forward to point guard. He really blossomed thanks to head coach Pat Kennedy, who had taken over the team the season prior. Under the new coach, the player got 15 pounds lighter and became a true team leader. This transformation was jokingly ascribed by Kennedy to his player's "outstanding discipline on the court and in the food line."[1] McCloud left the Seminoles as the third all-time leading scorer in school history. Due to his 6'6" frame and an ability to distribute the ball—4.2 assists per game in his senior year—McCloud was seen as a moderate version of Magic Johnson, even though Johnson was an NCAA champion and averaged twice as many assists as McCloud during his final year at Michigan State. McCloud was actually strongly considered by the Lakers' local rivals, the permanently underachieving Clippers, for the second pick of the 1989 NBA draft. The previous year, the team shot just 23 percent from three and was last in the league with 2.9 attempts per game, which explains why they were desperate for a shooter.

The Clippers eventually drafted Duke forward Danny Ferry (38.8 percent from three in college), even though the team already had Danny Manning and Ken Norman playing the same position. Granted, unlike Norman or Manning, Ferry could also shoot from the outside, but the team's primary need was at shooting guard. Once selected, Ferry refused to play in Los Angeles and decided to move overseas to Serie A. He was traded to the Cavaliers during the season, but joined the team only after honoring his contract in Italy. In that exchange, the Clippers finally got their shooter in Ron Harper, who would later sacrifice his shots for a place next to Michael Jordan in the starting backcourt of the 1996–1998 NBA champions, the Chicago Bulls.

McCloud would also go on to play in Italy after his first unsuccessful, four-year stint in the NBA. McCloud's and Ferry's names were linked later on as they were among the top candidates for the 1995–96 Most Improved Player Award. Ferry eventually ended up third in voting—*ex aequo* with teammate Terrell Brandon—with 6 votes while McCloud was second with 23 votes. The award went to the Romanian center of the Washington Bullets, Gheorghe Muresan, who got 50 votes of the 113 available. At the beginning of that season, both Ferry and McCloud were still considered busts.

Before McCloud's 1995–96 campaign turned into one of the more surprising comeback stories of the '90s NBA, there were high expectations surrounding the FSU player, after which came the eventual disappointment. The Clippers may have passed on him, but with fellow point guards Tim Hardaway, Mookie Blaylock and B.J. Armstrong still available, the Indiana Pacers drafted McCloud at number seven in the 1989 NBA draft to serve as the team's playmaker of the future, complementing shooters Reggie Miller and Chuck Person.

Adding a third scorer to these two seems ill conceived from today's perspective, considering how both men are remembered primarily for their ability to shoot the three, but even then, McCloud was a somewhat odd addition. Miller and Person were still developing as players, yet they averaged a combined 5.9 three-point shot attempts per game the season prior, which was very close to the 6.6 overall league average per team at the time. This made McCloud's primary ability of shooting the ball from long distance superfluous before he even put on a Pacers jersey. The coaches were not ready to rely so heavily on three-point shooting just yet. Along with Rik Smits at center, the team had a promising core—the eldest of the three, Person, was 24—of players acquired through three consecutive drafts. Picking McCloud put a stop to that successful streak, but even without his contributions, the Pacers turned into one of the best Eastern Conference teams of the '90s.

In his rookie year, McCloud was nagged by injuries, which limited him to just 44 games. In his debut, he entered the court during the final minute of the blowout win in the season opener against the Hawks. The rookie played minor minutes for the Pacers and soon turned into a punching bag, the lowlight of his season coming in a game against the Boston Celtics, during which McCloud was inserted for the final minutes to guard Larry Bird. When he saw who was guarding him, Bird felt disrespected, so he turned towards the Pacers bench and yelled: "hey, I know you guys are desperate, but can't you find someone who at least has a prayer?"[2]

The following season, McCloud saw his minutes and production increase, as he played in 74 games, averaged 4.6 points and attempted 1.7 three-point shots per game, twice the number as during his rookie campaign. Apart from injuries, his development was stopped by personal tragedy. His mother died of a heart attack on Valentine's Day 1991. His father, the reverend George McCloud, Sr., committed suicide just four months later in the bedroom of the family home, with his son actually in the house. In two years' time, plagued by injuries and weight problems, the player was out of the NBA. Reminiscing about that time. McCloud said he was not "strong enough to deal with all the hurt."[3] After two years he would return to a different league, one that would allow him to finally exhibit his shooting ability, partially thanks to a particular rule change.

On October 7, 1993, Michael Jordan announced his retirement from professional basketball, accompanied by his teammates, his wife and league commissioner David Stern. During the news conference the most recognizable NBA player of all time stated that he just was not motivated

Few players have benefited from the shortening of the three-point line in 1994–97 more than George McCloud (2001).

enough to play and had nothing left to prove, although personal tragedy to a certain point also influenced his decision— his father was murdered that same year, on the 23rd of July. Jordan's retirement meant that the title race was once again open, with no clear favorite. In 1993–94, for the first time in league history, ten teams finished with at least 50 regular season wins. From the seven concluding playoff series—conference semifinals, conference finals and finals—only two were not settled during Game Sevens.

Still, the 1994 NBA Finals enjoyed the lowest viewership numbers since the Pistons beat the Blazers in 1990. The average number of viewers per game plummeted from 27 million enjoying the Chicago-Phoenix series to a little over 17 million, even though the finals starred two evenly matched teams and were decided in seven games. Obviously, some people tuning in during the previous three seasons were Michael Jordan fans more than basketball fans, but there were other factors at play as well. The viewership numbers ultimately convinced commissioner Stern that the league was in need of a rule change, otherwise the numbers would keep declining. The popular belief was that the NBA would once again become attractive for casual fans if the teams would score more points.

The points per game averages have been steadily declining since the mid–80s, when teams used to average over 110 points per game. And in the 1993–94 season, they dropped by almost four points, from 105.3 to 101.5. There was also the issue of the quality of the games. One of the most dominant teams in the Eastern Conference during the '90s were the New York Knicks, who played a hard-nosed and equally hard to watch brand of basketball, reliant on conditioning and defense. Their game was so team-oriented that despite leading the league in defensive rating—an estimate of points allowed per 100 possessions—and opponent effective field goal percentage in the 1992–93 and 1993–94 seasons, only two players made the NBA All-Defensive teams during that period: John Starks made the second team in 1992–93 and Charles Oakley first team in 1993–94.

Since the summer of 1991, the Knicks had been coached by Pat Riley, who won four NBA championships with Magic Johnson and Kareem Abdul-Jabbar in Los Angeles in the '80s. Under Riley, the Lakers played what became known as "Showtime basketball." The idea was first introduced by coach Jack McKinney, who took over the team in 1979 only to leave after 13 games following a bicycle accident which left him in a coma for three weeks. But McKinney's offensive schemes were used by the interim head coach, Paul Westhead, and resulted in the Lakers winning the championship in 1980. Team owner Jerry Buss was particularly obsessed with Showtime, as he considered it to be a basketball philosophy and a way to fill arenas. Showtime was entertainment at its finest: fast-paced sports combined with short-skirted Laker girls and courtside celebrities like Jack Nicholson or Michael Douglas.

Riley was promoted from assistant to head coach at the beginning of the 1981–82 season, following an ultimatum issued by Magic Johnson. After being officially named head coach after the 1979–80 championship season, Westhead enforced a more conventional and conservative style of play, which the players did not respond particularly well to, resulting in Johnson publicly asking in November 1981 to be traded if things did not change. With Westhead out, Riley immediately reintroduced the old system, catering to his players' strengths.

Riley just as quickly recognized the strengths of his New York players, such as Patrick Ewing, Charles Oakley and Anthony Mason, and understood that they were not made for Showtime basketball. Unlike the Lakers', the Knicks' roster consisted of strong, scrappy players, so this time his team was playing what rival Phil Jackson characterized as "ugly ball."[4] Riley took the Knicks from 39 to 51 wins in his first season as head coach, and in the 1992–93 season, the team's record improved to 60 wins, while he won Coach of the Year for the second time in his career. During his third season as head coach, he led the team to the finals, where the Knicks faced off against the Rockets.

In the 1994 NBA Finals, "every game was decided in the final two minutes, but no team scored more than 93 points in any of the seven games. Forty percent shooting was an accomplishment; in four of the seven games, the losing team's field goal percentage was in the 30s."[5] The broadcast of Game Five was interrupted by a car chase involving the police and O.J. Simpson. Even some fans in attendance redirected their attention from the basketball court to available television screens, oblivious to the fact that their team was back in the finals after 21 years. The car chase and the subsequent trial of the former football player, concerning the deaths of his ex-wife and her friend, marked the beginning of a new craze—celebrity journalism.[6]

The Rockets won the series despite averaging 86 points during those seven games, and their best player was Hakeem Olajuwon, who was named both Most Valuable Player and Defensive Player of the Year. The team was second in defensive ratings during that season. Riley himself said: "when defense gave a team a chance to get to the Finals, it became like anything else—other teams were going to start playing defense."[7] The presence of the Knicks and the Rockets in the finals stood as proof that defensive play led to postseason success.

An exception to the rule were the Seattle SuperSonics, who had won the most games during that season, but fell to the eight-seed Denver Nuggets. That was one of the biggest upsets in NBA playoffs history, the first time a team placed so low eliminated the best regular season team in the conference. Both teams featured two of the best defenders of all time in point guard Gary Payton and center Dikembe Mutombo. In the top six defensive teams were also the Atlanta Hawks, second in the league in steals and fifth in rebounds, and the Jordan-less Chicago Bulls, now led by Scottie Pippen, another all time defensive great.

Less-talented teams, like Mike Fratello's Cleveland Cavaliers, also focused primarily on controlling the ball and rebounding. Even with rule changes in place, the Cavs continued to slow their pace until it reached

82.3 possessions per game in the 1995–96 season, which was 10.3 percent slower than the league average. The Cavaliers went 1–12 in the postseason during Fratello's tenure as head coach, making the playoffs four times in six years and never reaching the second round. Grant Hughes of *Bleacher Report* refers to that time in Cavs history as "the unwatchable era."[8]

With so many teams playing such unappealing basketball, league ownership tried to make the NBA more attractive, primarily by shortening the three-point line. The number of three-pointers per game was slowly growing since 1979, but it was believed that making the three easier, at least in theory, should translate into a rapid increase in the number of long-distance shots. This assumption turned out to be true, as the number of three-point attempts per game rose from 9.9 in 1993–94 to 15.3 in 1994–95, while the league average in points per game went from 101.5 to … 101.4. As the number of attempts grew, the points per game continued to decline and after three seasons, the league decided to restore the original three-point line. With 96.9 points per game, the 1996–97 average was actually the lowest since 1954–55, the first NBA season with the shot clock. Two seasons later, in the lockout-shortened 1998–99 season, teams would average just 91.6 points per game.

The original distance of the three-point line was 23.75 feet at the arc and 22 feet at the corners. Before the 1994–95 season, it was shortened to 22 feet around the entire basket, almost the same as the 22.2 feet in international men's competitions regulated by FIBA (*Fédération Internationale de Basketball*). Other rules that were supposed to "fix" the problem of low scoring included: limited hand-checking, increasing fines for technical fouls, and monitoring taunting. The changes allowed the players to stop relying so heavily on penetrating the lane and moved the game further away from the basket. Some players saw that development as an opportunity to become vital points of their teams' offense.

In 1994–95, John Starks of the New York Knicks led the league in three-point shots made and attempted with 217 and 611 respectively, shooting almost twice as much as in 1993–94. Starks was 45th in three-point percentage, but that did not stop him from letting it fly from long range. In 1993–94, Dan Majerle led the league in three-point shot attempts with 503; Houston's Vernon Maxwell was second with 403. In 1994–95, with the same amount of shots, "Mad Max" would not even make it to the top 15. Clyde Drexler, who became Maxwell's teammate via a mid-season trade with the Blazers, and once the season was over would eventually reach that elusive NBA championship, attempted a career-high 408 three-point shots during that season. Esteemed shooters like Glen Rice, Nick Van Exel and Nick Anderson all set career highs in three-point attempts when the line was closer to the basket. Majerle attempted 548 shots in 1994–95, but his accuracy went down by 2 percent when compared to the prior season. Chicago Bulls' Steve Kerr led the league in percentage with 52.4 percent, improving his accuracy by over 10 percent from the prior season.

Another player who benefited from the change was the second-most accurate three-point shooter in the 1994–95 season, Detlef Schrempf, who was a decent-long distance shooter throughout his career (38.4 percent) but also holds the record for the lowest amount of points scored during the 3-Point Contest with five in 1988, tied two years later by Michael Jordan. During the 1994–95 season, he finally got to shoot from long distance more than once per game for the first time in his professional career, and finished the season with 2.2 attempts per game, making 51.4 percent of his shots. Schrempf joined the Pacers in February of 1989 from the Mavericks and left the team around the same time as McCloud. Unlike McCloud, while on the team, Schrempf enjoyed considerable success and won back-to-back Sixth Man of the Year awards in 1991 and 1992. A year later he was traded to the Sonics.

McCloud's career took a different path, as he was released by the Pacers and played in the 1993–94 season for the Serie A team Scavolini Pesaro, who finished the regular season and the playoffs only behind Virtus Bologna. In Italy, McCloud got used to different spacing and positioning associated with the shortened three-point line, which was especially important from the perspective of a long-distance shooter. He averaged 18.8 points per game and shot 42.3 percent from three. When he rejoined the NBA in January of 1995, after starting the season on the CBA's Rapid City Thrillers, he was better adjusted to the new rules, which allowed him to play the brand of basketball he preferred. The coach who encouraged him to shoot at will was Dick Motta, who enjoyed the most success before the three-point line had been introduced in the NBA, and was known as one of the most demanding basketball coaches ever.

Dick Motta got his first (and only) Coach of the Year award for his work during the 1970–71 season, in which he led the Chicago Bulls to the playoffs for the first time in the team's five-year history. Seven years later, Motta won his first (and only) NBA championship with the Washington Bullets. Motta bought out his contract with the Bulls to join the Bullets and in two seasons led the team to its first (and only) title, beating the Sonics in 1978. A year later, they would once again face off against the Sonics, only this time they would come out on the losing end. Motta moved from Washington to Dallas before the 1980–81 season, to coach the expansion Mavericks.

Not having talent on the same level as he inherited in Washington, Motta was able to lead the Mavericks to the playoffs in his fourth season as head coach, despite numerous arguments with the team's best player, Mark Aguirre. He resigned after his seventh season at the helm, following criticism from Mavericks' fans that he was openly talking with the Clippers and the Knicks about taking over one of those teams. Before the 1994–95 season, he came back to Dallas. The team had made the playoffs only once since he left, in 1990, and was easily eliminated by the Blazers in the first round. Motta was returning to a much different, inexperienced Mavericks team and "suddenly the youngest team in the league had the oldest coach."[9]

However, Motta was now also a different coach, still a mentor, eager to win, but more relaxed and easy-going. He was taking over for disciplinarian Quinn Buckner, who led the Mavs to just 13 wins the season before while clashing with the team's best players. Motta had a history of being tough on his superstars as well—apart from Aguirre, who eventually embraced Motta's coaching style and complex personality, he was critical of Hall of Famer and Bullets' legend Wes Unseld for his inability to shoot the ball—the difference was that his Mavericks managed to make the playoffs five years in a row, while Buckner was fired after just one year at the helm.

Motta was supposed to groom the promising duo of Jim Jackson and Jamal Mashburn, both selected with fourth picks in the 1993 and 1994 NBA drafts, both scorers and dunkers, possessing a very similar skillset and equally inflated egos. After Motta's appointment, with the second pick the team added Jason Kidd, a versatile point guard from California who was characterized as a potential superstar and future Hall of Famer were he to improve his shooting. Kidd ended his Hall of Fame career with 1,988 three-point shots made.

In the previous season, Mashburn and Jackson both averaged the same number of points (19.2), steals (1.1) and almost the same number of rebounds (4.7 and 4.5, respectively) per game. With Kidd, they formed "The Three J's" and earned comparisons with "The Triplets"—Troy Aikman, Michael Irvin and Emmitt Smith, three football players drafted by the Dallas Cowboys, who became the core of the three-time (two by then) NFL championship winning team. Motta, then 63 years old, decided to try out an unconventional—by his standards—approach toward his young players:

> All the players had heard stories of Motta's screaming, yelling, chair-kicking scenes. Yet when they reported for the first minicamp, they found that Motta had set up a pool table, a Ping-Pong table and a daily spread of food for them. He said his main ambition was to make the game "fun" again. (Really?) He told the young Mavs that if they would only listen to him, he would teach them to play the game the way it's supposed be played. And if they did that, Motta told them, they would win.[10]

In the following season, the team improved their overall record by 23 wins by relying on fast-paced basketball and a generally offensive approach—they led the league in field goal attempts, were ninth in points per game, but 24th in points allowed per game. The season before, they were last in points per game and 17th in points allowed.

Kidd, the eventual co–Rookie of the Year—with Grant Hill—was already becoming a leader on the Mavericks. His primary ability was his court vision, which quickly turned him into one of the greatest passers the NBA has ever seen; however, he was also capable of scoring and rebounding the ball, and in his rookie year he led the league in triple-doubles, with four. While this was far from Oscar Robertson's 1960–61 first-year record of 26, Kidd would finish his career with 107, good for third overall at the time of his retirement, behind Robertson and Magic Johnson.

Kidd's statement game as a rookie came against the inner-state rivals and NBA champions, the Houston Rockets. The teams had split their previous four meetings, and in their final game Kidd took over the offense, something he had been sometimes reluctant to do earlier in the season. Part of the reason for that was his teammates' unwillingness to share the limelight (and the ball). In an earlier game against the Utah Jazz, after scoring three times in a row on John Stockton, Kidd asked the coaching staff not to call a play for him for the fourth time because Jackson and Mashburn would get angry.[11]

In the April game against the Rockets, Jackson was absent with an injury, while Kidd went for 38 points, 10 assists and 11 rebounds, leading his team to a double-overtime victory. He made eight three-pointers, including two crucial running shots which sent the game to overtime. Tellingly, after the second game-tying shot went in, Kidd was congratulated by all of his teammates except Mashburn, who had a game-high 42 points that night. One of the first to pat him on the behind was George McCloud, who had joined the Mavericks team by the end of January 1995 from the CBA. When Jackson went down with a season-ending ankle injury in February, McCloud's minutes and role on the team increased. He even started three games, one of them being against the Rockets, during which he scored 25 points and went 3 for 6 from three. In March and April, the team won more games than it lost and fell short of reaching the playoffs by just five games.

Capable of playing four positions, McCloud served a vital role on the innovative, injury-ridden Mavericks. They played like few teams before them had done. Motta allowed his players to run, attack the opposing basket and shoot at will. Before its inception, the coach considered the three-point shot a gimmick, but hoped that "it'll prove to be interesting."[12] Now he had the perfect players to fully utilize the long-distance shot. He was mellow and calm, as if he understood that his younger players were going to make mistakes. Older players, such as McCloud, also benefited from that approach and the following season turned out to be the best of McCloud's career.

The 1995–96 season was the last full season of the Mavericks' talented core together, even though for Jamal Mashburn it ended after just 18 games. The small forward averaged 23.4 points per game, slightly less than the season before, but still enough to lead the team in that category. His absence was part of the reason why the Mavericks regressed to 26–56 despite still playing the same, entertaining type of basketball—second in pace, first in three-pointers made and attempted. A season later they were sixth in pace, 15th and 20th in three-point makes and attempts. On the flipside, Mashburn's injury may be the sole explanation as to how the Mavericks were able to keep Jackson, Mashburn and Kidd on the same team for one more season. At its start, with Mashburn still healthy, the team was experiencing serious locker room chemistry issues and the coach accused both him and Jackson of polarizing the team by not talking, as well as not passing to each other. By stating that "they can get in the fetal position and go back to Mama, or they can come back and be pros,"[13] Dick Motta began again showing signs of his former, mean self.

Motta's frustration was understandable, as one of the most talented teams of the '90s was quickly deteriorating due to egotism on his very eyes. Jackson was probably the most troublesome of the three; during his rookie season, he did not agree to Dallas' contract proposal and held out until March 1993, playing in only 24 games in his first year. When he came back after the calf injury in February 1994, he was displeased with Mashburn taking too many shots, at least in his opinion.

This time it was Mashburn's injury that somewhat solved the ball-sharing problem, but Jason Kidd, who had served as voice of reason the season before, was now openly talking to the media about the conflict between both players: "why shouldn't I just go buy my own boat and have everybody jump on my boat instead of everybody getting in their boat, when we don't know who's steering the boat?" Jackson replied in a hostile manner, deepening the Mavericks' chemistry issues: "he makes enough money, if he wants to buy his own boat, let him buy it. Buy 20 of them. Buy a yacht. I hope he has an anchor and some life rafts."[14] By February of 1996, coach Motta was willing to trade both Jackson and Mashburn, planning to rebuild the team around his young point guard. However, it was Motta who left the Mavericks by season's end, as the team was sold to a new owner. Donald Carter, the former owner, had been a friend of Motta's, and Motta had taken over the team as a personal favor to him; under the new ownership, Motta left despite Kidd's urges to stay.[15]

The team's first ever owner and first ever coach were both gone, while the toxic locker room atmosphere remained. Newly employed head coach Jim Cleamons had won four NBA championships as an assistant for the Chicago Bulls, working under Phil Jackson. He would end his career with nine titles, all while being on Jackson's staff on the Bulls and later on the Lakers. At the beginning of his tenure with the Mavericks, Cleamons was full of hope that Kidd, Jackson and Mashburn would mend their differences, so "during Cleamons's first week in Dallas, Kidd met with the coach to get acquainted and talk about the Mavs. Cleamons thought they had an understanding as to what the coach expected of his young star. But the next day Kidd stunned the Mavs' new management team by issuing a public ultimatum: Either he or Jackson had to go."[16]

Three-Pointer!

The coach and the three superstars attempted to solve their issues at the beginning of the 1996–97 season one last time, but Cleamons' insistence on playing the Bulls' signature triangle offense stalled the team's progress. The Mavericks were still losing games, and on December 26, Jason Kidd was traded to the Suns. There he once again excelled at playing small-ball basketball alongside point guards Kevin Johnson and Steve Nash and shooting guard Rex Chapman. Kidd would become one of the best point guards in league history and during the later stages of his career, he would return to the Mavericks to provide veteran leadership on a team headlined by Dirk Nowitzki.

In 2011, Kidd won his sole NBA championship as a member of the Mavericks, the team that traded him, along with Loren Meyer and Tony Dumas, to Phoenix for Sam Cassell, Michael Finley and A.C. Green. Kidd ended his career as a member of the New York Knicks, just one season deep into his three-year contract. In the playoffs, the 40-year-old Kidd averaged 0.9 points, two assists and one turnover, despite playing 20.6 minutes per game in 12 games. He shot 12 percent from the floor (3 for 25 overall), 17.6 percent from three, and had not made a single two-point shot. His jersey was eventually retired by the New Jersey Nets, whom he took to the 2002 and 2003 NBA Finals.

During Kidd's first time on the Mavericks, he was not particularly liked by interim general manager and minority owner Frank Zaccanelli, who considered the player a troublemaker. When Don Nelson took over, after Kidd was already gone, he was not fond of how Jackson and Mashburn conducted themselves on and off the court, and traded them away as well.[17] Mashburn went on to have a stellar career playing for the Miami Heat and the Charlotte/New Orleans Hornets, until it was cut short by a knee injury. Despite deliberately sitting out a year, Mashburn's knee never got better and he failed to appear in a single game for the Sixers, who traded for him in February of 2005. As for Jackson, once he left Dallas after four and a half seasons, he never stayed on a team longer than one and a half seasons, and he ended up playing for 11 different teams throughout his career, second-most in league history behind Chucky Brown, who played for 12 teams. Jackson was a very decent player, in high demand as one can guess from the number of teams that were willing to take him on.

McCloud was traded along with Jackson in 1997 to the New Jersey

Nets, but was immediately moved to the Lakers as Nets coach John Cal-
lipari did not see McCloud becoming a member of the team's rotation.[18]
During his last (half-)season with the Mavericks, he was still a vital contributor for the team, playing 29.4 minutes, scoring 13.7 points and attempting five three-pointers a game—it was fairly obvious that he had
to take less shots with both Jackson and Mashburn healthy. After the
1996–97 season was over, McCloud joined Kidd on the Suns, where he
would mostly come off the bench for two years. He then signed with the
Nuggets, where he played for three seasons. Before the 2002–03 season,
McCloud was traded to the Wizards, who placed him on waivers and released him. The next year he joined the Warriors, but was once again released without playing a single game. Two days later, McCloud officially
retired from professional basketball.

During the 2000–01 season, he set one last personal record, when
playing at point guard while starter Nick Van Exel was on the injured list.
His Nuggets won against the Bulls in overtime and McCloud ended the
game with 22 assists, reminding everyone that there was a time when he
was being compared to Magic Johnson. Still, his production never got
close to what he achieved in Dallas, which can be partially blamed on his
inconsistency, as well as the lack of trust in his abilities that he so benefited from under Motta. While these did not always translate into team
wins, McCloud's 1995–96 season stands out for numerous reasons. He was
able to set a number of NBA records, the last of which would remain un-
broken for 20 years.

The 1995–96 Mavericks can be regarded as a team ahead of its time,
albeit circumstances played a crucial part in its creation. The team was
playing the type of basketball NBA executives probably hoped for when
introducing the shortened three-point line—offensive, quick and entertaining. However, the Mavs were also plagued by injuries. While ten
players managed to play in over 58 games, which is the minimum to be
considered for league leaders in stats, only five appeared on the court in
over 68 games. Two of them were reserve point guard Scott Brooks and
rookie center Loren Meyer, who finished the season with averages of 5
points, 4.4 rebounds and 0.4 blocks. The other three were Jackson, Kidd
and McCloud.

With slow-paced, defensive ball not being much of an option with
that roster, Motta instructed his players to run the court and shoot when-

ever they were open. McCloud said about his time under Motta, "it was so much fun because you had freedom, it's not just one player that had the green light. Some games it was you, some games it wasn't you. But every game you shot. You had that opportunity."[19] Since the three-point shot was still not held in high regard, defenders were not as concerned with defending it. When Kidd was running with the ball, players would take their spots and immediately fire away after getting the kick out pass from the point guard. It was Kidd's extraordinary speed that made this type of play possible and thanks to it, the Mavs did not have to depend on the pick and roll, as was the case with most pass-first point guards.

Still, even when the shots did go in, the Mavericks failed to win games. Playing with a point guard, a center and three wing players impacted the team's defensive abilities, as it could not handle the forceful play of taller, stronger athletes. Even though the Mavericks led the NBA in three-point attempts per game with 24.9 (the second-placed Rockets shot for three 21.5 times per game) and completed, with an average of nine makes (followed once again by the Rockets with 7.8 completions per game), they were only 18th in the league in three-point shot percentage with 36 percent. Three teams—the Bullets, the Pistons and the Bulls—made over 40 percent of their three-point shot attempts that season.

McCloud was the player who contributed the most to the number of three-point shots per game taken by the Mavericks. In 34 games, he attempted ten or more shots; in 20 games he made at least five. In 21 games, he converted 50 percent or more of said attempts. In a game against the Phoenix Suns on December 16, 1995, he attempted 12 shots and made ten of them, shooting with an incredible percentage of 83.8. During said game, he made eight three-pointers in a row, while six came during a third-quarter comeback. McCloud's impressive performance took the game to overtime, but that was not enough to beat Charles Barkley and the Suns. With his tenth three-pointer, he tied the (then) NBA single-game record held by Brian Shaw and Joe Dumars. Shaw set the record by shooting from behind the old three-point line, placed further away from the basket, in a game against the Milwaukee Bucks in April 1993; Dumars tied the record in November 1994, when the line was already shortened. McCloud said after the game: "I still have my bad days, but I look ahead knowing the worst has already happened to me."[20]

Another notable occurrence during the 1995–96 season was Mc-

Cloud's record-setting streak of six games with five or more made three-point shots. It started on February 25, 1995, against the Raptors, and ended on March 5 with a different record-setting performance—this time regarding the number of three-point shot attempts in a single game. Both records have since been broken numerous times. In six consecutive games, McCloud went 5 for 12, 8 for 16, 8 for 14, 7 for 14, 5 for 16 and 7 for 20. His averages from that time were: 26.8 points, 7.2 rebounds, 3.5 steals, 3 assists and 1 block. The Mavericks won four of those six games. The streak ended with a loss to the Charlotte Hornets, during which McCloud made just two of his ten attempts. The 20 shots came in a game against the Nets, during which the Mavericks as a team also set a league record with 49 three-point shot attempts. They won that game 127–117, with Jackson draining five of nine, and Kidd ending the game with four out of eight made three-point shots.

Just three days after McCloud's streak ended, the team from Charlotte put to a close another concurrent three-point streak, as a different player came up one game short of tying the record just set by the Dallas Mavericks small forward. Dennis Scott of the Orlando Magic recorded five games with five or more three-point shots made by going 6 for 11, 8 for 16, 5 for 12, 8 for 15 and 5 for 6 during a stretch that lasted from February 28 to March 5, so the same day McCloud and the Mavs played the Nets. On March 8 in Orlando, Scott went four of six against the Hornets. He lost that "rivalry" with McCloud, but set another record later on in the season, by making 11 three-point shots (in 17 attempts) against the Hawks. The last shot was assisted by Brian Shaw, one of the holders of the previous record.

Selected with the fourth pick in the 1990 NBA draft by the Magic, Scott was not as unlikely a candidate for three-point record books as McCloud. In the first eight years of his professional career, he never averaged less than four three-point shots per game. Nicknamed 3-D, Scott was primarily a long-distance scorer, whereas his defense left much to be desired—some joked that his nickname actually referred to his defense (D) which was rated three out of ten, and not to his number and first name.[21] In college, Scott had influenced Georgia Tech's style of play by convincing his coach that his three-point shot was worth the risk, and did likewise with Brian Hill, the coach of the Magic. During his best college season, as a junior, he averaged 27.7 points per game. His teammates used to joke about his ability to shoot from long distance, shouting: "layup!" whenever he released the ball from 19 feet and 9 inches, a distance Scott himself found "laughable."[22]

When Scott was younger, he wanted to play like Magic Johnson, but never possessed the speed and the court vision to play as a point guard. Luckily for him, his first pro team, the Magic, soon drafted an all-time great center and an All-Star point guard, so he could focus on what he did best—shooting the ball. Scott was a starter on the Orlando team that reached the 1995 NBA Finals, which featured Shaquille O'Neal, Anfernee Hardaway, Horace Grant and fellow long-distance shooter Nick Anderson. During that season, Scott made 150 three-pointers in 62 games, whereas during 1995–96, he set an NBA record with 267 makes in 82 games. It was beaten by Ray Allen ten years later.

McCloud made 257 threes during the 1995–96 season, coming up second in the league in makes behind Scott, but the number that stood out the most from that time were his 678 three-point field goal attempts. For 20 seasons, nobody attempted more three-point shots in a season, until Steph Curry's 2015–16 back-to-back MVP campaign, during which time he took 823 long-distance shots, 145 more than McCloud. The Mavericks' small forward set the long-lasting record against the Phoenix Suns on April 19, 1996, during

Dennis Scott set an NBA record with 11 three-pointers made during a single game in 1996 (1996).

the second to last game of the season. Three days earlier, McCloud went 0 for 8 against the Lakers and 5 for 8 the night before, against the Nuggets. Considering how streaky his shooting was, the game against the Suns was either going to be a very bad or an incredible shooting night. It turned out to be the former, as he went 0 for 6 from three and 3 for 14 overall. The Mavericks lost that game by 20 points.

McCloud's 1995–96 campaign stands out as one of the most unexpected shooting seasons in NBA history. While his stats were seen as an element of basketball trivia before the three-pointer became a staple of today's game, he was actually a player ahead of his time. The reason why this chapter ends with a missed shot—or rather six of those—is because that is what that Mavericks team was, a missed opportunity to revolutionize basketball. Had the same cast of players been assembled after the 2004–05 rule change—which moved the game away from the basket by introducing illegal defense (the defensive three-second violation), as well as disallowing hand-checking—it would have fared much better than it did ten years earlier.

The ascension of small-ball and the appearance of teams like the 2010s Golden State Warriors make the 1994–96 Mavericks a graceful topic of barroom, journalistic and TV debates, one of the "what-if" teams of all-time, yet they should not be reduced to just that. In a sense, Rob Mahoney is right by calling that Mavericks team "the Warriors—without the winning,"[23] but clearly their roster was built for a different type of game, more physical, less open. While it may be convenient to blame circumstances for their losses and ultimate demise, it is thanks to circumstances that they can be remembered so fondly in the first place. Even if their transition to small-ball happened by chance and not design, the Mavericks were the pioneers, the prophets of a new era of basketball, and these always need some time and perspective to be appreciated for their contributions to the game.

The Mavericks set a number of three-point records while playing a very entertaining brand of basketball. Most of these records were set by George McCloud, a small forward who should have been a point guard. A draft bust who was able to turn things around and become a vital part of his team's offense. A streaky shooter and unlikely starter who would not have been put in that position had another player not been injured.

February 8–9, 1997

Steve Kerr and Glen Rice
Dominate the All-Star Weekend

Steve Kerr was an integral part of two teams that have won the most single-season games in NBA history. On the 1995–96 Bulls, he was the reserve point guard, playing 23.4 minutes per game, attempting 2.9 threes on 51.5 percent accuracy, while on the 2015–16 Warriors, he coached a team led by a duo of exceptional three-point shooters, Steph Curry and Klay Thompson. Serving as the only link between the two teams, it was inevitable for Kerr to share his thoughts on which team would win the hypothetical confrontation: the 72–10 Bulls or the 73–9 Warriors? While the players who played in the '90s were almost unanimously convinced that the Bulls would pretty much sweep the Warriors, Kerr himself was reluctant to give a definite answer, stressing the way the game had changed since the time he played as the reason why such a debate did not make much sense.[1]

Indeed, in 2016 the game was quite different than when the Bulls dominated the NBA. Kerr carved out a niche for himself as a very useful role player precisely because players like him were so uncommon in the early '90s NBA. The 6'3", skinny guard, who was not particularly athletic or fast, is remembered only for his three-point shooting. He joined the league with the 50th pick in the 1988 NBA draft after a successful career at the University of Arizona, where he already made a name for himself as a sharpshooter—with the three-point line being introduced to the league only in his last NCAA season, he was attempting 5.2 and making 3 three-pointers a game, immediately setting the (still-standing) league record for accuracy. Kerr made 57.3 percent of his long-distance attempts as a senior. Actually, before his final NCAA game, Kerr was making 59.9 percent from three, before going 2 for 12 in the semifinal game against Kansas, lost by the Arizona Wildcats. Interestingly, Steph Curry, who would enjoy the most success as a professional athlete while playing under Kerr, also set an NCAA long-distance shooting record, for the most three-pointers made during a single-season, with 162 at Davidson.

Upon entering the NBA though, Kerr had to fight tooth and nail for his place in the league, just like he first had at college, where he went almost unrecruited due to being skinny, slow and unable to jump particularly high.[2] After an unsuccessful rookie season on the Suns, he joined the Cavs, where he would serve as a backup to Mark Price, one of the best pure shooters in league history. Price made 976 threes with 40.2 percent accuracy throughout his NBA career, the first nine years of which he spent on the Cavaliers. Price and center Brad Daugherty were supposed to lead the team from Ohio to NBA glory, but they struggled with injuries to such an extent that, despite participating in a total of nine All-Star games and making the 1992 Eastern Conference Finals, the team felt somewhat of a disappointment when it came to reaching its potential. Their peak also coincided with the rise of Michael Jordan and his Chicago Bulls, the most dominant team of the decade.

Price was the second player ever, after "founder" Larry Bird, to join the 50–40–90 club, entry to which is only available to professional players who have made over 50 percent of their field-goals, 40 percent of their threes and 90 percent of their free-throws during a single season. Price achieved that in the 1988–89 season, the one before Kerr became his backup. Other members of the club include Reggie Miller, Steve Nash (four times), Steph Curry and WNBA's Elena Delle Donne.

Price also won the 3-Point Contest twice, in 1993 and 1994. During the second contest, he faced off against Kerr, who was picked up by the Bulls in the summer of the previous year, after another uneventful season in the league, this time for the Orlando Magic. On the Jordan-less Bulls, Kerr became an important part of the offense. Coming off the bench, as he usually did—Kerr started only 30 games of the 910 he played in the league—he played the most minutes (24.8) and had the highest points per game average (8.6) of his career. He even made it to the second round of the 1994 3-Point Contest, but scored just 13 points, 4 less than Dana Barros and 8 less than Price. In the final round, Price made 24 points, beating Barros by 11.

Mark Price was a shoot-first point guard who was way ahead of his time (1993).

Kerr once again appeared in the contest a year later, but this time he did not make it out of the first round, while the final featured Reggie Miller and Glen Rice, who both scored 19 points in the previous phase. Rice won 16–15, becoming the second Miami Heat player to earn an individual trophy during the All-Star Weekend after Harold Miner, who won two Slam Dunk Contests in 1993 and 1995. Even though he was a superstar in college, it seemed that Miner earned the nickname "Baby Jordan" solely for his dunking ability, as he was out of the NBA after just four seasons.

Rice entered the NBA a year later than Kerr, in 1989, with the fourth pick in the draft, and, unlike Kerr, never had to struggle for playing time, as he was named the starter immediately in his rookie year. Rice, like Kerr, earned the reputation as one of the best three-point shooters in the NCAA. In his senior year, he released 5.2 three-point shot attempts per game and made 51.6 percent of them. In his final college game, Rice scored 34 points and led the Michigan Wolverines to their first (and only) NCAA championship. His number was retired by the team.

In 1996, Kerr would once again lose in the first round of the 3-Point Contest, the winner that time being Tim Legler of the Washington Bullets. Legler became the first player in the competition's history to score 20 or more points in each of the three rounds. His wife, Jennifer, pregnant at the time, was induced early so that her husband could participate in the contest. Her reasoning was that "because Tim had been cut from more teams than he'd made in the National Basketball Association, and that this was one of his few moments to shine, the sacrifice was worth it."[3] It turned out to be a good decision, as her husband delivered the best performance of his career during the best season of his career—Legler not only finished the season as the league leader in three-point shot accuracy (52.2 percent) but was also voted second for the Sixth Man of the Year award.

Legler went undrafted in the 1988 draft bounced between teams from the USBL, the CBA, the WBL, the NBA, as well as play in Europe, starting each season on a different team. The turning point of his career came when he was signed by the Warriors at the end of the 1994–95 season. By making 52 percent of his threes in the 24 games he got to play, at age 28, he finally proved to NBA teams that he was able to contribute on the highest level. After appearing in a career-high 77 games in the 1995–96 season, over the next four years, due to knee injuries, Legler appeared in just 76 games. He subsequently retired from professional basketball and became a high school women's basketball coach, and later on a TV analyst.

Kerr ended up behind Legler in accuracy that season, making 51.5 percent of his long-distance attempts in 1995–96. A season earlier, Kerr was the one who led the league with 52.4 percent accuracy. He achieved that even though Jordan's return for the last 17 games of the 1994-95 regular season disrupted the flow of the game for the Bulls. Instead of playing in accordance to the system which allowed the team to remain competitive in the East, Jordan demanded the ball and played one-on-one basketball, with the rest of the team often serving pretty much as spectators.

Jordan was highly critical of Kerr at first, as if he was testing his toughness, like he had done with several teammates in the past. During a preseason workout, Kerr and Jordan got into a heated argument, which ended in a fistfight, the first of Kerr's adult life. Jordan gave him a black eye, but by the time Kerr returned home, there was already an apology waiting on his answering machine. By standing up to Jordan, Kerr gained his respect and the two did not have any problems afterward. Seeing the seriousness with which Kerr approached the game, Jordan finally started showing belief in Kerr's ability.[4]

He trusted Kerr to the point that he passed him the ball during the final seconds of Game Six of the 1997 NBA Finals. That alone put Kerr in the same category as John Paxson, whom Jordan also trusted in crucial moments of important games. With Game Six tied at 86 and the Bulls leading the series 3-2, they had 28 seconds to make a basket and then try to stop the Jazz from scoring in front of their home crowd in Salt Lake City. After Coach Jackson called a timeout, Jordan approached Kerr about being ready for a pass if he was double-teamed by Bryon Russell and John Stockton. As this was exactly what happened, Kerr immediately moved close to the free throw line. Jordan noticed him and passed him the ball, Kerr caught the pass and nailed the shot, leaving 5.4 seconds on the game clock. The Jazz called a timeout and still stood a chance at tying the game, but Pippen tipped the inbound pass, then slid in the ball's direction and tipped it again to Kukoc, who dunked it, sealing the Bulls' fifth NBA championship, the second of Kerr's career.

The 1996–97 season would prove special for another reason for Kerr, as it was during the 1997 All-Star Weekend that he finally won the 3-Point

Contest. The competition took place in the middle of the celebrations of the 50th anniversary of the founding of the NBA. Other participants in the contest were: Legler, Rice, Walt Williams, John Stockton, Dale Ellis, Terry Mills (Rice's teammate at Michigan) and Sam Perkins. Kerr and the first three entered the second round of the competition. Rice was playing for the Hornets at the time, having being traded with Matt Geiger, Khalid Reeves and a first round pick (which would turn into Tony Delk) in November 1995 for Alonzo Mourning, LeRon Ellis and Pete Myers. The trade occurred the day after Heat coach Pat Riley assured Rice that he would not be moved.[5] Rice played for the Heat for six seasons and the team made the playoffs just twice, both times losing in the first round. He was averaging 19.3 points per game and making 38.6 percent of his threes, up to that point being by far the best player in franchise history.

Walt Williams was the small forward brought in by Miami mid-season to partially fill the role that Rice used to play on the team, as their previous starting small forward, Billy Owens, was not much of a long-distance shooter. Williams shot 45.5 percent from three, averaging 12 points and 4 rebounds in the 28 regular season games he played for the Heat, but the team renounced his free-agent rights as it was facing salary cap restrictions. Williams then signed with the Raptors for the veteran's minimum, becoming the first player representing the capital of Canada in the 3-Point Contest. He ended his career with 976 threes and 37.9 percent efficiency from long distance. Both Rice and Williams failed to make it to the final round of the 1997 3-Point Contest.

Kerr won, scoring 22 points, 4 more than the returning champion, Legler. After winning, Kerr did not participate in the competition again, and after the 1997–98 season he left the Bulls, as the team was rebuilding following the inevitable breakup of the championship core. The next season, the team was so bad that they were nicknamed the "Replace-a-Bulls." Ron Harper and Toni Kukoc were the only notable players that came back from the previous season, with Jordan and Jackson now retired, Pippen on the Rockets, Rodman on the Lakers, and Luc Longley on the Suns. Kerr, the only other player to average over 20 minutes per game, joined the San Antonio Spurs, where he would get less playing time, yet still contribute in a rather limited role. The Spurs won the 1999 NBA championship in the lockout-shortened season, but Kerr did not play much in the playoffs. He made just three three-pointers during that title run.

Three-Pointer!

In the semifinals against the Lakers, Kerr did not even step on the court, while his team swept the physically imposing LA roster, consisting of the likes of O'Neal, Horry, Bryant and Glen Rice. The last one was brought in before the 1999 season for fan-favorite Eddie Jones. Other players involved in the trade were: the Lakers' Elden Campbell, a center who was made expendable after O'Neal joined the team the season before; the Hornets' J.R. Reid and B.J. Armstrong. Armstrong did not play a single game for the Lakers and was signed again by the Hornets. A career 42.5 percent three-point shooter, Armstrong would have been useful a year later, when Phil Jackson took over the team. Armstrong played for Jackson on the Bulls and won three NBA championships. He made 436 three-pointers throughout his career.

Jones was traded because he was playing the same position as Kobe Bryant, who was projected to be a much better player than the elder shooting guard. Apart from Jones, around the same time the team also got rid of point guard Nick Van Exel, another solid three-point shooter. Van Exel made 1,528 three-pointers on 35.7 percent accuracy during the 12 seasons he played in the NBA. Jones would make the All-Star team three times, as a member of the Hornets and the Heat, and the 1999–2000 season would be the best of his career. He averaged 20.1 points per game and lead the league with 2.7 steals. Throughout his career Jones made 1,546 threes, shooting with 37.3 percent accuracy.

However, at the time of the trade between the Lakers and the Hornets, it was Rice who was the best player involved. He was coming off three consecutive All-Star Game appearances and two All-NBA selections. The most memorable performance of his career actually came during the 1997 All-Star Game, one night after he failed to reach the final round of the 3-Point Contest. Rice was selected as a reserve in the East and he made All-Star history by scoring 20 points in the third quarter, 24 total in the second half—both All-Star records when it came to points scored during a quarter and a half. Rice finished the game with 26 points, going 4 of 7 from three. He made such an impression with his shooting display that even though his teammate, Michael Jordan, recorded the first triple-double in All-Star history, it was Rice who was voted the game's Most Valuable Player. Jordan actually noticed that Rice was in the zone and encouraged the small forward to keep shooting. After the game Rice said, "Sometimes you see the basketball going in before you release it; you

Glen Rice was one of the best scorers of the '90s, who ended his career with 40 percent of his three-point shots made (1997).

feel everything you throw up is going in and it's one of the greatest feelings you can imagine. I love to shoot."[6]

During his three seasons in Charlotte, Rice averaged 23.5 points per game and shot 44.4 percent from three. Upon his move to Los Angeles, he was supposed to be the third superstar next to Shaq and Kobe, complementing them with his shooting, something the team had been missing in the previous playoffs. The Lakers made the 1998 Western Conference Finals, but were swept by the Jazz who shot 51.4 percent from the floor, including 53.3 percent from three. By comparison, the Lakers made 39.9 percent of their shots, 25.7 percent from the outside. In the 1999 playoffs, their first with Rice on the roster, the team got better in that department, but that time they were swept by the Spurs. Interim coach Kurt Rambis got fired and the team hired Phil Jackson, just one year after his official retirement from coaching professional basketball.

Jackson immediately recognized that the team needed veteran leadership in order to succeed and urged team general manager Jerry West to bring in Scottie Pippen from the Rockets. At the time, Pippen was basically an elder version of Eddie Jones—a lockdown defender who could also bring the ball upcourt and put numbers on the board. The fundamental difference was that unlike any member of the Lakers roster, Pippen had championship experience. Team owner Jerry Buss did not agree to the trade only due to salary cap reasons, as the $67 million Pippen was owed for the next four years of the five-year deal he had signed as a member of the Bulls, would severely limit the team's flexibility in constructing the rest of the roster.

The trade was supposed to involve Rice, who was demanding a long-term deal worth $14 million per season and was about to enter his contract year. Jackson was also interested in bringing in the Knicks' Latrell Sprewell, another player similar in stature and style of play to Jones. Sprewell however, unlike the well-liked Jones, had a reputation as a troublemaker after choking his coach at Golden State, P.J. Carlesimo, during a 1997 practice. The fact that the Knicks were shopping him around despite making the 1999 NBA Finals, in large part due to his contributions, was telling. Sprewell remained on the Knicks until the summer of 2003. In a February 4, 2003, game against the Clippers, he set an NBA record by making nine out of nine three-point shot attempts on the way to a 38-point night. In the summer, he was traded to the Timberwolves and in his first season there, along with Kevin Garnett and Sam Cassell, Sprewell took the team to the Western Conference Finals for the first time in franchise history. A year later, after failing to make the playoffs, he rejected a three-year, $21-million contract extension. Starting the 2005–06 season without a team, he refused to sign for less than $5 million, oblivious to multiple suitors approaching him. He soon went bankrupt, despite earning over $100 million during his professional career.

Unable to get who he wanted, Jackson eventually settled on Rice as the team's starting small forward. The Lakers won the 2000 championship, with Rice playing over 30 minutes per game that season but attempting almost twice as fewer three-point shots—2.9 to 5.0—as the year before, due to Jackson's triangle offense. The style of play took the ball out of his hands and turned him into a catch-and-shoot player, a role he did not feel comfortable with, as his offensive repertoire also included post-up plays and drives.[7] In the NBA Finals against the Pacers, Rice would sit out crucial moments of some games in favor of reserve forward Rick Fox, who was a worse shooter, but a better defender. In no way was Fox a bad shooter though, as he made 771 three-pointers in the 13 seasons he played in the NBA, making 34.9 percent of his long-distance shots as a member of the Celtics and the Lakers.

In Game One of the 2000 NBA Finals, Rice went one of eight from the floor. In Game Three, he scored just seven points, making three field-goals on nine attempts. He played around 27 minutes in both games, while in Game Two he scored 21 points and made five of six three-point attempts in 34 minutes. Rice's wife complained to the press during the series, referencing the aforementioned failed trade for Pippen and his husband's varying playing time: "It's all a mind game. It's all about control. Jackson did not get his way with the general manager or the owner about trading Glen, so who pays for it? Glen does."[8] Jackson did not want to address that issue during team meetings. O'Neal also approached Rice after Game Five in which the Lakers lost, making the series 3–2, and admitted that Rice was treated unfairly, yet needed to perform as the team was just one game away from winning the title.[9] Rice went made all three of his three-point attempts, scored a total of 16 points and grabbed six rebounds; the Lakers won by five points. In the summer, he was traded to the Knicks in a blockbuster trade that brought Patrick Ewing to the Sonics and Horace Grant to the Lakers. After a season on the Knicks, Rice would play for the Rockets and the Clippers, before retiring in 2004. He ended his career with 1,559 three-pointers made with 40 percent accuracy.

Steve Kerr had retired a year before, after winning his fifth NBA championship with the Spurs. In Game Six of the 2003 Western Conference Finals, Kerr delivered one last signature performance, in 13 minutes going four out of four from three. Three of those threes came in two minutes of the Spurs' 23–0 fourth quarter run against the Mavericks, who had entered the quarter leading 69–56. The team from San Antonio won that game and headed to the NBA Finals, where it made easy work of the Nets. The 37-year-old point guard made 726 three-pointers with 45.4 percent accuracy during his NBA career. He remains the all-time league leader in career three-point shooting percentage.

While Rice's story lacks a basketball-related second chapter, Kerr remains one of the most influential people in shaping today's NBA, as he is now the head coach of the team that turned the three-point shot into the deadliest tool to date. Under Kerr, the Warriors went to the NBA Finals five seasons in a row and won three championships. Klay Thompson, the Warriors shooting guard, set the league record for most three-pointers made in a single game with 14, scoring 52 points against the Chicago Bulls on October 30, 2018. Steph Curry made 402 three-pointers during the 2015–16 season, also an NBA record. During the January 5, 2019, game against the Sacramento Kings, both teams set the league single-game record for three-pointers made with 41. Those are just a few incredible performances by Kerr's team.

While these would not have been possible without such talented shooters, Kerr is also partially responsible for them, as it was the former role player who transformed the Warriors. Mark Jackson made the Warriors a playoff team and during his last season, the team won 51 games but was tenth in points per game and fifth in pace. When Kerr took over in the 2014–15 season, the Warriors improved their record by 16 wins, ending the season first overall. They were also first in pace and points per game. More importantly, they won the NBA championship. A season later, the Warriors set an NBA record of three-pointers made during a single season by a team with 1,077 and recorded the best start in regular season history, going 24–0.

While Rice did not transform the league with his coaching, he made more than enough of an impact on the game with his long-distance shooting. For a brief period, from 1996 to 1998, he was one of the best small forwards in the NBA. Kerr never earned that distinction; he was not even one of the best players on his team. Such different players as Kerr and Rice were united through the act of three-point shooting, which made the 1997 All-Star Weekend memorable for both of them. On All-Star Saturday and Sunday, Kerr and Rice won individual trophies thanks to their shooting abilities, and are forever remembered when discussing the historical occasion that was the assembly of the 50 best players in league history for its 50th anniversary.[10]

May 26, 2002

Robert "Big Shot Rob" Horry Strikes Again

While in the history of the league there are some teams who have won championships without great superstars, like the 2004 Detroit Pistons or the 1979 Seattle SuperSonics, not a single team has won a title without role players. Michael Jordan would not have won his third NBA championship without John Paxson's huge shot in Game Six of the 1993 Finals, just as Dirk Nowitzki would not have won his without great performances by J.J. Barea or Jason Terry in the 2011 Finals. The term "role players" signifies athletes who are excelling while serving a supporting role on the roster, either due to their lack of talent or the willingness to sacrifice their abilities for the good of the team. Former MVPs Bob McAdoo and Bill Walton were role players on their championship teams in the same way Udonis Haslem and Rick Fox were on theirs. Every team needs players willing to do the dirty work, who do not care about appearing in the stat sheets, nor look for the spotlight, but are always reliable when called upon. John Havlicek or Don Nelson—just to name two from a group of esteemed role players—were so important for the Boston Celtics' success that the team retired their jerseys, with the former even entering the Hall of Fame as a player (while the latter made it as a coach).

Both were undeniably great athletes, however, their success as players came before the introduction of the three-point line in the NBA, so it is hard to visualize how much success they would have in the modern game. If I were to point out the best role player in modern NBA history, from 1979 onward, no one comes close to Robert Horry, who won seven NBA championships, two on the Rockets, three on the Lakers and two on the Spurs. From 1992 to 2008, Horry made a name for himself by hitting big shots in important games, earning the moniker "Big Shot Rob."

The clutch three became a vital part of his legacy. Even though he made 795 three-pointers on 34.1 percent accuracy in 16 seasons in the NBA, he is mostly synonymous with long-distance shots in crucial moments of games. Horry started his career on the Rockets, selected with the 11th pick in the 1992 draft, which was a perfect situation for a future role player. He joined a good team that was just on the brink of greatness.

In the 1990s, the Houston Rockets had somewhat of a knack for immortalizing role players by giving them the ball in crucial moments of games. Rudy Tomjanovich, who coached the team from 1992 to 2003, showed enormous trust in his players' abilities, regardless of if they were superstars or benchwarmers. A five-time All-Star himself, Tomjanovich had a great career, which is probably why he understood the importance of role players for team success. In Game Four of the 1997 Western Conference Finals, the aging Rockets faced off against the Utah Jazz in what would turn out to be the last deep playoff run for that team. Hakeem Olajuwon already had two NBA championships, the second won with Clyde Drexler, who joined the team during the 1994–95 season from the Portland Trail Blazers. In the summer of 1996, the team added Charles Barkley, who was still trying to win his first title at age 33, to the roster. The Rockets had the oldest starting five in the NBA, as four—the aging superstars plus Mario Elie—of the five starters were at least 33 years old, but the team was still a problem for the much younger Seattle SuperSonics and Los Angeles Lakers.

The Barkley trade seemed to invigorate the Rockets after a disappointing 1996 playoffs, even though the team lost two young starters in Sam Cassell and Robert Horry, as well as bench players Chucky Brown and Mark Bryant, to the Suns in order to bring him in. The Rockets were actually eighth in pace during that season and seventh in offensive rating. In the series, they faced off against the Utah Jazz, whose three main stars—Karl Malone, John Stockton and Jeff Hornacek—were also either 33 or 34 years old, but they were surrounded by younger and simply better role players.

While Malone and Stockton were the source of identity for the Jazz, they were only able to reach the finals following the addiction of Hornacek. The shooter perfectly complemented the duo with his outside scoring ability—40.3 percent from three throughout his career, 828 three-pointers made. The Jazz also had talented reserves in Howard Eisley and Shandon Anderson, and starting small forward Bryon Russell, a 1993 second round pick, who was having the best season of his career to that point, starting 81 games and shooting 40.9 percent from three. While both teams were relying on veteran players, the team from Utah had young and athletic players on the bench while the Rockets did not. The eldest player on both rosters was Eddie Johnson, then 37, drafted by the Kings in 1981, when they were still playing in Kansas City.

The small forward averaged more than 20 points per game for three seasons and during the last of those, 1989, he won the Sixth Man of the Year award. The Rockets signed Johnson in the middle of the 1996–97 season, after he was released by the Nuggets, who had acquired him from the Pacers. Shooting 38.8 percent from three and averaging 11.5 points per game, Johnson was one of the most important bench players for the Rockets that season. During the final minutes of Game Four, with the score tied 92–92, the team from Houston had the chance to tie the series with 6.7 seconds left.

The inbound pass went to Matt Maloney, the only player who not only played in, but also started all 82 regular season games for the Rockets in the 1996–97 season. Maloney was an undrafted rookie, who was signed to fill a spot on the roster from the CBA, similar to Sam Mack and Emanual Davis, who were also signed by the Rockets after successful stints in the inferior basketball league. All three were at least above-average three-point shooters, as the team was looking for affordable players to whom the three superstars could kick the ball out. Maloney was not even supposed to be on the Rockets; he was released before the season by the Golden State Warriors, but Houston's projected starter, Brent Price, went down with a knee injury and, following Barkley's recommendation, the team signed Maloney.[1]

Brent Price was the younger brother of Mark, also an established scorer, who became a starter on the Washington Bullets in the 1995–96 season, but was made expandable when the team acquired Rod Strickland from Portland in a move that would shape the future for both franchises. The Blazers in return got Rasheed Wallace, a rookie power forward who became a starter after Chris Webber went down with an injury that would limit his input during that season to just 15 games. Strickland became a vital part of the Bullets/Wizards teams, even leading the league in assists in the 1997–98 season. Wallace was the heart and soul of the Trail Blazers team that would reach the 2001 Western Conference Finals. Brent Price was out of the NBA after five more seasons. He would still remain a solid three-point shooter, ending his career with 38.7 percent from the outside, but could never remain healthy enough to earn a starting spot on the Rockets, the Grizzlies or the Kings.

Maloney, similar to Price, was a good three-point shooter, making 40.4 percent as a rookie. He also set franchise rookie records for three-pointers made (154) and attempted (381), earning a selection to the All-Rookie Second Team in a very stacked draft class of 1996, considered one of the most talented ever. It was, however, during the playoffs where Maloney made a name for himself, battling against All-Rookie First Team sensation Stephon Marbury and his Timberwolves, and world-class defender Gary Payton and the Sonics. During the two series, Maloney made 43 threes, helping his team reach the Conference Finals against the Jazz.

In the series, however, he was dominated by John Stockton, the veteran point guard and future Hall of Famer, who held Maloney to 6.5 points per game in the series, while himself averaging 20.5. Since he was having a bad series, Maloney was not expected to take that shot. The other players on the court were Olajuwon, Drexler, Barkley and Johnson, with the last two standing behind the three-point line. Barkley was probably standing there as a decoy, luring Karl Malone away from the basket, as Barkley himself was one of the worst three-point shooters in NBA history. Throughout his career, Barkley made just 26.6 percent of his threes, so 538 out of 2,020 attempts, a surprisingly high number considering how poorly he shot the ball. Barkley was capable of scoring a game-winner—like in Game Six of the 1993 NBA Western Conference Semifinals against the Spurs, where he sealed the series with a deep two over David Robinson— just not from three-point land.

As Drexler and then Maloney were double-teamed, the latter passed the ball to Johnson, who was standing alone behind the three-point line, and with a buzzer-beating shot he won the game for the Rockets. John Stockton would return the favor in Game Six of the series, sending his team to the finals after making the game 103–100 with a buzzer-beating three of his own. Despite being a career 38.4 percent three-point shooter, Stockton made just 845 threes throughout his career. In only one season, 1994–95, did he make more than 100 three-pointers. The reason for that was Stockton's pass-first mentality. During Stockton's 19 seasons on the Jazz, he made 15,806 assists, the most by any player in NBA history.

Maloney got his place on the roster mostly due to Price's injury, but partially also because the Rockets released their reserve point guard, Kenny Smith, in the summer of 1996. Nicknamed "The Jet," Smith has spent the first three years of his professional career on mediocre Kings and Hawks teams. He was traded from Atlanta to Houston in the 1990 offseason and during his first year on the Rockets noted his best individual season, averaging 17.7 points and 7.1 assists per game. Smith actually finished one place above his new teammate, Hakeem Olajuwon, in MVP voting, getting five points, good for 17th place. Smith's numbers would drop during each of his six seasons on the Rockets when it came to points and assists—he averaged 8.5 points and 3.6 assists during his final season in Houston. A career 39.9 percent three-point shooter, in Game One of the 1995 Finals, Smith set an NBA record by making seven three-pointers in a single game, allowing the team to win the game by a close margin. The Rockets would sweep the Orlando Magic in the series.

Apart from Smith and Olajuwon, the Rockets' starting line-up consisted of the unpredictable shooting guard Vernon Maxwell, athletic dunker Otis Thorpe, and Robert Horry, the forementioned 6'10" role player who could rebound, pass and shoot in crunch time. Horry was a quintessential team player, so unselfish that he angered the man who brought him to Houston, coach Rudy Tomjanovich: "It got to where he was so sensitive to everybody else's needs that he was neglecting his own."[2] Horry was actually not supposed to be on the championship roster, as the team traded him along with fellow 6'10" long-distance shooter, Matt Bullard—38.4 percent from three during his career—on February 4, 1994, to the Detroit Pistons for Sean Elliott, the Spurs' lifer, playing his only season outside of San Antonio. After two days the deal was canceled, as Elliott failed his physical and both players returned to Houston.

Horry's game was severely impacted by the non-trade, as he not only averaged more points, but also shot for three more freely—during the whole season he made 44 threes, while in the 1994 playoffs alone he made 34. In the 1995 playoffs, Horry drained exactly 44 three-point shots. When the Rockets' front office said that their reasons for trading for Elliott was that they needed more scoring, Horry gave them exactly that. He now had the support of the coach and the best player on the team, Olajuwon, as both took a liking to Horry and his team-first attitude.[3] After his career was over, Horry, despite playing with O'Neal, Duncan and Bryant, and for Phil Jackson and Gregg Popovich, regarded Olajuwon and Tomjanovich as the best player and the best coach he had ever worked with.

Despite Horry's improvements, and despite the three-point shot that clinched the Rockets' win in Game Three of the 1995 Finals, the Rockets traded Horry again, this time for Charles Barkley, to the Suns. Horry was unhappy seeing limited playing time on the Suns and, after being taken out of a game against the Celtics, threw a towel in Danny Ainge's face during the latter's first (and only) stint as head coach. He was traded soon afterward to the Lakers for Cedric Ceballos, who was also displeased with his role on his team. Horry was a starter only during his first season and a half on the Lakers, settling for the role of the sixth man for the rest of his career.

While it might be argued that during the regular season Horry tended to cruise at least a little bit—as he himself had admitted[4]—in the playoffs he was one of the most important players on the court. He was not afraid to make a risky play, attempt a block or a shot, when other players were hesitant to make a mistake. Already in his first playoff run as a Laker, in Game Two of the 1997 Western Conference Semifinals against the Jazz, Horry went 7 out of 7 from three, but the team lost the game and the series, so his performance was somewhat forgotten. After Game Three of the 2001 NBA Finals, in which Horry scored 15 points, 7 of those in the last minute of the game, he explained how he was able to keep a cool head in deciding moments: "The fear factor comes from Houston.... We played so many elimination games. The most ever in a finals run. So you go out there and just play. You got to be fearless."[5] Both the Lakers and the Sixers had won one game each in the series, and Horry's performance allowed the team to build the momentum to win their second NBA championship in a row. The Lakers were so dominant that year that they had lost only one game, Game One of the Finals, during their playoff run.

It was, however, in the 2002 playoffs that Horry stated the case for the indispensability of role players for team success. First, he made a big play in the first round against the Blazers. This was no longer the Blazers team that had caused the Lakers so many problems in the 2000 Western Conference Finals. The team from Los Angeles won the first two games, but was about to lose the third one, as the team from Portland was leading

91–89 in front of the home crowd, with ten seconds left. After Brian Shaw inbounded the ball, Kobe Bryant was dribbling behind the three-point line, only to drive inside and kick the ball out to Horry for a corner three. He made that shot, and with 2.1 seconds left, the Lakers were up by one point. They did not surrender the lead and headed to the next round of the playoffs.

The moment that would define Horry's career came in the Western Conference Finals, when the Lakers faced off against the Sacramento Kings, who won the team-record 61 games, three more than the Lakers, that season. The in-state rivalry was fueled by the cities' close proximity to each other, and the fact that, despite being the fourth-largest city in the state, Sacramento and not Los Angeles is the capital of California. Lakers coach Phil Jackson capitalized on those animosities by calling Sacramento "semi-civilized," "redneck in some form or fashion" and "a cow town." Kings fans responded to these insults by bringing cowbells into the arena.[6] Most of Jackson's attention as a coach was devoted to containing the bumpy relationship between O'Neal and Bryant. Other players did not communicate with their coach that much. For example, Horry, who played under Jackson for four seasons, reportedly had just one off-court conversation with the coach, about the towel incident in Phoenix that got him traded.[7] Whereas the Lakers were basically two superstars surrounded by role players, the Kings were a team, sharing the ball and playing organized defense.

That season the Kings were first in pace, second in rebounds and points, third in steals, and fourth in assists per game. The team was only ninth in three-point percentage, despite having some of the best three-point shooters in the game in Peja Stojaković (41.6 percent that season), Mike Bibby (37 percent), Doug Christie (35.2 percent) and Hedo Türkoğlu (36.8 percent). Christie was already a veteran and had played for the Lakers, the New York Knicks and the Toronto Raptors before joining the Kings, where he became one of the best defensive guards in the league, making the All-Defensive Team in four out of the four and a half seasons he spent in Sacramento. In the middle of the 2004–05 season, Christie was traded to the Magic. He retired a year later with 805 three-pointers made and 35.4 percent accuracy.

Türkoğlu was a reserve who was slowly growing into his own, but with Stojaković and Chris Webber on the team, he did not have a chance

Robert Horry became known as "Big Shot Rob" due to his late-game heroics involving long-distance shots (2002).

to get much playing time. He would finally become a starter on the Spurs in the 2003–04 season, and a year later would be traded to the Magic, where he would form a pair of frontcourt long-distance shooters with Rashard Lewis. Both were important elements of Orlando's strategy of surrounding center Dwight Howard with outside shooters, a mixture that would prove successful in the 2008–09 season, when the Magic reached the NBA Finals, only to lose to Bryant's Lakers. Türkoğlu retired with 1,246 threes made and a 38.4 percent three-point shooting average.

Bibby was the only member of the Kings' starting line-up brought in before the 2001–02 season, traded for fan favorite, Jason Williams. Nicknamed "White Chocolate," Williams was probably the flashiest player in the league at the time, capable of dishing out impressive and efficient passes at any given moment. However, he was not a great shooter and noted 2.9 turnovers per game during his three seasons in Sacramento. The Kings traded him for Bibby, who was also turnover-prone (three per game during his three years in Vancouver), but was more disciplined and able to score more points. Bibby and Williams were both selected in the 1998 draft, the former with the second pick and the latter with the seventh. Both would also play for the Miami Heat in later years; however, while Williams was able to win the title for the team from South Beach with Shaquille O'Neal and Dwyane Wade, Bibby failed to do the same with Wade, LeBron James and Chris Bosh. Williams would play his part in their title run, scoring 21 points on 10 for 12 shooting during Game Six, the last of the 2006 Eastern Conference Finals, against the Pistons.

Bibby was brought in mid-season in 2011 by the Heat, after being traded by the Hawks to the Wizards, and bought out by the team from Washington. The Heat was disappointed with the production of their point guards, Eddie House (privately Bibby's brother-in-law), Carlos Arroyo and Mario Chalmers. Bibby started all but one of the Heat's postseason games, but his team would ultimately fall in the finals to the Dallas Mavericks, who also had a starter from the 2002 Kings on their roster, small forward Peja Stojaković. Stojaković joined the team from Texas around the same time as Bibby joined the Heat, and in similar circumstances as well—after starting the season on the Hornets, then being traded to the Raptors, his contract was bought out, and the shooter was picked up by the Mavericks. The Mavs were struggling with filling the small forward position after Caron Butler went down with a season-ending injury after just 29 games. Stojaković was 34 years old, Bibby was 33. Both retired by the end of the season, but it was Stojaković who retired as a champion, with the team from Dallas beating the "Heatles" 4–2.

Stojaković's contributions to the title were rather humble, as he did not score a single three-pointer—and a total of two points—in the finals during the first four games, and would not even enter the court during the last two. However, he had one exceptional performance in the 2011 playoffs, against the Lakers, going six for six from three in Game Four of the Conference Semifinals, completing the sweep of the reigning champions. Stojaković was finally able to overcome the team from LA in the postseason for the first time in his career, making up for his disappointing performance in the 2002 Conference Finals.

Then he did not play in the first four games of the series due to a sprained ankle, and performed poorly during the three games he took the court, making just one of ten threes and scoring a total of 20 points. Bibby, on the other hand, was the reason why the team got close to eliminating the reigning champions in the first place, averaging 22.7 points and 4.4 assists per game throughout the seven-game series, second on the team in both, behind Chris Webber, the only superstar on the Kings, who was making 24.3 and 6.3 respectively.

With the Kings leading 2–1, Game Four would prove to be pivotal— had the Kings won, they would have home court advantage in two games and three more occasions to put away the Lakers. Instead, the series would turn out to be one of the most controversial ever, due to bad officiating. In Game Five, O'Neal shot just one free throw, which was unusual, considering how often he was fouled by opposing players. The "Hack-a-Shaq" strategy, which was based on the assumption that it was better to send O'Neal to the free throw line than to just allow him to dunk the ball, was sometimes the only way of stopping O'Neal from scoring, considering how bad he was from the line (52.7 percent).

After openly complaining to the media, O'Neal shot 17 free throws and made 13 in Game Six, while in Game Seven he made 11 of 15, proving that in the series he was simply unstoppable. While the number of free throws made by O'Neal was slightly above his career postseason average of 10.7 attempts, the more problematic thing was that the Lakers shot 27 free throws in the fourth quarter of Game Six alone, 40 in total, while the

Kings attempted 21 during the whole game. The Lakers made 34 of said free-throws and won the game 106–102.

The Lakers won Game Seven in overtime, 112–106. Kings' players and journalists alike have criticized the officials for their questionable calls, and some have even raised accusations against the league, suggesting that it wanted to, firstly, prolong such an interesting series, and, secondly, have the Lakers emerge victorious in order to have at least one big-market team in the finals, with the opponents being the New Jersey Nets.[8] The Lakers swept the Nets and earned their third NBA championship.

It must be stated here that without Robert Horry's big shot in Game Four there would be no conspiracy theories, as it seems more than certain that the Kings would get one more win against the Lakers given three occasions to do so. In Game Four, with seven seconds left, the Kings were leading 99–97, squandering almost all of the 24-point lead that they held at one point in the game. Similarly to Game Three from the first round series against the Blazers, Kobe Bryant had the ball and was driving into the lane to tie the score. The Kings' defense was all over him, but he still somehow managed to shoot the ball. He missed, and during the fight for the rebound, the ball was swiped by Kings center, Vlade Divac, toward the top of the key, where it bounced farther away from the basket and reached the three-point line. Horry caught it, and with 0.8 second left, released the shot. He scored, the Lakers won 100–99, tied the series, and eventually headed to the NBA Finals for the third time in a row.

The Lakers did win the NBA championship that year, but a year later they fell to the Spurs in the Conference Semifinals. In the offseason, they signed Karl Malone, who left the Utah Jazz after 18 seasons, a year after playing his last in the league with John Stockton, with whom Malone formed an on-court partnership that lasted for 17 years. Malone seemed in great physical shape despite being 40 years old, but the season turned out to be the worst of his career, as he appeared in only 42 games due to injuries, and his scoring average was the lowest of his career. Horry himself claimed that Jackson wanted to bring in Malone ever since he took over the team.[9] In order to create the salary cap space necessary to sign Malone, Horry was released and signed with the Lakers' biggest rivals, the Spurs. Since Michael Jordan's second retirement in 1998 up until 2005, either the Lakers or the Spurs would represent the Western Conference in the NBA Finals.

In the 2005 NBA Finals, Horry would once again appear as Big Shot Rob, making 18 of his 21 points in the fourth quarter and overtime of Game Five against the Pistons, the last three coming with his team down 93–95. With 9.4 seconds left, Horry inbounded the ball to Manu Ginobili, who was immediately double-teamed, leaving Horry open to shoot for three, which was exactly what he did. In that game Horry made four out of five three-pointers, despite a shoulder injury. Tim Duncan, Spurs legend, was the starting power forward on that team, and described his teammate's crunch-time heroics as "probably the greatest performance I've ever been a part of."[10] The Spurs took the 3–2 lead in the series and would eventually win the championship, Horry's sixth.

The seventh came in 2007. This one was marred by some controversy though, as during Game Four of the Western Conference Finals Horry checked Steve Nash, the point guard of the Phoenix Suns, into the scorers' table. Outraged Suns players Amar'e Stoudemire and Boris Diaw left the bench, both earning one-game suspensions. Horry was suspended for two games. The foul changed the momentum of the series, which was tied 2–2, and effectively limited the Suns' chances at reaching the NBA Finals. The move can be seen as the consequence of Horry's willingness to do anything his team needed of him in order to win. Whether it was shooting a three-pointer or fouling the best player of the opposing team, Horry was dependable, no matter the circumstances.

Taking into account his seven championship rings and the number of big time moments he amassed during his playing career, it should not be an overstatement to say that he was the best role player since the introduction of the three-point line in the NBA, maybe even in the history of the league. When talking about his achievements, Horry said, "I always joke around that it is a matter of luck … but I would like to think it has a little bit to do with some of my skill."[11] While luck had to play some part in Horry reaching the status he enjoys today, he did more than his fair share in helping it. His capacity to make important plays in important games highlighted how crucial role players were for team success. The fact that most of these were three-pointers proved that shooters could easily find a niche—and a spot on the roster—in the NBA as long as they were not afraid to shoot.

February 18, 2006

Dirk Nowitzki Becomes the Tallest Three-Point Contest Winner Ever

In Kirk Goldsberry's *Sprawlball*, the book on how the three-point shot transformed today's basketball and moved the game away from the basket, Kevin Love is presented as the face of the change regarding the power forward position. During his first years in the NBA, Love was a double-double machine, averaging 15.2 rebounds in his third season in the league. In that season, he averaged less than three three-point shot attempts per game. Still, that was much more than during his rookie year, when he took a total of 19 shots from the outside. In his fifth NBA season, Love played in just 18 games, but he was already changing his game, rebounding less and shooting from long range instead. Ever since the 2012–13 season, Love has not attempted less than five three-pointers per game, whether as a member of the Timberwolves or the Cavaliers. "Power forwards used to spend all their time in the paint, or very close to it, but those days are gone. This trend is not unique to Kevin Love: the league is now chock-full of exemplar power forwards who spend more time away from the rim than close to it."[1] While it can be argued that Love is representative of said change, he is not the first, nor the best, power forward/center to make long-distance shots a vital element of his game. That honor belongs to Dirk Nowitzki, a 7'0" lanky power forward born in West Germany.

Nowitzki was obviously not the first big man with a sweet shot. That was Bob McAdoo, a 6'9" center selected with the second pick in the 1972 NBA draft. Shawn Fury writes that "players like Dirk Nowitzki and Kevin Durant are the heirs to McAdoo's game and style, but even forty years after he outshot everyone in the league there's still never been a center who performed like he did from the perimeter. And few players have been as unappreciated."[2] McAdoo won the MVP award in 1975, while a member of the Buffalo Braves (now the Los Angeles Clippers), and was the league's best scorer for three years in a row (1974–76). In 2000, he was inducted into the Basketball Hall of Fame.

And yet, McAdoo was unappreciated during his playing career, because he was expected to score, yet constantly criticized for the way he did it—mostly outside the paint. He was traded by numerous teams because coaches did not know quite how to play him. A center who preferred to shoot from mid-range rather than make his points near the basket was unheard of around that time. Between the years 1979 and 1981, McAdoo was a member of five NBA teams. He was called a "malingerer" and urged to retire by the Pistons front office.[3] Once picked up by the Lakers, he became a vital contributor from the bench on two championship teams, next to Kareem Abdul-Jabbar and Magic Johnson. While Pat Riley was the one who finally embraced McAdoo for who he was, for the best years of his career the player rarely had that type of support. The same cannot be said of Dirk Nowitzki, who was allowed to play basketball his way from the start of his NBA career and in consequence. influenced the NBA like few players before him.

While Nowitzki had the Mavericks' staff full support, in his first season he was considered a bust by fans and journalists:

> As he lumbered through a difficult rookie season, no end of pundits pointed out the apparent lack of wisdom in Dallas selecting Nowitzki in the draft instead of the still-available Pierce, the all-American forward from the University of Kansas who was acclimatizing just fine in Boston, eventually averaging 16.5 points a game and finishing third in voting for the league's Rookie of the Year. Nowitzki averaged just 8.2 points a game and shot a career-low 40.5 percent from the floor.[4]

He was acquired via a draft-day trade with the Milwaukee Bucks. With the sixth pick in the 1998 draft, the Mavericks selected Robert "Tractor" Traylor, a 6'9" center from Michigan whose playing weight was 300 pounds. They immediately traded him to Milwaukee for the seventh pick, Nowitzki, and the 19th pick, Pat Garrity. Garrity was included in a trade package with Martin Muursepp, Bubba Wells and a first round pick that brought Steve Nash from the Phoenix Suns to Dallas. Pierce was selected with the tenth pick by the Celtics.

The success that the small forward instantly enjoyed cast a large shadow on Nowitzki's performance as a rookie. It was inconceivable that he was not only taken in front of Pierce, but actually even traded for Traylor, who was a proven talent on American soil. Around that time, only 38 non–American players were playing in the league, but only one of said players was a teenager who did not even have first league experience on a professional level—his hometown team, the Würzburg X-Rays, was playing in the 2. Basketball Bundesliga, German second division.

During his first season in Dallas, Nowitzki struggled and was booed by his own crowd. He was uneven, going zero for five from the floor in his first and six for ten in his second NBA game, foreshadowing how difficult it would be for him to stabilize his form during his rookie year. The Mavericks had not made the playoffs since 1990 and in the 1996–97 season Don Nelson traded away potential superstars Jim Jackson and Jamal Mashburn (Jason Kidd was traded earlier), not getting much in return—apart from Michael Finley—for players who simply did not get along with each other.

In the 1999 season, the fans took out their frustrations on the two newcomers, Nowitzki and Nash. Some players, however, could see the glimpses of future success that the German would enjoy in the league, as he had some solid showings during his rookie year. Nick Van Exel, then of the Denver Nuggets, stopped Nowitzki after a game against the Mavericks and said to him: "Man, you're going to be a good player, man. You just keep balling. You're going to figure this shit out, and you're going to be a good player."[5] When Van Exel joined the Mavericks a couple of years later, Nowitzki reminded him of the encouragement he had received from the point guard.

The fact that Nowitzki was even selected by an NBA franchise was the result of incredible circumstances. The German started playing basketball at 13 and fell in love with the sport one year later, after watching the Dream Team dominate at the Olympics in Barcelona. Back then, Nowitzki wore number 14 to honor Charles Barkley, who wore it in Barcelona. Once he joined the Mavericks, Nowitzki decided on the number 41, because 14 was taken by journeyman point guard Robert Pack. Barkley was among five legendary players—next to Scottie Pippen, Larry Bird, Shawn Kemp and Detlef Schrempf—who stood in the middle of the American Airlines Center during Nowitzki's last NBA game and congratulated him on his career. Barkley reminisced about a Nike Hoop Heroes exhibition game during which an 18-year-old Nowitzki scored 42 points.[6] After the game, Barkley urged Nowitzki to go to an American college—preferably Auburn, his alma mater—but Nowitzki refused, saying that an NCAA coach would try to change his game.[7] And it was Nowitzki's game that made him such a promising prospect in the first place.

Coach Holger Geschwindner is the man most responsible—obviously next to Nowitzki—for his extraordinary career. While Nowitzki was naturally gifted as an athlete, both of his parents represented Germany in either handball (father) or basketball (mother), it was Geschwindner, the former captain of West Germany basketball team, who devoted a lot of time and work into turning the tall teenager into an NBA-worthy player.[8] The primary focus of their training was Nowitzki's shooting. Geschwindner used the technology available at the time to project the optimal shooting angle and urged his player to use finesse instead of strength. He is responsible for the German's extraordinarily high shooting arc. But Geschwindner also understood that the physical aspect of the shot was not the whole thing—he also forced Nowitzki to finish high school, taught him to think strategically and pushed him to pursue other interests that went beyond basketball. The player's inborn humility helped him, as he quickly learned to fully trust his coach. And he did not have to wait too long for the results.

Just one year after he shone in the game against the NBA pros, Nowitzki was invited to a Nike Hoop Summit that took place in San Antonio to join a group of international teenagers who would face off against American high school players. The decision to go was spontaneous, as the power forward considered himself not ready yet to fly to the United States. His coach, however, thought otherwise. Nowitzki scored 33 points and grabbed 14 rebounds, receiving 36 college scholarships on the basis of that sole game, but more importantly, his coach formed a relationship with Donnie Nelson, then the assistant manager to his father, Don, on the Dallas Mavericks. Don had taken over as the coach and general manager in 1997, just after the team traded away its best player, Jason Kidd, to the Phoenix Suns.

One of the players that the Mavericks received in that trade was Michael Finley, who would become the team leader until Nowitzki matured. Finley had spent eight and a half seasons on the Mavericks, averaging 20 or more points for five seasons in a row. Don Nelson referred to Finley as the team's "centerpiece," while Michael Jordan himself handpicked him, along with Ray Allen, Vin Baker, Eddie Jones and Derek Anderson, to be a member of the "starting five" of the first faces of the Jordan Brand. Finley earned comparisons to the early Jordan for his explosive style of play and scoring ability, but also for working with the same personal trainer and being a leader of a really bad team.[9] Just like Jordan's Bulls in his early years, Finley's Mavericks were a dormant team, in no small part thanks to Don Nelson, who had traded away all the potential superstars.

Nelson's stint with the Mavericks came almost a year after he was fired by the New York Knicks. After Pat Riley suddenly left them in 1995, the team confusingly employed Nelson, who from the start was a bad fit for the likes of Patrick Ewing and Charles Oakley. At one point, Nelson proposed the team trade the aging Ewing for Shaquille O'Neal, who was rumored to leave Orlando for either the Lakers or the Knicks in the up-coming offseason. It was a deal that from today's perspective would have made sense for both teams, as the Magic would at least get something in return for O'Neal, who joined the Lakers in the summer of 1996 as a free agent. However, word of the trade got out to Ewing, and Nelson was soon gone, while the Magic fell apart. Nelson's up-tempo style of play known as Nellie Ball was not what the Knicks' players were used to, and they openly rebelled against their head coach.

The Celtics' legend—Nelson won five championships as a player in Boston, the team retired his number 19 jersey to honor his contribu-tions—was a visionary coach, whose style would greatly fit today's NBA. It was Nelson who introduced the idea of a point forward, a small forward who could dribble the ball, allowing both guard positions on the floor to be taken by shooters and not a shooter and a passer, as was generally the rule. While he never won a championship as a coach, he inspired other prominent NBA coaches, like Eric Spoelstra, Mike D'Antoni or Steve Kerr to rely on smaller, fast-paced players, instead of flooring a regular line-up with a tall center who would slow down the offense.

Jon Kasten, the general manager of the Atlanta Hawks, was one of the first to introduce the idea of overpaying for mediocre players with above-average height. He infamously signed an average NBA center, Jon Koncak, to a six-year, $13-million deal, which was more than Larry Bird, Magic Johnson or Michael Jordan were receiving at the time. Even though Koncak was well-liked by his teammates, he became known around the league as Jon Contract, and a point of reference for underpaid stars. Kasten said, after signing the player in 1989, "you look at every freaking body you can over six-ten ... but in 20 to 30 years we'll have five seven-footers on the floor on one team. Somebody will."[10]

Nelson went in the opposite direction and was able to achieve considerable success with the Milwaukee Bucks, and later with the Golden State Warriors. During his first tenure, the team from the Bay Area was led by "Run TMC"—a fast-paced (hence the "run") trio of Tim Hardaway, Mitch Richmond and Chris Mullin. All three were great shooters. Chris Mullin remains a true Warriors legend, a left-handed scorer who averaged 20 or more points per game for six seasons in a row. He made 815 three-pointers with 38.4 percent accuracy during his 16 seasons in the league, three of which he spent on the Pacers—for the rest of his career he stayed in Golden State. While he served primarily as a small forward or shooting guard, in Nelson's system he actually played long stretches at power forward. The team's playmaker, Tim Hardaway, ended his career with 1,542 three-pointers made with 35.5 percent accuracy. He was one of the best point guards of the decade, making the All-NBA team five times, twice on the Warriors, three times on the Heat. Apart from his shooting, he was known for the crossover dribble.

Hardaway's backcourt partner and close friend, Mitch Richmond, was on the Warriors for just three seasons, but that was enough for him to make an impact on the fans in the Bay Area. Richmond spent most of his career in another California city, Sacramento, playing for the Kings. He ended his career on the Lakers, where he won his sole NBA championship, the only member of Run TMC to do so. Richmond averaged 20 or more points per game for ten consecutive seasons. On the first day of the 1990–91 season, Richmond was traded to the Kings for rookie Billie Owens, who possessed the height that was supposed to make the Warriors even better—there was constant pressure on Nelson to make the team bigger and he eventually obliged. When discussing the move, the coach called it "the toughest [he has] ever made."[11]

Šarūnas Marčiulionis, a bench player who joined the NBA thanks to incredible circumstances, was also a part of that roster. Thanks to the Richmond trade, he got more playing time and exploded for 18.9 points per game, but a season later, 1992–93, a leg injury severely limited his playing ability. After returning from that injury a year and a half later, he was not the same player anymore. It is hard to say if his biggest legacy is being the first Soviet player to join the NBA (along with Alexander Volkov) or introducing the Americans to the Eurostep, which became the go-to dribble move of current players like Manu Ginobili and James Harden.[12]

Marčiulionis arrived in the NBA thanks to his connection with Donnie Nelson, who became his close friend after the Lithuanian superstar scored 40 points on him during a game between the Soviets and the basketball team representing Athletes in Action, an American Christian sports organization. As a member of the team, Nelson traveled around the world and established connections which would later help him find interesting basketball prospects. Marčiulionis was the first player that he was enamored by.

Arvydas Sabonis, a fellow Lithuanian, was still playing for the USSR national team at that time, and was the first Soviet player drafted by an NBA team—24th pick in the 1986 NBA draft, after the Hawks' 77th pick in the 1985 draft was voided because of the player being under 21 years old—but he did not play in the league until 1995, when he was already past his prime and dealing with injuries. It was his colleague, Marčiulionis, who paved the way for future European stars and prospects. Still, Sabonis was able to play six solid seasons for the Blazers at center, showing incredible court vision, dribbling and passing ability for a player his size, and he even came back from retirement in 2002–03 at age 38 for one more, albeit not so successful, season.

In Sabonis' final year in Spain before joining the Blazers, while playing for Real Madrid, the 7'3" center attempted 2.2 three-point shots per game, making 33.8 percent of his attempts. During the previous three seasons, he made over 40 percent of them. In his second season in the NBA, he would attempt 1.9 long-distance shots per game, but he ended his career in America with an average of slightly less than one three-point shot per game. While he was not the player he was when drafted, Sabonis was also never able to show his long-distance shooting skills on a scale which suited his abilities.

Nobody in the USSR knew that Sabonis was actually drafted; the player learned about the honor after reading about it in a magazine.[13] He could not join the league anyway, because of the Cold War. In 1989, as the Iron Curtain fell, apart from Marčiulionis, other Eastern European players entered the NBA as well. Among them were Drazen Petrovic, Vlade

Divac and another Soviet player, Alexander Volkov, who spent two seasons on the Atlanta Hawks before going back to Europe. Divac would play for 16 years in the league and have his number retired by the Sacramento Kings. In 2002, the Kings came very close to eliminating the Lakers in Game Seven of the Western Conference Finals, just like Sabonis' Blazers a year earlier. Petrovic established himself as a great scorer—43.7 percent from three during his NBA career. He died in a car crash when he was only 28.

Arvydas Sabonis was never allowed to fully utilize his long-distance shooting skills in the NBA (1996).

The 1991–92 season was Petrovic's breakthrough, as he not only became a starter on the Nets, but also came up second in voting for the Most Improved Player of the Year award behind Pervis Ellison, the first pick of the 1989 NBA draft. Ellison enjoyed only two full, healthy seasons in the league, the first being the one in which he beat out the Yugoslavian shooting guard in the voting for the award. Sarunas Marčiulionis got two votes for the award, but he was also second in voting for the Sixth Man of the Year that season.

The winner of the award for the second time in a row was Detlef Schrempf, the most successful European player in NBA history up until Dirk Nowitzki turned into a superstar. Just like Nowitzki, Schrempf came from West Germany, was selected as a lottery pick (eight in 1985), started his NBA career with the Mavericks, and struggled during his early years in the league. The difference was that unlike Nowitzki, Schrempf played in the NCAA for four years and had already adjusted to the American lifestyle. Early on, Coach Motta was really careful about evaluating his player's potential: "In terms of development he's only a college sophomore. If he wants to be an All-Star, he will be."[14] Schrempf made the All-Star team three times, once as a member of the Pacers and twice on the Sonics.

Schrempf shared the locker room and the court on the Mavericks and the Sonics with another player ahead of his time, who, although shorter than Schrempf, played at center. Sam Perkins, who obviously was not European, played in a way similar to European big men in his later years. During his first eight seasons in the NBA, Perkins was allowed to attempt one or more threes per game only once, even though he was a capable shooter. In Game One of the 1991 NBA Finals, Perkins made the winning three-point shot in the sole game won by the Lakers against the Bulls in the series. It was only after he joined the Sonics at age 31 that his shooting ability was incorporated into the offense by coach George Karl. Perkins responded to that trust by elevating his scoring percentage. When he joined the Sonics, he made around 25 percent of his shots, while during his five and a half seasons in Seattle he made over 38 percent of his threes. He ended his career as a 36.2 percent three-point shooter. No centers played like that at the time, which prompted two-time Defensive Player of the Year award winner Hakeem Olajuwon to say, "defending Sam can be a big headache."[15]

Perkins would have been an even bigger headache in today's game. In 1989, he was almost traded by the Mavericks, along with Schrempf and Dale Ellis, to the Celtics for Kevin McHale. It remains one of the ultimate what-if questions of the three-point era: what would have happened if these three great three-point shooters teamed up with Larry Bird? Would they sacrifice their long-distance scoring abilities or would they be allowed to shoot at will, starting the three-point evolution twenty years earlier? The German and Perkins met again in Seattle and became the captains—along with Nate McMillan—of a Sonics team that made it to the 1996 NBA Finals. While Schrempf was somewhat encouraged to shoot for three, and he made two appearances in the 3-Point Contest in 1987 and 1988, Perkins was invited to participate only once, in 1996. He became the first center to appear in the competition.

Schrempf joined the league along with another player from Dirk's homeland, Uwe Blab, a 7'2" center who was selected with the 17th pick the same year as Schrempf, and by the same team, the Mavericks. Blab played for them, the Warriors and the Spurs. He even started 33 games for the 1989–90 Warriors, but played just 12 minutes per game, averaging 2.1 points and 2.5 rebounds. Blab was useful for tip-offs and playing defense; however, he was not a player fit to play Nellie Ball, unlike Marčiulionis, who at 6'5" could play three positions, dribble the ball and shoot from long distance.

Donnie Nelson was instrumental in bringing Marčiulionis to his father's team, as he was quick to recognize that with his skillset he would be a perfect fit for the Warriors. As the people in the Soviet republics were given more freedom, and finally allowed to travel to Western countries, Nelson started handling all the necessary paperwork to bring the player to the United States. Even though the Soviet government supposedly took 75 percent of the $3.9 million earned for his first professional contract, Marčiulionis was happy to finally be able to play in the NBA. He did not know the language or the culture and he relied heavily on Donnie Nelson, who became his personal translator.[16]

Thanks to Nelson's hard work and his father's trust, Marčiulionis changed the perception of European players in the United States. Nelson called Nowitzki the beneficiary of "the Jackie Robinson years of the first Europeans. Guys like Drazen and Sarunas Marčiulionis took the razzing, took the beating, [put up with] all the stereotypes of how they couldn't play in the league."[17] Even after Nowitzki was selected, European players were regarded as "soft," despite strong showings by the aforementioned athletes. His rookie season largely contributed to that perception. But after a summer of rigorous workouts in his homeland, Nowitzki was a better, more mature and confident player.

His progress was influenced by a number of factors, the two most important being his growing friendship with point guard Steve Nash, and Mark Cuban's acquisition of the team in the middle of the 1999–2000 season. Nash, just like Nowitzki, was struggling during his first season on the Mavericks. Donnie Nelson was the one behind the idea of bringing Nash to Dallas, whose selection he suggested to the Phoenix Suns in 1998, while working as an assistant coach in Arizona. The team actually wanted to trade up in order to select Kobe Bryant, but nobody was interested in the packages offered by general manager Danny Ainge.

Nash was a rather interesting prospect, a Canadian born in South Africa, playing for the university of Santa Clara and holding a degree in sociology. He received only one scholarship offer from a Division I college, but once he got there, he was compared to NBA legend John Stockton, who was also white, physically unimposing and had a pass-first mentality. However, Stockton was a world-class defender and a reliant long-distance shooter, and while Nash would eventually turn into an even more trustworthy scorer, making the exclusive 50–40–90 club four times, his defense would remain his biggest weakness. That progress seemed almost impossible judging from Nash's early showings as a member of the Mavericks.

Even before Nash played in an official game for the team, he suffered a back injury during a pickup game, which would impact his future in more ways than one. The back issues clearly slowed down Nash's development into the MVP-type player he would eventually become, and made the Mavericks hesitant to resign him, opening the door for the Suns to bring him back and put him at the center of their offensive rotation. During his first two years in Arizona, Nash was a backup to Kevin Johnson and Jason Kidd. During his second season there, his minutes and his role increased, but there was no chance for him to win the starting role over Kidd, who was then one season away from becoming the best point guard in the NBA, and earning the title of the league assists leader for three years in a row. So Nash moved to the Mavericks, and he immediately found a kindred spirit in Nowitzki.

The two players warmed to each other because of their shared love for soccer, as Nowitzki was German, hence his love of the beautiful game was fairly obvious, whereas Nash's father was a professional soccer player and his early travels were the result of his dad's playing career. Nash's younger brother, Martin, followed in his father's footsteps and even earned 38 caps for Canada. Nash and Nowitzki lived next to each other, arrived together to training and drank (reasonable amounts of) beer in their free time. Micheal Finley said of his fellow co-stars half-jokingly that "they see each other, like, twenty hours a day."[18] Interestingly, their personalities could not have been more different. The German was shy and quiet, the Canadian outspoken and outgoing.

While in Nash's later years, he would become a consummate bachelor, making headlines because of his flings with Geri Halliwell or Elizabeth Hurley, Nowitzki's personal life was relatively unknown until his fiancée was arrested in his house on charges of fraud and document forgery. The woman had used multiple identities, introducing herself to Nowitzki as a

Brazilian even though she was from St. Louis.[19] In 2009, the famously private player was involved in a scandal and the people of Dallas responded by showing him public support by calling talk shows, writing letters and making online comments.[20] At some point, the woman claimed to be pregnant, with the narrative being that Nowitzki allowed the future mother of his child to stay behind bars, but her pregnancy turned out to be a lie, and one of the German's most vocal supporters, team owner Mark Cuban, reacted by calling it "good news" on Twitter.

Cuban bought the majority stake on the Mavericks on January 4, 2000, and immediately made his presence felt. Before his arrival, the team had not been to the playoffs for nine seasons, and after the acquisition, things looked to remain unchanged, at least at first. While after the move the Mavericks did not make the postseason once again, they went on a 31–19 run to close out the season, and missed the playoffs by just four wins, finishing ninth in the Western Conference. The lack of success prior to his arrival is what actually propelled Cuban to buy the Mavericks: "I thought to myself that I could do a better job than this. It's pretty typical to this day, if I walk into a business that I think is mismanaged, to think through what I would do differently."[21] One of the most important moves made by Cuban was retaining the services of Don Nelson and his son. His improvements included a first-class plane, a dietitian, a traveling therapist and a group of developmental coaches.[22]

He was also the one involved in trade negotiations, signing and trading for players chosen by Nelson and his son. One such player was Dennis Rodman, a Dallas native who played in just 12 games for the Mavericks, before being released by the team. Rodman was critical of the owner being too involved in team management, which was what Cuban obviously did, attending every game, shouting at the opposition, referees and sometimes even his own players. Rodman called these actions "dumb" and compared Cuban to Jerry Jones, the owner of the Dallas Cowboys, whose ego destroyed one of the most talented NFL teams of the 1990s.[23] Interestingly, Rodman lived in Cuban's guesthouse for a while, but was forced to move out after the league accused the Mavericks of breaking the league's salary cap rules.[24] After some time, however, Rodman thanked Cuban for the chance when no other team wanted to sign him, while Cuban said that he "learned a lot about dealing with the media and PR" from Rodman.[25]

Three-Pointer!

The biggest fallout of Cuban's career as a team owner was with Don Nelson, who resigned mid-season in 2005 after observing that the players were responding better to assistant Avery Johnson than their coach.[26] Nelson was also unhappy with Cuban not re-signing Nash, as the owner considered Nash's back problems too big of a risk to offer the player as much money as he demanded. Cuban offered Nash $20 million less than the $65 million for six years he agreed to with the Suns. Nelson turned Nash into an All-Star, substantially improving his passing and shooting. The coach called the move a setback, saying: "we lost a big part of our team and we don't have anything to fill it."[27]

With the point guard duties shared by John Terry (who was actually a shooting guard), rookie Devin Harris (who was the fifth pick in the 2005 draft, but was supposed to learn from Steve Nash during his first NBA season) and veteran Darrell Armstrong, the team won 42 games and was on its way to win 50 or more for the fifth season in a row—they would go on to enjoy 11 such seasons—but Nelson still decided to step down, unhappy with the on-court product. A year later, he was once again named coach of the Golden State Warriors and in the 2007 playoffs his team, which barely made it to the postseason, eliminated the first seeded Mavericks who ended the 2006-07 season with 67 wins and 15 losses.

Under Nelson, Nowitzki developed into one of the best shooters in NBA history, completely redefining the power forward position. However, due to lack of team success—the Mavericks have reached the Conference Finals only once and were twice eliminated from the playoffs by their in-state rivals, the San Antonio Spurs—Nowitzki was never considered a true leader. Leading by example, constantly working on his game, being polite and humble—those characteristics seemed to not be enough. When Johnson took over, he wanted Nowitzki to become more like Tim Duncan, the leader of the San Antonio Spurs, who were able to win three NBA championships during Nelson's tenure in Dallas.

Similar to Nowitzki, Duncan was a silent leader, a rebounder and a scorer, but he played closer to the basket and was a reliable defender. Johnson demanded Nowitzki attack the glass, block shots and take charges—things not earlier expected of him. During his playing career, Johnson was the point guard for San Antonio Spurs for nine seasons and was nicknamed "The Little General" because of his size, attitude and the fact that he shared the court with "The Admiral" David Robinson. Johnson won one championship with the Spurs and the team retired his number. Johnson thought that in order to achieve the same success as the Spurs, his team should mimic them as closely as possible.

The problem with that assumption was that Nowitzki was always a different type of player than any other power forward and center in NBA history. Big men like Duncan were groomed to play at center as well as power forward, making their living in the paint, while Nowitzki began his NBA career as a small forward, away from the basket. Duncan had great teammates from the beginning, as he got to regularly work out with and learn from David Robinson, Sean Elliot and Johnson, while the best player on the Mavericks during Nowitzki's first two seasons was Michael Finley, who was then still trying to find his footing in the NBA.

In their first playoff series, the Mavericks trio of Finley, Nash and Nowitzki faced off against the aging Utah Jazz, which from today's perspective should be seen as a duel between the new and the old guards. Stockton and Malone were on their way out as the best point guard and power forward in the game, respectively. Malone is actually second on the all-time scoring list with 36,928 career points, while Nowitzki is sixth with 31,560 points, 141 more than seventh place Wilt Chamberlain. As promising as the series seems from a narrative perspective, it was not until the 2003–04 season that Nowitzki started to play most of his minutes as a four. That was also the last season of Karl Malone's career, spent chasing that elusive championship ring as a member of the Los Angeles Lakers.

The Jazz-Mavericks series was not a direct duel of legends and future greats, mostly since power forward Juwan Howard was the one who played against Malone. Meanwhile, Nowitzki attempted a series-high 35 three-pointers, converting 12. Finley made 13 of his three-point shots and Nash 11 of his. With two of the three elimination games being won by a total of four points by the Mavs, it must be pointed out that the series was decided by long-distance shooting. In that season, Nowitzki attempted almost five (4.8) three-point shots per game, exactly one and a half more than the second long-distance shooter on the team, Howard Eisley, a long-time reserve of John Stockton.

While Nowitzki's offensive production was constantly rising, Finley's was steadily declining. He finished the 2004–05 season with the lowest points per game average (15.4) since his second year in the league. Nash left the team in the summer of 2004, and just a year later the shooting guard was gone as well. With a chance to escape luxury tax, the Mavericks first tried to sell Finley, and when their attempts failed, they released him, getting rid of his three-year, $51.8-million contract in the process.

Finley joined the Spurs because they were the reigning NBA champions and he considered them his biggest shot at winning a title. One of the teams he snubbed was the Miami Heat, who at the time was creating its own championship roster, surrounding Dwayne Wade and Shaquille O'Neal with veterans like Gary Payton, Antoine Walker and James Posey. The Heat would turn out to be the 2006 NBA championship winners, overpowering the team that released Finley before the season.

The 2005–06 season was exceptional, not only because the Mavericks were able to tie the then team-best record with 60 regular season wins, but also because the team finally beat the Spurs and Nash's Suns on their way to the NBA Finals. Nowitzki was the team's sole superstar, a development which seemed unfathomable in the past. During the season he was averaging the highest average of points per game of his career with 26.6, and making a career-high 40.6 percent of his three-point shots, a number he would beat in only 4 of his next 13 seasons in the league. The first sign that this season was going to be different came during the All-Star Weekend in Houston. There, the German finally proved that he could perform when it counted.

On February 18, 2006, Nowitzki participated for the third time in his career in the 3-Point Contest. He made his debut in the competition in 2000, a year after the contest was canceled due to the lockout-shortened NBA season. Nowitzki was the fourth European player ever to get invited to the competition, after Detlef Schrempf (1987, 1988), Rimas Kurtinaitis (1989) and Drazen Petrovic (1992). Kurtinaitis was a curious case, as he never played in an actual NBA game, nor was he on the roster of an NBA team. His trip to the USA was an eventful one, as Charles Barkley proposed to take him to a strip club the day before the contest, but canceled the invitation once he discovered that Kurtinaitis wanted to take his wife along with him. "The best three-point shooter in the Soviet Union" finished last with only nine points, yet he made an everlasting impression on NBA players and executives, showing his worldliness with statements like: "my home is exactly like Indiana, except without Bobby Knight."[28] While

Kurtinaitis spoke hopefully about joining the league, as 1989 was the first year that American professional players were allowed to participate in international competitions and Eastern Europeans were able to finally join the league as well, the contest would remain his only performance on an NBA court.

Nowitzki scored 18 points in the opening round of the 2000 contest, and got into the final round with Ray Allen and returning 1998 champion, Jeff Hornacek. The formula now featured two rounds, with the three best participants from the first round entering the final one. The Utah Jazz shooting guard won that contest by scoring just 13 out of 30 possible points. Allen had 10 points and Nowitzki 11. Nowitzki returned to compete a year later, and once again he made it to the final round with Allen. The third finalist was Peja Stojaković. With ten points, Nowitzki was last, scoring seven points less than the Serbian winger and nine less than Allen.

In his third appearance in the competition, in 2006, Nowitzki barely made it to the final round with 14 points. In fact, he released his last shot past the buzzer and it actually should not have counted. In the final round, he scored 18, beating Allen by three points and Gilbert Arenas by two. Nowitzki became the second European player to win the competition, his future teammate on the 2011 NBA championship team, Stojaković, being the first one. With that win, Nowitzki became the tallest player ever to win the contest, paving the way for other power forwards and centers to shoot from long distance.

Nowitzki ended his career with 1,982 three-pointers made. With his ability to stretch the court, he is representative of other big men, like the 6'10" Rashard Lewis (1,787 career three-pointers made) or the 7'0" Andrea Bargnani (507 career three-pointers made), who benefited from his early-career struggles and the ridicule he had to endure. In the present-day NBA, it is almost required of big men to shoot from long range, as proven by the shooting evolution of players like Brook Lopez (from 0.2 the season prior to 5.2 threes attempted per game in 2015–16) or Marc Gasol (from 0.1 the season before to 3.6 three-point shot attempts per game in 2016–17).

Nowitzki revolutionized the game of basketball thanks to the success he enjoyed as an individual player and a teammate. His 2007 MVP trophy and his 2011 NBA championship justify the belief that a tall player does not have to play under the basket to be properly utilized. The three-point shot was such a vital element of his game that out of respect, despite having the worst three-point shooting percentage since his rookie year (31.2 percent) and noting career lows in every statistical category, he was invited to participate in the 2019 contest during his last NBA season. He scored 17 points, one point shy of reaching the final round.

June 18, 2013

Ray Allen Makes the Most Famous Shot of His Career

Ray Allen played for 18 seasons in the NBA, was selected to ten All-Star teams, won two championships, and set the record for career regular season three-point field goals made and attempted with 2,973 and 7,429, respectively. He also starred in *He Got Game*, a Spike Lee movie about a high school basketball prospect who ponders whether to go to college or turn pro. He was a starter on the Milwaukee Bucks, the Seattle SuperSonics, the Boston Celtics, and for two seasons came from the bench on the Miami Heat. It was, however, while on the team from Florida that Allen performed the play he is most remembered for. Even though he made 3,358 career three-pointers during his NBA career (385 coming in the postseason), none was more important and significant than the corner three Allen drained during the last seconds of Game Six of the 2013 NBA Finals against the San Antonio Spurs.

The shot was so emblematic that the player opens his autobiography, aptly titled *From the Outside*, with the description of the last 19.4 seconds of the game between the Heat and the Spurs. The Spurs were leading the series 3–2, and the game 95–92. That was the first evenly fought game of the 2013 Finals, as all of the previous ones were decided by at least ten points. The most devastating loss came in Game Three, which the Spurs won 113–77, outscoring the Heat in the second half 63–33. Danny Green made seven three-pointers, Gary Neal made six, and the whole team set an NBA Finals record with 16 made during a single game. Both players were reliable shooters and their coach, Gregg Popovich, made great use of their ability to shoot from long distance, even though he himself hated, and probably still hates, the play.

Three-Pointer!

The Spurs teams ran by Popovich featured such great three-point shooters as: Vinny Del Negro (35.9 percent career three-point percentage), Nick Van Exel (35.7 percent), Bruce Bowen (39.3 percent), Brent Barry (40.5 percent), Matt Bonner (41.4 percent) and Steve Kerr (45.4 percent), yet Popovich openly criticized the shot for taking the beauty out of basketball: "I hate it, but I always have, I've hated the three for 20 years.... There's no basketball anymore, there's no beauty in it. It's pretty boring. But it is what it is and you need to work with it."[1] It is hard to say if Popovich was honest or just playing the role of the grouch, as he often does during interviews. Whether criticizing the idea of happiness or stating that his winning record as head coach was more important to him than his grandchildren, he is always interesting to listen to, regularly providing reporters with snappy and entertaining soundbites.

Erik Spoelstra, the coach of the Heat, is the complete opposite of Popovich. Not as charismatic or outspoken, Spoelstra seems like a man destined to be in the background. For years he was perceived as the extension of Pat Riley, the *de facto* leader of the team and the creator of Heat culture. Whereas other teams rested their star players—Popovich once famously did not play Tim Duncan, citing his old age as the reason why he was left out of the roster—and gave them some time off, the Heat always organized exhausting workouts and long shootarounds. The Heat are almost obsessed with keeping their players in top shape, and always playing hard, no matter the score. They even differentiate between regular shape and "Miami Heat Shape," meaning the best possible shape of a player's career. Spoelstra joined the team in 1995, some time before Riley, as a video coordinator. He climbed through the ranks and eventually took over as head coach in 2008.

At the beginning of his tenure, the belief was that Riley, not Spoelstra, was responsible for the way the team played. In 2010, a frustrated LeBron James bumped into Spoelstra during a timeout and the next day he suggested to Riley, serving as team president since 1995, that he should return as head coach, as he already did once in 2005. This action shows how little respect the players had for their relatively young coach.[2] However, it was Spoelstra who was responsible for the Miami Heat's success during James' time there, as he ultimately ushered in the small ball era, becoming the first coach to win an NBA championship playing without an actual center. It was his idea to play power forward Chris Bosh in the middle, and move LeBron James, a nominal small forward, to the power forward position. This freed up an extra spot on the court for another shooter, like Shane Battier, James Jones, Mike Miller, Rashard Lewis or Ray Allen.

Shane Battier was for years known as a "no-stats All-Star" for his ability to make his teams better despite not contributing significant numbers in terms of points, rebounds, assists or other important statistical categories. Rockets general manager Daryl Morey used to call Battier "Lego." because thanks to him all the pieces on the court would fit together.[3] Apart from being a great defender, Battier was also a reliable long-distance shooter, ending his career with 38.4 percent from three. He won two NBA championships as a member of the Heat and was a member of two out of four teams who won the most regular season games in a row (27 games as a member of the 2012–13 Heat, second on the list, and 22 games on the 2007–08 Rockets, fourth all-time).

James Jones was another locker room presence that was crucial for the Heat's playoff success. He had a high basketball IQ and was always willing to get to know all the players on the rosters of his teams in order to learn how to communicate with them. LeBron James respected Jones so much he not only took Jones with himo the Cleveland Cavaliers after he left the Heat in the 2014 free agency, but he also called him his "favorite player of all time."[4] Nicknamed "Champ," Jones provided veteran leadership on the Heat and the Cavs, and was lauded as a great teammate by players as various as Kyrie Irving and Kevin Love. Not once did Jones average ten points per game during a season, but he ended his career with 776 three-pointers made (1.1 per game) with a 40.1 percent shooting average.

Mike Miller left the Heat after the second championship season in 2013, and was signed by the Cavs after LeBron returned to his homestate team. Miller was selected with the fifth pick in the 2000 NBA draft, one of the weakest in league history. Only three players from that draft would go on to become All-Stars (in the same season, 2003–2004), and only one would be selected to an All-NBA team (Michael Redd, the 43rd pick). While the class did include a couple of great three-point shooters in Miller, Redd, Hedo Türkoğlu (38.4 percent), Jamal Crawford (34.8 percent) and Quentin Richardson (35.5 percent), the only individual awards the players would receive were either for the Most Improved Player of the

Year (Türkoğlu in 2008) or Sixth Man of the Year (Miller in 2006, Craw-ford in 2010, 2014, and 2016).

Miller was the 2001 Rookie of the Year, earning a starting spot on the Orlando Magic only because Grant Hill, one of the players who was supposed to carry the torch after Michael Jordan's second retirement, suffered an ankle injury that forever limited his basketball abilities. In his first year as a pro, Miller averaged just 11.9 points, 4 rebounds and 1.7 assists per game, but already had established himself as one of the most accurate three-point shooters in the league, making 40.7 percent of his three-point attempts. In 2010 Miller signed a five-year, $25-million contract with the Heat, thanks to James, Wade, Bosh, as well as Udonis Haslem, who took significant pay cuts in order to give the team some sal-ary cap flexibility. Haslem sacrificed around $14 million in the 2010 free agency, which he would have gotten from the Mavericks or the Nuggets, to stay on the Heat. Miller himself claimed that the fact that the Heat am-nestied him after three years, in a move which saved the team $17 million dollars in luxury taxes, was one of the reasons James did not decide to stay in Miami.[5]

Rashard Lewis was still a rarity when he made a name for himself in the league—a long-distance shooter with finesse in a 6'10" frame. Selected straight out of high school with the 32nd pick in the 1998 draft, Lewis be-came a starter during his third season in the NBA. For four and a half sea-sons, Lewis and Allen played on the Sonics, and both left the team during the 2007 offseason. The team would relocate to Oklahoma City the next year, following a failed attempt to get the Washington legislature to fund a new arena, presumably worth $500 million. The group that purchased the Sonics from Starbucks chairman Howard Schultz claimed that their intention was not to relocate the team, but e-mails obtained later by Seat-tle lawyers proved otherwise. Schultz filed a lawsuit; however, the fact that the ownership group led by Aubrey McClendon, Tom Ward and Clayton Bennett lied about their initial intentions, was not enough in court, and the suit was dropped.[6]

Allen and Lewis were both traded by the new Sonics general man-ager, Sam Presti. Allen was traded to the Celtics on the same night that the team drafted Kevin Durant, even though earlier in the month Presti took Allen out to lunch to discuss the future of the team.[7] Lewis was traded soon afterwards to the Orlando Magic for a second-round draft pick, following a career season by the forward. The Sonics won just 31 games, but Lewis averaged 22.4 points and grabbed 6.6 rebounds in 60 games. That was his third season with 20 or more points per game. Both Lewis and Allen missed a substantial amount of games in 2006–07 due to injuries.

Even though he did not make the All-NBA team even once during his career, Lewis signed a six-year deal with the Magic for $118.2 million. His production would steadily decline and despite being a starter on the Orlando team that would make the trip to the 2009 NBA Finals, his contract stands out as one of the worst in league history. By his second season in Orlando, he was mentioned in discussions about the most overpaid players in the NBA. On the road to the last series of the 2009 season, his team would beat Allen and his Boston Celtics in the Conference Semifinals. After the win Lewis said, "Not only was it fun to beat the Boston Celtics, but to beat Ray Allen, to top him, to try to get a championship ring, to go to the Finals. He'd been there. He's done it before. But I felt like it was my time."[8]

After being traded to the Wizards and the Hornets, Lewis was waived and signed a two-year deal worth just $2.8 million with the Heat. During the 2013 playoff run, his role on the Heat would be fairly limited, as he would play just 4.3 minutes per game, second-to-last on the team. As many other players on championship teams, Lewis had to sacrifice his minutes and his shots in order to win the ultimate prize. During his second season in Miami, his role on the team increased, but the Heat failed to win their third NBA championship in a row, this time falling to the Spurs 1–4. He ended his career that year, after failing a physical for the Mavericks.

Allen, by comparison, played 24.9 minutes per game during the Heat's 2013 playoff run, and made the most threes on the team in the postseason with 39. As noted previously, none was as important as the last shot made in regular time of Game Six of the finals. With 28.2 seconds left, the Spurs were leading 94–89. Some Heat fans were already leaving the arena, the court was being surrounded with yellow tape, and the Larry O'Brien Trophy was brought out in order for the Spurs to celebrate their fifth NBA championship. The Heat did not make a field goal in over four minutes. When LeBron James got open following a successful Ray Allen screen, he shot for three and missed. None of the Spurs' players could secure the rebound, Allen pushed the ball towards Mike Miller, who threw it to James, still waiting behind the line. He once again shot for three, but this time the ball went in. The Heat were trailing just 92–94 with 20.1 seconds to go. It would be the only three-pointer James would make in the game, missing the other four attempts. Up until the fourth quarter, he had experienced a bad shooting night, making just 3 of his 12 shots. He noted two crucial turnovers in the last minute of the game as well, and ye he finished the game with 32 points (nine coming from free throws), 10 rebounds and 11 assists.

Three-point shooting had been the biggest flaw of James' game during the early years of his career. He was undoubtedly an extraordinary athlete, but a rather disappointing shooter, at least in comparison to his other abilities—in his rookie year, he shot 33.9 percent from mid-range and 29 percent from three. In the 2007–08 season, he was the best scorer in the league with 30 points per game, making just 31.5 percent of his attempts from three, but 68 percent of his shots in the paint. It was only after he joined the Heat that he started to really improve his three-point shooting, making 36.9 percent of his attempts from beyond the arc during the four years he spent in South Beach. In the 2012–13 season, he noted his career best three-point percentage, 40.6 percent, the only time he made more than 40 percent of his attempts from beyond the arc. In this game, however, he made just one of five threes.

During the next play, the Heat quickly fouled Kawhi Leonard, who made only one of two free-throws, and with 12.1 seconds left, James once again got open and shot for the three. He missed. The 6'11" Chris Bosh, being the tallest player on the court, grabbed the ball. Both James and Mario Chalmers, the team's starting point guard, were open, standing behind the line as the Spurs were gathering under the basket. Chalmers' claim to fame was the clutch shot he made during his last game in college, the 2008 NCAA title game in which his Kansas Jayhawks faced off against the Memphis Tigers. The Tigers led by three points with 10.8 seconds left. Chalmers got the ball and released the three with 2.1 seconds left, tying the score, while his team won in overtime. The play made the cover of *Sports Illustrated*, with the description: "Mario's Miracle." On June 18, 2013, Chalmers was having a solid game and would finish with four out of five three-pointers made, 20 points overall. But once Bosh grabbed the ball, he had his sights set on Allen.

Allen caught the ball as he was still backing up to get behind the three-point line, with Tony Parker running with his hands up to stop him. This was a situation Ray Allen had actually prepared himself for since his early years in the league. As a member of the Bucks, Allen came up with a drill in which he would start by being on his knees, back or stomach. Then he would quickly get up, catch the ball and shoot. "The point was to develop the muscle memory of getting off a good shot when there's chaos around you."[9] Allen being in that spot was also not an accident, as he had already moved to the left side of the basket as James was shooting for three. Why did not he wait behind the line? In order to trick Danny Green, who was guarding him. By moving nearer the basket, Allen made Green believe that he would not shoot for three, so Green did not bother to stand so close to him.

When Allen released the shot, James raised both of his hands into the air. He was no longer waiting for the ball, he was celebrating. After the game James said, "Thank you, Jesus," referring to the name of Allen's character in *He Got Game*.[10] It was not the first time the shooting guard had hit a vital three-pointer against the Spurs that season. In a November game in Miami, with 25.2 seconds left, the Spurs were leading 98–97. The game was surprisingly close despite the fact that the Spurs were playing without their nominal starting five. While Kawhi Leonard was out with an injury, Popovich did not dress Duncan, Parker, Ginobili and Green for the game, for which his team was fined $250,000. League commissioner David Stern argued that this was unfair to their opponents, the media, the league and the home fans, who were expecting to see the superstars in the Spurs' only regular season visit to the American Airlines Arena.[11] Still, the Spurs stood a good chance of actually winning the game until James drove inside and kicked the ball out to Allen, who buried the three, putting his team in front 100–98. The Heat would go on to win that game 105–100.

Making threes was always one of the main features of Ray Allen's game. While he was a quick and athletic player—he even participated in the 1997 Slam Dunk Contest—it was his shooting ability that distinguished him from the rest of his draft class. Allen finished his college career shooting 44.8 percent from three, improving his accuracy in each of his three seasons at UConn. He did not stay for the fourth year of college, openly questioning the idea of playing for next to nothing, while other people—namely, the NCAA and its sponsors—were profiting from his basketball abilities. He was actually considered to be among the players available in the 1995 NBA draft, but he decided to return for one more college season. During the 1995–96 season, Allen's coach, Jim Calhoun, tried to persuade him to stay by giving him paper clippings about the problems encountered by his college teammate, Donyell Marshall, who was struggling early in his NBA career.[12]

Donyell Marshall went from a bust to a reliable bench player partially thanks to his three-point shooting (2001).

The unanimous 1994 Big East Player of the Year, Marshall was selected in that year's draft by the Minnesota Timberwolves only behind Glenn Robinson, Grant Hill and Jason Kidd. From the beginning, his teammates questioned his work ethic, habits and defensive abilities, and the team traded him after just 40 games for Tom Gugliotta. After the trade, Marshall improved his game, blaming the lack of trust for his poor performances in Minnesota, stating that "with the Warriors, I knew my role and I knew how much I was going to play. That makes all the difference in the world."[13]

Marshall was never a star in the NBA, but he did tie one significant NBA record, that of three-pointers made in a single game, set by Kobe Bryant. On March 13, 2005, Marshall came from the bench for the Raptors in a game against the Sixers. He converted 12 of his 19 three-point attempts, making the most of the fact that his defenders, mostly Chris Webber and Samuel Delambert, stayed near the painted area. As he often did while sharing the court with Jalen Rose and Vince Carter, he would "just run to a spot near the line and wait for them to kick it out."[14]

Bryant set his record on January 7, 2003, going 12 for 18 against the Sonics, finishing the game with 45 points. This was a sign of things to come, as in February he went on a nine game streak of scoring 40 or more points. Bryant said, as if unimpressed by his own performance, that "the streak is a streak.... It's not going to win us any championships."[15] That was true, as that year the Lakers fell to the Spurs in the Western Conference Semifinals after winning three consecutive championships.

With his 12 made three-ponters, Bryant beat the record set by Dennis Scott in the 1995–96 season, albeit with the shortened three-point line. Bryant's record was tied, then beaten by Steph Curry, whose record was then beaten by his Warriors' teammate Klay Thompson. Bryant would go on to make 1,827 threes throughout his career with 32.9 percent shooting. On January 22, 2006, he scored 81 points against the Raptors, the most by a player in a single NBA game since the 100-point night by Wilt Chamberlain. Bryant also holds the league record for most career shots missed with 14,481, over a thousand more than the second-worst John Havlicek.

At some point in their careers, Bryant and Allen engaged in a competitive conflict. Allen, then on the Sonics, openly questioned Bryant's leadership after he forced the Lakers to trade away Shaquille O'Neal. He would quite accurately predict Bryant's future as the sole superstar on the

Lakers, stating that he would not be able to carry the team by himself, and would either ask for some help or for a trade.[16] That was exactly what happened, and Bryant almost joined the Chicago Bulls in 2007, but ultimately rejected the move because the Lakers wanted Joakim Noah, Ben Gordon and Luol Deng in exchange, making the Bulls unable to remain competitive.[17] Bryant stayed in Los Angeles, the Lakers brought in Pau Gasol and Lamar Odom, and he won two more championships to add to the three won with Shaq. One of them came against Allen and the Celtics.

The conflict had died out by that time, but the competitive fire remained. While Bryant congratulated Allen after he passed Reggie Miller on the all-time three-pointers made list in a February 10, 2011, game against the Lakers, Bryant was the one who emerged triumphant that day, as the Lakers won 92–86. Bryant supposedly "took no small joy in winning in Boston while also ruining the big night of Ray Allen."[18] However, after the game he said, "I'm truly happy for Ray … that's just unbelievable,"[19] which was a sign that both players had buried the hatchet, at least in the media.

Before their two meetings in the finals, before Bryant became the player that came the closest to emulate Jordan, Allen was the one Jordan almost single-handedly picked as his successor. Ray Allen was among the first five players to be signed by the Jordan Brand (while Bryant signed with Adidas); he was handsome, well-spoken, and played golf (which was Jordan's favorite past-time as well). He was a family man, an athletic dunker, and a shooter. He could be many things to many people, just like Jordan, which enhanced his marketability. While the name "Mike" was immediately associated with Jordan in basketball circles, so was "Ray." Timing was also on his side, as he was more developed as a player than Bryant when both of them entered the league. Their paths first crossed during the NBA draft, as Allen was almost part of a trade that would bring Bryant to Milwaukee.

Three teams were particularly interested in Allen—the Bucks, the Timberwolves and the Celtics, who were picking fourth, fifth and sixth, respectively. The first three picks were pretty much a lock, as the Sixers desperately wanted Allen Iverson, the most exciting player in the draft class. The Raptors were interested in drafting Kobe Bryant, but he did not want to move to Canada, so they settled on power forward Marcus Camby, who would become one of the best defenders in the league. The other player heavily considered by the Raptors was Shareef Abdur-Rahim, who was picked third by the Vancouver Grizzlies. The team was actually concerned with his availability at the third spot.[20]

The Boston Celtics really wanted Ray Allen, and Red Auerbach, the legendary president of the Celtics, even said to him that he will take him with the sixth pick if he is still available. The Bucks' general manager, Mike Dunleavy, also wanted Ray Allen, at least originally, but he picked Stephon Marbury, a point guard from Georgia Tech, only to trade him to the Timberwolves for their pick, Allen, who did not even want to work out for the team from Minnesota, and a future selection. Dunleavy wanted to trade the shooting guard to the Celtics for their pick and a selection in next year's draft. He would then trade the sixth pick to the Nets for their eight pick and another future pick. With the eighth pick, Dunleavy intended to draft Kobe Bryant. If everything would have worked out, he would have had Kobe Bryant and three extra picks, but the moves were blocked by team owner, Herb Kohl, who thought they were simply too risky.[21] Allen, on the other hand, was a sure thing. While he welcomed the idea of being drafted so early, on that night Allen broke down and cried, hurt that he was traded, hence unwanted, without even playing a single NBA game.[22]

His first NBA coach was Chris Ford, the recorded maker of the first three-pointer in league history. While Allen was not very appreciative of Ford and his methods, at least judging from his description of them in *From the Outside*, he acknowledged that it was Ford who first introduced him to the idea of routines, which became crucial for his career.[23] Thanks to Ford, Allen understood the importance of preparation, and would become famous in basketball circles for his work ethic, which bordered on obsession. What Allen supposedly lacked was fierce competitiveness, at least according to George Karl, the man who took over coaching duties from Ford, and was the one who finally led the Bucks to the playoffs.

Karl called Allen "Barbie Doll" in a profile for *Sports Illustrated* because of the way he cared about how he was perceived, on and off the court.[24] The head coach picked his best player to be the whipping boy, but this was actually Karl's accusation towards the whole team, as it had too many players who "could laugh during a game, and you rarely see a great player crack a smile ... I wanted a lot more focus and passion. I wanted losses to hurt."[25] The ones that hurt the most were the four losses in the 2001 Eastern Conference Finals against Allen Iverson and the 76ers.

In 2000–01, the Bucks noted their best regular season record since 1986, winning 52 games, and got out of the first round of the playoffs for the first time since 1989. They made it all the way to the Eastern Conference Finals, where they faced off against league MVP Allen Iverson in a series which was marred by bad officiating. Bill Simmons points out that "Philly's wins in Games 1 and 4 swung on a controversial lane violation and two egregious no-calls. The Sixers finished with advantages of 186–120 in free throws, 12–3 in technicals and 5–0 in flagrant fouls. Glenn Robinson, one of Milwaukee's top-two scorers, didn't even attempt a free throw until Game 5."[26] It was after that game that Allen complained to the press, calling the league "a marketing machine," and that its best interest was that the reigning MVP from a more marketable team should face off against the Lakers, and not a small market team like the Bucks.

In that season, the Lakers played the Bucks two times and lost both games. Karl backed up his player and the team was fined $85,000 by the NBA. Allen exploded for 41 points in Game Six, making six three-pointers on the way to a tie in the series. Team center Scott Williams was suspended hours before Game Seven as the league changed the foul he committed on Iverson during the previous game to a flagrant two. The Sixers won 108–91 behind a great game by Iverson, who scored the series-high 44 points.

The next season, the Bucks got better on paper, as they retained the same roster plus brought in Anthony Mason, who was coming off an All-Star season on the Miami Heat. Mason, however, disrupted team chemistry and the Bucks did not even make the 2002 playoffs. Glenn Robinson was traded after the season, while Allen left after a mid-season trade to the Sonics for Desmond Mason and Gary Payton, Karl's favorite player, who was then 33 years old. Karl wrote afterwards that "it was a relief to see Ray gone … he was too good and too well paid to be under my control and he knew it."[27] Even though Karl knew Payton would not stay on the Bucks once the season was over, as the point guard was chasing his first championship ring, he still decided to trade Allen. The coach was fired after the Bucks did not make it past the first round of the playoffs that year.

Allen, on the other hand, enjoyed a couple of solid seasons in Seattle, but it was in Boston where he would spend "the most important time of [his] life because [he] had never won. And [he] was able to win."[28] During his five seasons on the Sonics, the team made the playoffs only

Ray Allen was one of the best three-point shooters in the history of the NBA. He still holds league records for most long-distance makes and attempts (2000).

once, while during the five seasons on the Celtics his team has reached at least the Conference Semifinals each year, and made it to the finals twice. The season prior to his arrival, 2006–07, the team had won just 24 games. In 2007–08, the Celtics improved their record to 66 wins with the aid of two superstars who joined Paul Pierce in Boston—Allen and Kevin Garnett.

Born in Inglewood, California, from his early years Pierce was a Lakers' fan, which was synonymous with being a Celtics hater in the '80s: "So, man, this whole thing has been ironic, just how my career went. You're a Lakers fan and you're a Boston Celtic and you win a championship in 2008 against the Lakers. It's just like it was supposed to happen this way."[29] Pierce played for the Celtics for 15 seasons and set various franchise records, two of them regarding overall three-pointers made and attempted, with 1,823 and 4,928, respectively. He ended his career with 2,143 three-pointers made on 36.8 percent shooting, and he would also go on to play for the Nets, the Wizards and the Clippers.

Pierce and Antoine Walker, a small forward picked instead of Allen in the 1996 NBA draft, were supposed to be the duo around which the Celtics would rebuild their dynasty. After failing to make a significant impact in the league through much of the '90s, the drafting of Walker in 1996 and Pierce in 1998 provided the team with a small forward-shooting guard tandem, which would eventually get the team not only into the playoffs, but even help it reach the Eastern Conference Finals in 2002, where they fell to the Nets. Walker was traded away a season later, after the team once again lost to the Nets, and the Celtics became Pierce's team, for better or worse.

It meant mostly the latter, as the Celtics did not make it out of the first round in the first two seasons, and even failed to make the playoffs during the next two. Pierce was a great player, but he was about to turn 30 and, if things would not change, he was in store for a few more losing seasons, surrounded by a cast of promising players who still needed some time to develop. When Danny Ainge, the Celtics' general manager, informed Pierce of his plans of trading the fifth pick in the 2007 NBA draft for Ray Allen, he said, "Shoot. I'd rather have Ray Allen than the fifth pick."[30]

On the 2007 draft night, Ainge traded for Ray Allen in a multi-player deal, and a month later brought in Kevin Garnett, three years removed from his MVP season. Garnett spent 12 years on the Timberwolves, being by far the best and most accomplished player in franchise history, which dates back to the 1989–90 season. The team made the playoffs for the first time in its history in the 1996–97 season, Garnett's second in the NBA, and would qualify there for eight years in a row, making it out of the first round only once.

After three seasons without even reaching the playoffs, Garnett, 31 at the time, was traded for three young players and a once-great shot blocker Theo Ratliff, whose career was marred by injuries. The aging superstars formed the second Big Three in Boston history, similarly to the 1980s trio of Bird, McHale and Parrish, and won an NBA championship in their first season together. In the 2007–08 season, the team won 66 games, 42 more than the year before. Obviously the Celtics were more than just the Big Three, as they also had on their roster: three-point shooter James Posey (34.9 percent, 1,035 made threes), great defender Tony Allen, and a young point guard/center duo of Rajon Rondo and Kendrick Perkins.

During their five years with Ray Allen at shooting guard, the Celtics would remain a dominant force in the East, despite the old age of their best players—the Big Three were all in their '30s when they joined forces. Team point guard, Rajon Rondo, then 24, said of Allen, "They say they're getting old, but our older guys take great care of their bodies.... Ray is always on the treadmill, he's always in the pool. He's in the best shape of his life, and he runs the most on the court of anybody on our team."[31] Rondo would actually turn out to be the main reason why Allen decided to leave the Celtics.

The point guard was at first supposed to be a part of the trade package that would bring Allen to Boston, and Minnesota wanted him in exchange for Garnett as well, but Ainge refused to trade the 21-year-old player just before his second season in the NBA. On both teams Rondo would probably have been a bench player, as the Sonics had Luke Ridnour and Earl Watson, while the Timberwolves had Marko Jarić and Randy Foye.[32] The Celtics put him on the court, though, with three future Hall of Famers, and Rondo more than held his own. With time, however, relationships between teammates started to deteriorate.

Allen describes the 2011–12 season as "the most stressful by far" in Boston.[33] Ever since his rookie year, Rajon Rondo was causing locker room tensions, arguing with every player on the roster and every member of the coaching staff. However, Rondo's court vision and understanding of the game—which allowed him to note 11 or more assists during three seasons in a row in Boston, as well as lead the league in that statistical category three times—were enough of a reason to put up with him. At least up until the summer of 2011, when Ainge discussed trading Rondo to the Hornets for Chris Paul. After the Celtics backed out of the deal, team coach Doc Rivers and Ainge decided to give the current roster one more try. Rondo responded to that vote of confidence by not passing the ball to Allen as often as he used to, since Allen was especially critical of Rondo. This caused a problem and the solution proposed by Rivers was not to criticize Rondo, but rather bring Allen off the bench, and limit their time together on the court, to which Allen (35 years old at the time) did not respond kindly.

By the 2012 trade deadline, Allen was traded to the Memphis Grizzlies, but the deal fell through. Allen knew that the team wanted to get rid of him, yet he still wanted to stay in Boston after the season, which culminated in the second playoff loss in a row to the Miami Heat. When Allen's contract was up, he was immediately contacted by the Grizzlies, while the Celtics took their time with re-signing him. They offered him $12 million for two years, while Allen asked for $24 million for three.[34] Seeing how he was undervalued by his team, with his role on the roster limited, Allen joined the Celtics' biggest rivals, the Miami Heat, even though the team offered him far less money ($6 million for two years) and a role as a reserve. The Heat, however, went to the NBA Finals for two years in a row and stood a better chance of winning the title.

The Celtics team treated Allen as a traitor. Garnett refused to shake his hand before the first meeting of both franchises, during the first game of the 2012–13 regular season, Allen's achievements for the Celtics somewhat forgotten. In Game Two of the 2008 finals, Allen set an NBA record with eight threes scored in a game in such an important series (Steph Curry beat that record in 2018). That was an incredible performance, yet it is that one three-pointer made for the Heat that is the biggest highlight of Allen's career. Throughout the 2012–13 season, Allen did not start a single game, yet was fifth in minutes behind the Heat's own Big Three of James, Wade and Bosh, as well as point guard Mario Chalmers. The same was the case in the playoffs, where Allen remained the fifth member of the rotation. His numbers and shooting percentage also stayed on the same level.

June 18, 2013

When Allen hit that corner three and took the game to overtime, it was an ideal culmination of a career of an exceptional shooter, one of the best in the history of the league. The 37-year-old was the perfect bridge between the old school era of physical basketball, filled with paint-dominating big men and guards shooting from mid-range, and the one that was already beginning, brimmed with players posing a threat to his individual game, season and career three-point shooting records. Allen, the Heat and the Spurs would appear in the finals one year later. After that season, the three-point craze would take over the league on a never before seen scale.

March 8, 2015

*Steph Curry Proves That He Can Score
from Anywhere on the Court*

Writing about still active athletes is problematic, as one season, and sometimes even one play, may significantly alter the perception of their career narratives. For a good example of the importance of a particular moment, one must look no further than the previous chapter, the central part of which is Ray Allen's three-point shot against the Spurs, which he took in his 17th NBA season, when he was 38 years old. Without that shot, Allen would still be remembered as one of the best shooters in league history, but that shot is the one play he is best remembered *for*.

That uncertainty is why the four significant three-point shooters analyzed in this chapter—Steph Curry, Klay Thompson, James Harden and Kyle Korver—will be discussed together, with special emphasis put on Curry, the one player most responsible for the three-point craze that has swept the present-day NBA. The fact that seemingly every player is now trying to transform into a long-distance threat can be "blamed" on most of the players mentioned in this book, but none contributed to the general appeal of the three-point shot more than Curry, and none is more synonymous with its modern prevalence.

The 2019–20 season opened with the reigning champions, the Toronto Raptors, taking on the New Orleans Pelicans on October 23, 2019. It took the teams less than two minutes to fire the first three-point shots of the season. The Raptors' small forward OG Anunoby made his shot with 10 minutes and 17 seconds left until the end of the first quarter, while the Pelicans' Lonzo Ball answered during the next play, just six seconds later, with a three of his own. During the whole game, the Raptors attempted 40 threes and the Pelicans took 45, so 85 in total. Of three-pointers attempted,

33 of them were makes. Forty years earlier, on October 12, 1979, during the first NBA game in which a three-point shot was made, the Rockets and the Celtics attempted 13 long-distance shots in total, and only two of those went in. Nothing is more representative of the way the three-pointer has changed how basketball is played than those numbers.

Before he became the head coach of two of the best three-point shooters in league history, Curry and Thompson, Steve Kerr himself was skeptical about the steadily growing importance of shooting from long distance: "It doesn't make for great basketball if everyone is just jacking up 3s trying to even up the odds. I'd like to see it used efficiently and with a purpose. There are a lot of guys shooting it that shouldn't be. It can definitely get out of hand."[1] Depending upon what one considers to be "out of hand," the rise of three-point attempts from 2.8 in the 1979–80 season to 32 per game in the 2018–19 season may be regarded as significant, but even more impressive is how their number rose from "just" 18.4 in the 2011–12 season. In this chapter I try, based on the examples of the forementioned four players, to retrace what exactly happened in those seven seasons that caused the number of three-point attempts per game to almost double.

In the 2011–12 season, Steph Curry came up second in three-point shot accuracy with 45.5 percent, despite appearing in just 26 of the 66 games of the lockout-shortened season. After that season, the Warriors signed Curry to a four-year, $44-million contract, which earned them a substantial amount of criticism for spending so much money on an often-injured player. Granted, Curry had proven that he could shoot the ball, he was even runner-up in the Rookie of the Year voting in the 2009–10 season, but the injuries could have put his steadily developing career on hold and, in consequence, his team would still have remained one of the most dysfunctional and ridiculed in the league, a reputation it deservedly earned since the early '90s and the dismantling of Run TMC (Tim Hardaway, Mitch Richmond and Chris Mullin).

The Warriors selected Curry in the 2009 NBA draft with the seventh overall pick, behind players as various as Blake Griffin, James Harden, Hasheem Thabeet and Jonny Flynn. The fact that Curry would even be a lottery pick was inconceivable a couple of years earlier, when he was considered too small and weak to even play college basketball as anything other than a walk-on. It was only in his sophomore year in high school that the 5'6" Curry learned to shoot the ball differently than from the hip. Virginia Tech was the only major program that considered bringing in Curry, but passed on him due to his size. Curry eventually joined David-son College, situated 30 minutes outside of Charlotte, where he went to high school.

Curry was born in Akron, Ohio, which is also the birthplace of LeBron James, whom Curry would face in four consecutive NBA Finals. They were actually born at the same hospital.[2] The future sharpshooter moved to Charlotte before his first birthday, as his father was selected by the Hornets in the NBA expansion draft. The Cavaliers were the second team that had given up on Dell Curry after just one season, the first being the Utah Jazz, who had selected him with the 15th pick in the 1986 NBA draft. Coming from Virginia Tech, Curry made just four three-pointers throughout his college career, as the line was still in its experimentation stages in the NCAA.

The move to the Hornets would turn out to be the best thing for his career, and Curry senior would spend ten seasons in Charlotte. Despite starting just a total of 77 games for the Hornets, he was an important ele-ment of the team, earning the 1994 Sixth Man of the Year award. Primarily a shooter, Curry finished his NBA career with 1,245 three-pointers made on 40.2 percent accuracy. In the 1999 season, he led the league in three-point percentage, making 47.6 percent of his long-distance shots during his sole season on the Bucks. Both of his sons, Steph and Seth, became NBA play-ers who are also appreciated primarily for their long-distance shooting. Dell and his wife are now famous for cheering them on from the stands, even wearing custom-made jerseys with both of their numbers when they face-off against each other.

The elder, Stephen, would eventually grow to be 6'3" during the three years spent at Davidson. For two seasons, he played as a shooting guard next to Jason Richards. During the two seasons Richards was passing to Curry (among others), Richards averaged 7.7 assists per game. He even led the NCAA in assists in his senior season with an average of 8.1. That season saw the Wildcats go on a "Cinderella run," beating big-ger college programs: Gonzaga, Georgetown and Wisconsin, before fall-ing to Kansas by just two points in the Midwest Regional Final. In the first of these two games, the team was able to win thanks to Curry-led comebacks. LeBron James was actually in the stands as Curry and his

Dell Curry, seen ca. 1994, was himself a very good three-point shooter, but his older son, Steph, will retire as the greatest three-point shooter of all time.

teammates played against Winsconsin, and even gave Curry his auto-graphed jersey.

During the next season, Curry was moved from shooting guard to point guard, but since he was primarily a scorer, in the draft he was passed over in favor of natural passers, Ricky Rubio and Jonny Flynn, the fifth and sixth picks in the 2009 draft, both curiously selected by the Minnesota Timberwolves. Curry was considered not athletic or explosive enough to make an instant impact in the NBA. The fans in New York re-acted with boos when the Warriors picked Curry with the seventh pick, as they were hoping that their team, picking next, would land him. Instead, the combo-guard joined the Warriors, who had reached the playoffs only once in the past 15 seasons, and was tasked with forming a success-ful backcourt with Monta Ellis. Ellis, like Curry, was 6'3" and was also a combo-guard, considered primarily a scorer. However, while Curry did most of his damage from long distance, Ellis focused on driving inside and scoring from mid-range.

Before Curry even played a game for the Warriors, starting small forward Stephen Jackson demanded a trade after criticizing the team for getting younger instead of better, while Ellis stated that he did not want to share backcourt duties with Curry due to the similarities between the two.[3] What Jackson and Ellis did not know, or just chose to ignore, was Curry's work ethic—in high school he would take 1,000 shots a day *before* team practice. In their first season together, Ellis averaged a career-high 25.5 points, while Curry averaged 17.5 points and 5.9 assists per game. The team was still not very good and won only 26 games.

During his rookie season, Curry (as well as the rest of the league) witnessed the setting of an important three-point record by an already established shooter—in the 52 games he played for the Utah Jazz, Kyle Korver made a humble 59 three-pointers, but on just 110 attempts, so 53.6 percent, better than Kerr's 52.3 percent in 1994–95, and Legler's 52.2 percent in 1995–96. In the 2009–10 season, Korver led the league in three-point percentage for the first time in his career. He would repeat that achievement three more times and appear in one All-Star Game as a member of the Atlanta Hawks. Throughout his career, Korver was pri-marily a bench player, and he averaged more than 14 points a game during a season only once.

Taken late in the second round, with the 51st pick of the 2003 draft,

Korver became the first rookie ever to participate in the 3-Point Contest, despite not playing big minutes for the Sixers. The best player on the team at the time, Allen Iverson, took Korver under his wing and urged him to shoot, providing him with the ball whenever Korver was open.[4] In consequence, Korver became synonymous with catch-and-shoot basketball, turning into one of the fastest shooters in the game. Kirk Goldsberry notes that Korver's average pop time—the time it takes to catch the ball and release it—from the 2013–14 up to the 2016–17 season was 0.68 seconds, while the league average was 0.83. During that period, Korver led the league three times in three-point shot accuracy and made 45.5 percent of his shots. However, this number also includes the shots he had to create for himself. If we were to focus only on "pure" catch-and-shoot percentage, Korver's accuracy from that period would rise to 52.1 percent.[5]

The second player on that list of catch-and-shooters is Golden State's Klay Thompson, who made 46.8 percent of such three-point attempts in said four seasons. He joined the NBA in 2011, whereas in the previous draft the Warriors selected center Ekpe Udoh with the sixth pick. Udoh would turn out to be an important trade piece during the 2011–12 season, in a move that sent him, Kwame Brown and Monta Ellis to Milwaukee, in exchange for the often-injured center Andrew Bogut and Stephen Jackson. A disgruntled Jackson was traded after just nine games during Curry's rookie year to the Charlotte Bobcats, and after two seasons in North Carolina he joined the Bucks, only to be traded again mid-season to the Warriors, who immediately shipped him to the Spurs. Ellis was demanding a trade before the 2011–12 season even began, after the Warriors drafted Klay Thompson with the 11th pick to take his spot as the starting shooting guard.

Thompson, just like Curry, was the son of a former NBA player, his father being Mychal Thompson, a two-time league champion who played as either power forward or center for the Blazers, the Spurs and the Lakers. Furthermore, Klay Thompson was also a shooter who ended his three-year stint at Washington State with 242 three-pointers made with 39 percent accuracy. The difference between the two Warriors was that Curry preferred to create his own shots, while Thompson was primarily a spot-up shooter. More importantly, with his 6'7" frame and defensive ability, he would solve the problem of the Warriors' undersized backcourt. Along with Curry, they would soon become known as the "Splash Brothers," a moniker they earned for their ability to fire from long distance.

In his rookie year, Thompson shot 41.4 percent from three and was named to the All-Rookie First Team. He did not play much with Curry though, since during said season the point guard went down with a series of ankle injuries. His absence put the Warriors in the draft lottery again. That time, the team picked small forward Harrison Barnes. More importantly, in the second round of the 2012 draft, the Warriors selected Draymond Green, who in three seasons would transform from benchwarmer to one of the most versatile players in the league. While never statistically dominant and potentially undersized as a power forward, Green became the heart and soul of the team, as he was willing to do anything necessary to win. The front office obviously understood his importance to the way Golden State played basketball, and offered him a five-year, $82-million contract in the summer of 2015, after the team won its first NBA championship since 1975, its fourth overall. In 2019, Green signed a four-year, $100 million extension.

Prior to Thompson's rookie year, one more important thing happened—the team appointed Mark Jackson as head coach. In the three seasons he was in the Bay Area, the former point guard improved the team's defense, and took it to the playoffs for two consecutive seasons, something that had not happened since 1992. He would, however, clash with management, refuse to give credit to his assistants, and ignore the importance of practice and preparation. That is why after three seasons, Jackson was fired and the team appointed Steve Kerr to his first coaching job.

Kerr was not a complete rookie though; he had front office experience as the general manager of the Suns from 2007 to 2010. Kerr fired coach Mike D'Antoni, who refused to work on team defense—the biggest deficiency of the Suns ever since D'Antoni and Steve Nash joined the team in the summer of 2004. He also traded fan favorite Sean Marion and brought in Shaquille O'Neal, who was already past his prime and could not keep up with his teammates, who were used to playing up-tempo basketball under D'Antoni. In what would turn out to be Kerr's last season in Phoenix, the Suns surprisingly made the Western Conference Finals, but he left anyway, stating that he wanted to spend more time with his family, who had stayed in San Jose. He described the three years as follows: "I wasn't very good at the job, but I learned a ton. The biggest thing I learned was organizational dynamics and the relationships within an organization that are so important: owner, GM, coach, top players. Those relationships have to all be in line."[6]

While the Warriors wanted precisely someone who understood the inner-workings of an NBA franchise, Kerr was also a better fit for them than Jackson, due to his experiences as a basketball player: "While Jackson made NBA hay as one of the game's most brutish point guards at the height of one of the league's most physical eras, Kerr made his hay avoiding the paint and spacing the floor. Both played the guard position, but they played it in very different ways."[7] Jackson was one of the best passers in league history (10,334 career assists, fourth all-time), who did not care much about working on his jumpshot, while Kerr was one of the purest shooters ever (45.4 percent career three-point accuracy, first all-time). His past alone was reason enough to think that he would be able to relate to such shooters as Curry and Thompson.

However, the New York Knicks also had their eyes on Kerr, and they stood a strong chance of landing him, as his former coach, Phil Jackson, was their team president. Luckily for the Warriors, joining the Knicks would require Kerr to move to the other side of the country, and the team actually offered him less money than the Warriors—$13 million for three years to Golden State's $22 million for five years.[8] The Knicks also had a worse roster than the Warriors. Interestingly, the team could also start the season without their second-best player, as in the summer preceding their first championship run, the Warriors almost traded Klay Thompson and Harrison Barnes to Minnesota for Kevin Love. Love finished the 2013–14 season averaging 26.1 points and 12.5 rebounds per game, while shooting 37.6 percent from three. He was one of the biggest stars in the NBA despite never appearing in the playoffs. Thompson, on the other hand, was scoring 18.4 points per game and shooting 41.7 percent from three, but his team has just lost in the first round of the playoffs to the Clippers, led by power forward Blake Griffin.

The move made a lot of sense, but it was vetoed by NBA legend and team advisor, Jerry West. West won the award for the Executive of the Year two times: in 1995, when working for the Lakers, and in 2004, while on the Memphis Grizzlies. Known as "the Logo," due to the fact that it is

West's silhouette that has been serving as the league logo since 1969, he is an NBA Hall of Famer and a great shooter who won only one championship as a player but eight as team executive (six with the Lakers and two with the Warriors). He was responsible for bringing in Shaquille O'Neal to the Lakers, Kevin Durant to the Warriors, and Kawhi Leonard and Paul George to the Clippers.

The veto meant that the Timberwolves had to find a different suitor for Love, who would eventually join the Cleveland Cavaliers. The team had just signed LeBron James, who was coming back to his homestate team after four seasons and two NBA championships with the Miami Heat. Love became an important part of Cleveland's playoff success, averaging 14.7 points (41.4 percent from three) and 8.8 rebounds per game. He also performed one of the most important plays of the 2016 finals, stopping Steph Curry from scoring in the last minute of Game Seven.

With 53 seconds left in the game, Curry had the ball behind the three-point line, with Kevin Love defending him one-on-one. The Cavs' point guard, Kyrie Irving, had just drained a three-pointer and made the score 92–89 for the team from Ohio. Curry had a chance to tie the game, but Love—knowing that he would be attempting a shot from long distance rather than trying to get past him and attempt a two-pointer—stood his ground and forced Curry to take a bad shot. When reminiscing about that play, Curry said, "That was a shot where I was not under control. And it cost us a championship."[9] The best team in regular season history failed to win the title, which in a way made all of Curry's achievements during that season somewhat in vain.

That was a shame, because some of his personal records were almost historical landmarks, as the 2015–16 season was one of the most dominant by a basketball player in the 21st century. The fact that Curry became the first unanimous MVP in league history, winning the award for the second year in a row, should serve as sufficient proof of his greatness. In his rookie year, only 6.2 of Curry's 17.5 points per game came from beyond the arc. Six years later, as he won the scoring title, it was 15.2 of his 30.1 points per game that came from three-point range.[10] The NBA record for three-pointers made during a single campaign—set by Curry himself during the previous season—was 286. In his second MVP season, Curry made 402. In his fourth NBA season (2012–13), he made 272 threes, beating Ray Allen's single-season record of 269, set in 2005–06. In a way, from 2012 to 2017 Curry was in a league of his own when it came to three-point shooting. His teammate, Klay Thompson, was close, especially in 2015–16, which he finished with 276 three-pointers made—so 678 threes made by the same backcourt in one season, another record—but he was still behind Curry.

Curry's distinguishing feature was his ability to create his own shot— Kerr trusted Curry so much that he granted him the freedom to do whatever he considered right on the court, which in turn allowed the Warriors to win three NBA championships in five seasons. It also inspired another team, the Houston Rockets, to implement the same strategy with their star player, James Harden. The success enjoyed by the Rockets, in turn, influenced the whole of the NBA. It is estimated that around 85 percent of NBA triples are assisted, which is what made Curry all the more special— by the 2012–13 season, out of his total 272 threes, 105 were unassisted.[11] Pure shooters like Korver or Thompson did not need to hold onto the ball in order to be efficient, they just had to get in position in order to shoot. When it came to Curry, he did not even need to follow his regular shooting motion to cause damage.

Case in point, one of the greatest shots ever made by Curry— which is already something, considering that there is a whole bunch to choose from, and with each season the number is still growing—in a regular-season home game against the Clippers on March 8, 2015. In the third quarter, with the Warriors leading by ten points against their biggest rivals in the Western Conference, Curry got a pass behind the three-point line from center Andrew Bogut, who immediately tried to set the screen. With Thompson cutting behind Bogut as well, Curry found himself surrounded by three Clippers, who left both Thompson and Green open to shoot the three. Instead of passing the ball, Curry pretended to drive into the two Clippers standing in front of him, with Chris Paul, one of the best point guards in the league, behind him, only to step back behind the three-point line and shoot. The ball went through the net. While the shot itself could be seen as disrespectful, the behind-the-back dribble just in front of Paul, with Curry's back turned toward the point guard, was even more so. Kerr raised his hands in a gesture questioning his player's decision making, only to burst out laughing and shake his head after the ball went in.

Three-Pointer!

The Warriors won the NBA title that season, but failed to repeat due to an incredible play by LeBron James and his Cavs. The Warriors' post-season was already in jeopardy after they went 1–3 against the Oklahoma City Thunder in the 2016 Western Conference Finals. Led by Kevin Durant and Russell Westbrook, the Thunder seemed to be on their way to the their second NBA Finals appearance. The first occurred in 2012 and the trio of Durant, Westbrook and James Harden was overpowered by the Miami Heat led by James, Wade and Bosh. Harden was traded after that series to the Rockets, with the team not having enough cap space to offer him a max contract, which he was rightfully expecting.

The Rockets offered Harden $60 million for four seasons, $7 million more than the Thunder, and the 2012 Sixth Man of the Year was off to become the lone star in Houston. The move was a consequence of the reliance on big men that was still considered a common-sense approach around the league. Two seasons earlier, the Thunder acquired center Kendrick Perkins from the Celtics and immediately signed him to a four-year, $36-million contract. That move, as pointed out by *Bleacher Report*'s Dan Favale, "forced the Thunder's hand" when it came to Harden,[12] successfully limiting the team's cap flexibility.

Harden was selected in the 2009 draft four spots in front of Curry, only behind Blake Griffin and Hasheem Thabeet. Thabeet, the second pick, stands as a prime example of drafting need instead of potential, as well as height in front of talent. Already in his rookie season, he was assigned to the G-League, at the time the highest pick to be treated that way.[13] The third pick in that draft, Harden, was brought in from the bench by the Thunder, and would eventually start just seven games for the team from Oklahoma during his three seasons there. After averaging 19 points per game for two seasons at Arizona State, Harden, just like Curry, was raising concerns for his lack of athleticism, aggressiveness and speed. Unlike Curry, he was primarily criticized for "disappearing" in crucial moments of the NCAA tournament.[14]

It was only during his third season in the NBA that Harden proved he could be just as good, if not better, than Durant and Westbrook. Team coach Scott Brooks, in an interview with Chris Mannix, said that Harden himself personally urged him to play as a reserve, presumably because he got more touches than when forced to share the ball with his other, then more-established, teammates.[15] That Thunder team made the NBA Finals in 2012, but Harden—as was feared he would do—disappointed in the series, shot 37.5 percent from the floor, and averaged just 12.4 points and 3.6 assists in the five-game series. After the finals, Harden was traded along with Daequan Cook (a career 35.9 percent three-point shooter, 2009 NBA 3-Point Contest winner), Cole Aldrich, and Lazar Hayward for Kevin Martin and Jeremy Lamb, two first-round picks and one second-round pick.

Westbrook's and Durant's Thunder would reach the Western Conference Finals one more time, in 2016, and they would even get a commanding 3–1 lead against the record-setting Warriors. The Thunder outscored the Warriors during the series, and it was assumed that the recently begun jump-shooting era was coming to a close, due to the physical and athletic Thunder. However, in the last three games, the Warriors had proven that they were indeed the best team in the league. It was especially evident in Game Six, where 63 out of 108 points scored by the Warriors came from behind the three-point line. In that game, Klay Thompson made a playoff-record 11 threes, finishing the game with 41 points. After beating the Thunder, the Warriors once again faced the Cavs and that time it was the team from Golden State that gave up a 3–1 lead. LeBron James had finally delivered on his promise to bring the NBA championship to Ohio, while the Warriors were about to face an important decision regarding their roster.

Immediately after the 2016 Game Seven loss, Draymond Green made two phone calls: one to team general manager, Bob Myers, about recruiting Kevin Durant, and the other to Durant himself, letting him know that the Warriors would try to sign him.[16] Durant was a four-time NBA scoring champion, the 2013–14 MVP, and one of the best players in the league. He was also a solid three-point shooter (38 percent accuracy up to that point) and a big who could stretch the floor. However, he lacked an NBA championship, which would solidify his legacy as an all-time great. He would go on to win two with the Warriors but failed to win a third due to injuries that happened to him and Klay Thompson during the 2019 playoffs. The Warriors finished their incredible reign with five consecutive NBA Finals appearances. They would not have achieved that without Durant, who rightfully won two Finals MVP trophies and drained important three-point daggers in the last minutes of Game Threes in both the 2017 and 2018 Finals. He joined the Brooklyn Nets in the 2019 free agency.

Three-Pointer!

During the previous Western Conference Finals, the Warriors were just one game away from failing to reach the 2018 finals as they encountered their toughest challengers yet—the Houston Rockets, led by James Harden and Chris Paul. While Harden's superstar status had been undeniable since his first season in Houston, when he finished with averages of 25.9 points and 5.8 assists, he posed quite a problem for general manager Daryl Morey, as each attempt at building a successful roster around him did not give sufficient results. Morey was the first general manager in the NBA to use analytics and spreadsheets in evaluating team performance, following what was called the Moneyball approach, implemented by baseball general manager Billy Beane. It was Morey who, in his search for the most efficient shot, encouraged his players to disregard the mid-range shots in favor of three-pointers. In Harden's first season in Houston, the Rockets attempted 73.6 percent of their shots from either behind the arc or inside the restricted area.[17]

In the 2013–14 season, Morey brought in center Dwight Howard, who was coming off a hugely disappointing year in Los Angeles, where the Lakers were supposed to challenge the Miami Heat for an NBA championship. Howard played alongside Kobe Bryant and Steve Nash, but the team—following two coaching changes and eventually settling on Mike D'Antoni—barely made the 2013 playoffs, and were swept by the Spurs in the First Round of the 2013 playoffs. The next season, with Howard at center, despite winning 54 games, the Rockets fell to the Blazers in the first round. A year later, the Rockets won 56 games and reached the 2015 Western Conference Finals, where they fell to the Warriors. In the 2015–16 season, they barely made the playoffs and were once again eliminated by the Warriors, this time in the first round. Even though the team wanted to retain him, Howard opted out of the last year of his contract and joined the Atlanta Hawks.

The move turned out to be a blessing for the Rockets, who brought in Mike D'Antoni as head coach. D'Antoni's first decision was to assign playmaking duties to James Harden, who led the league in assists with 11.2 per game and averaged 29.1 points, the most in his career up to that point, but the team fell 2–4 to the Spurs in the Western Conference Semifinals. In the summer, Morey traded for Chris Paul from the Clippers and D'Antoni adjusted his team's offense to his two best players. Instead of relying on fast-paced basketball, which led to considerable success in Phoenix,

D'Antoni slowed things down, and the Rockets fell from third the before to 13th in pace in 2017–18. The team was also dead last in pass per game.

One thing that did not change was the team's reliance on three-point shooting. For the second season in a row, they led the league in three-point shot attempts. In 2016–17, the Rockets attempted 40.3 threes a game, a season later they shot from long distance 42.3 times a night, while in 2018–19 they once again beat their record with 45.38. This all came despite the team never ranking higher than 12th in three-point shot accuracy in the D'Antoni era. Even though Harden played next to Chris Paul, who led the league in assists four times during his illustrious NBA career, Harden was the league-leader in unassisted threes in 2017–18 with 564, 7.8 per game. In that season, he created a total of 1,177 threes (attempts plus assisted shots for his teammates).[18]

Putting another point guard next to Harden was a risky move by the Rockets, whose offensive plan up to that point was for their star player to dribble the ball, while the other four were either setting screens or trying to get open in order to release a quick shot. Paul, however, turned out to be a great addition to the roster. A career 37 percent three-point shooter before he joined the Rockets, the point guard said he had a better chance at winning the NBA championship in Houston than in San Antonio, the other team that was heavily recruiting him. Harden was personally involved in convincing Paul that their partnership would work.[19] And in their first season together it did—the Rockets were the best team in the league in the regular season, winning 65 games. The 2017–18 Rockets were the first team in NBA history to attempt more three-point shots than twos throughout the whole season. Harden won the 2018 MVP race, averaging 30.4 points, 8.8 assists and 5.4 rebounds.

In the previous season, Harden's stats were even more impressive (29.1 points, 11.2 assists and 8.1 rebounds per game) but he lost the award to his former teammate, Russell Westbrook, who, now the sole superstar in OKC, was averaging 31.6 points, 10.4 assists and 10.7 rebounds—the first player to average a triple-double throughout the whole season since Oscar Robertson in 1961–62. Westbrook would actually average a triple-double for three seasons in a row before joining Harden in Houston, where he was traded for Paul. Pairing Westbrook and Harden raised a lot of concerns,

erent brand of basketball than the one preferred
rimarily an inside and mid-range scorer, with the
ıe biggest flaw of his offensive game. During the 11
ıtbrook made 30.8 percent of his long-distance shots,
/ent him from attempting 2,995 regular-season threes
ıder.

ıl and Harden had a major falling out following the last
game ᴜ   J19 playoffs, they made it to the 2018 Western Conference
Finals, where they faced off against the Golden State Warriors. In an
evenly-matched series, the Rockets even took a 3–2 lead, but with 22.4
seconds left on the game clock in a Game Five victory, Paul suffered a
hamstring injury which kept him out of the rest of the series. The Warriors were able to win both games and headed to the NBA Finals, where
they swept the Cleveland Cavaliers.

While the Rockets' and the Warriors' success was proof of the ef-
fectiveness of the style of play heavily reliant on three-point shooting,
Game Seven of that 2018 series was a prime example of what happens
when a team depends on long-distance shots too much. The Rockets had
home-court advantage, the reigning MVP on their roster, as well as esteemed shooters: shooting guard Eric Gordon (37.6 percent from three
up to the 2018–19 season), small forward Trevor Ariza (35.3 percent) and
power forward Ryan Anderson (38.2 percent). However, they simply did
not have luck, as they attempted 44 threes during the game and made only
seven. Both teams released 83 three-point shots, one every 34.7 seconds,[20]
but the Warriors made 16 of their 39, so 41 percent, while the Rockets
made 15.9 percent of their attempts. At one stretch during the game, the
Rockets missed 27 three-point shots in a row, yet they still continued to
fire away, as if there was no other way to win a game in the modern-day
NBA.

Instead of serving as a lesson, the game actually inspired teams to
shoot from long distance even more, as proven by the 2019-20 season
opener and the 85 total attempts by the Raptors and the Pelicans. Maybe
there is no other way to win, since the basketball era dating from 1979
onward is often referred to as the three-point era. The name indeed signifies that there is no getting around the long-distance shot. It seems almost unthinkable from today's perspective that in the beginning, teams
and players were reluctant to just release the ball whenever open behind

the three-point line. So reluctant in fact, that the 1979–80 Atlanta Hawks set the NBA record for the lowest amount of long-distance shots released per game in a single season with 0.91. While the number of three-point attempts seems to constantly rise, it is more than certain that the Hawks' record will never be broken.

Chapter Notes

Introduction

1. Kirk Goldsberry, *Sprawlball*. Boston and New York: Houghton Mifflin Harcourt, 2019, p. 11.
2. The contest was at that time called the Three-point Shootout, but to avoid any confusion, in this book it is referred to by its current (2020) name, the "3-Point Contest."
3. SLAM Staff, "Dale Ellis: I'm the Best Shooter of All Time." *SLAM Online*. Jul. 5, 2011. Web.
4. *Sportslingo*. "Pure Shooter." Web.
5. Pasha Malla, "How the Jump Shot Brought Individualism to Basketball." *The New Yorker*. Mar. 14, 2016. Web.
6. Felix Gilette, "Sideshow Bob." *Slate*. Jun. 16, 2005. Web.
7. Jeff Walker, "A Tribute to Antoine Walker—Employee Number 8." *SB Nation*. Sept. 2, 2015. Web.
8. Shawn Fury, *Rise and Fire*. New York: Flatiron Books, 2016, p. 266.

October 12, 1979

1. Ira Berkow, "Perspective; Mikan Ruled an Era and Changed the Rules." *New York Times*, Mar. 11, 2001, section 8, p. 11.
2. Hot Rod Hundley, *You Gotta Love It Baby*. Champaign: Sports Publishing. 1998, p. 179.
3. Scott Morrow Johnson, *Phog: The Most Influential Man in Basketball*. Lincoln: University of Nebraska Press, 2016.
4. Howard Hobson, *Scientific Basketball*. New York: Prentice-Hall, 1949, p. 210.
5. Hobson, p. 7.
6. Hobson, p. 58–59.
7. Fury, p. 39–40.
8. Fury, p. 43.
9. Hobson, p. 113.
10. Terry Pluto, *Loose Balls: The Short Wild Life of the American Basketball Association*. New York: Simon & Schuster, 1990, p. 70.
11. Hobson, p. 114.
12. Hobson, p. 115.
13. Charley Rosen, *The Chosen Game: A Jewish Basketball History*. Lincoln and London: University of Nebraska Press, 2017, p. 41.
14. Jerry Crowe, "How Basketball Became Three-Dimensional." *Los Angeles Times*. May 6, 2008. Web.
15. Murry R. Nelson, *Abe Saperstein and the American Basketball League, 1960–1963*. Jefferson: McFarland, 2013, p. 12.
16. Fury, p. 42.
17. Crowe.
18. Nelson, p. 111.
19. Howard Beck, "Bowing to Body Clocks, N.B.A. Teams Sleep In." *New York Times*, Dec. 19, 2009. Web.

20. Pluto, p. 70.

21. The rule states that the player is not allowed to spend more than three consecutive seconds in the opponent's restricted area, also known as "the Key."

22. Goldsberry, p. 191–194.

23. Pluto, p. 72.

24. Pluto, p. 75.

25. Goldsberry, p. 197.

26. Scott Osler, "Ex-Laker Haywood Tells of Plan He Had to Kill Westhead." *Los Angeles Times*, June 5, 1988. Web.

27. John Papanek, "There's an Ill Wind Blowing in the NBA." *Sports Illustrated*, Feb. 1979, p. 20.

28. Papanek, p. 21.

29. John Feinstein, *The Punch: One Night, Two Lives, and the Fight That Changed Basketball Forever*. Boston: Back Bay Books, 2002, p. 316.

30. Fury, p. 267.

31. David DuPree, "New Twist in NBA: The 3–Point Goal." *The Washington Post*, Oct. 11, 1979. Web.

32. Shaun Powell, "Doubt, Disdain Marked Most NBA Teams' First Forays Into 3–point Land." *NBA.com*, Feb. 21, 2017. Web.

33. Sam Goldaper, "N.B.A. Leaning to 3–Point Goal." *New York Times*, June 13, 1979, section D, p. 22.

34. Goldaper, "N.B.A. Leaning..."

35. Sam Goldaper, "N.B.A. Preview: New Faces and Some." *New York Times*, section S, p. 13.

36. Sam Goldaper, "More Teams Succeed by a Long Shot." *New York Times*, section D, p. 24.

37. Jack McCallum, "The Three-point Uproar." *Sports Illustrated*, Jan. 1987, p. 40.

February 6, 1988

1. Larry Bird, *Drive: The Story of My Life*. London: Bantam Books, 1989, p. xi–xii.

2. Fury, p. 234.

3. Baxter Holmes, "Larry Bird: 'I Knew I Wasn't Going to Last Long.'" *ESPN*. Dec. 6, 2016. Web.

4. George Vecsey, "I Can't Use It as an Excuse." *New York Times*. May 20, 1985, section C, p. 6.

5. David Halberstam. *Playing for Keeps. Michael Jordan & the World He Made*. New York: Broadway Books, 1999. p. 163.

6. *Drive*, p. 153.

7. Kelly Dwyer, "Anthony Mason Used to Act as a Bouncer at LL Cool J's Barbecues Because of Course." *Yahoo! Sports*, Dec. 2, 2013. Web.

8. Scott Horner, "Larry Bird Trash-Talking Stories Never Get Old." *Indy Star*, May 1, 2018. Web.

9. Charles Bethea, "Two of the World's Greatest Shooters Consider the Four-Point Shot." *The New Yorker*, May 20, 2016. Web.

10. *Drive*, p. 226.

11. Mike Wise, "Nothing but Net for Coach Bird." *New York Times*, Jan. 18, 1998, section 8, p. 1.

12. Bird, p. 53–54.

13. Reggie Miller, *I Love Being the Enemy*. New York: Simon & Schuster, 1995, p. 54.

14. ESPN Staff, "Bird: NBA 'a Black Man's Game.'" *ESPN*, Jun. 9, 2004. Web.

15. Roy S. Johnson, "Thomas Explains Comments on Bird." *New York Times*, Jun. 5, 1987, p. 20.

16. Ira Berkow, "The Coloring of Bird." *New York Times*, Jun. 2, 1987, section D, p. 27.

17. *Drive*, p. 185.

18. Halberstam, p. 165.

19. NBA.tv, "Open Court Short:

Trash Talk." *Open Court.* Air Time: Mar. 11, 2018.

20. Anthony Cotton, "Celtics Top Bullets in Overtime." *The Washington Post*, Nov. 8, 1988. Web.

21. *Drive*, p. 142.

22. Chad Finn, "An Oral History of Larry Bird's 60–point Game." *Boston.com*, Dec. 7, 2017. Web.

23. Ira Berkow, "When the Game Was All Business." *New York Times.* Feb. 5, 1998, section G, p. 6.

24. Drive, p. 222.

25. Sam Smith, *The Jordan Rules.* New York: Simon & Schuster, 1992, p. 148.

26. Donald McRae, "Craig Hodges: 'Jordan Didn't Speak Out Because He Didn't Know What to Say.'" *The Guardian.* Apr. 20, 2017. Web.

27. William C. Rhoden, "Hodges Criticizes Jordan for His Silence on Issues." *New York Times,* Jun. 5, 1992, section B, p. 12.

28. *Drive*, p. 228.

March 23, 1991

1. Bruce Anderson, "Scouting Reports: 14 Boston College." *Sports Illustrated.* Nov. 1983, p. 82.

2. Richard Hoffer, "Floor Leader." *Sports Illustrated.* Feb. 1997, p. 28–31.

3. Special to New York Times, "Adams String of 3–Pointers Ends at 79." *New York Times.* Jan. 25, 1989, section B, p. 10.

4. David Aldridge, "After Proving Them Wrong, Adams Returns to Right Bullets." *The Washington Post.* Sept. 28, 1991. Web.

5. Pluto, p. 77.

6. Bruce Newman, "This Joker Is Wild." *Sports Illustrated.* Nov, 1988, p. 104.

7. Sean Merchant, "Doug Moe: Nuggets Coach Not Comfortable with Attention." *Los Angeles Times*, Apr. 16, 1989. Web.

8. Aldrige, "After Proving Them Wrong..."

9. Fury, p. 229.

10. David Astramskas, "Michael Adams—The Man with the Ugliest Golden Shot Ever." *Ball Is Life.* Jan. 19, 2017. Web.

11. Tony Kornheiser, "Some Points of Note on Michael Adams." *Los Angeles Times.* Feb. 6, 1992. Web.

12. Clifton Brown, "3–Pointer Adds Dimension to N.B.A." *New York Times.* Feb. 5, 1990, section C, p. 1.

13. Rhiannon Walker, "The Day Denver Nuggets Guard Michael Adams Became the Shortest NBA Player to Record a Triple-Double." *The Undefeated.* Jan. 31, 2018. Web.

14. Hank Hersch. "Fast Break to Nowhere." *Sports Illustrated.* Nov, 1990. p. 37.

15. Scott Davis, "The Coach Who Designed the Offense That Changed the NBA Nearly Failed Before He Started." *Business Insider.* Dec. 3, 2017. Web.

16. UPI Archives, "Nuggets Trade Adams and Pick for Bullets' First-Round Selection." *UPI.* Jun. 11, 1991. Web.

17. Leigh Montville, "Mighty Mike." *Sports Illustrated.* Jan. 20, 1992, p. 50–53.

June 3, 1992

1. The player changed his first name in 1991 to its original, Arabic spelling, Hakeem. This is the only instance in the book where his first name is spelled that way, due to the fact that it was how it was spelled at the time he entered the NBA.

2. Jack McCallum, "Double Trouble, Houston Style." *Sports Illustrated.* Nov. 1984, p. 21.

3. Sam Goldaper, "N.B.A. Draft Is a Peek Into Future." *New York Times.* Jun. 17, 1984, section 5, p. 10.

4. Kelly Dwyer, "Sam Bowie Reveals That He Lied to Portland About Feeling Leg Pain Before the Infamous 1984 NBA Draft." *Yahoo! Sports*, Dec. 11, 2012. Web.

5. Lenny Carlos, "The Blazers with Clyde Drexler and Michael Jordan Is the NBA's Biggest 'What If.'" *Open Court.* Mar. 29, 2018. Web.

6. Sam Smith, "The Bulls Sit at Picking Sixth in the Draft, But What Are the Odds at Moving Up?" *NBA.com.* May 2, 2018. Web.

7. Sam Smith, *Jordan Rules*, p. 31.

8. Halberstam, p. 203.

9. Smith, *Jordan Rules*, p. 31.

10. Richard Hoffer, "A Cliffhanger." *Sports Illustrated.* Feb. 1993, p. 40.

11. Halberstam, p. 292.

12. There were actually two "episodes" bearing that title, both concerning series-winning shots, one against the Cavs in 1989, the other against the Jazz in 1998.

13. Naomi Klein, *No Logo.* Toronto: Vintage Canada, 2000, p. 50.

14. Smith, *Jordan Rules*, p. 158.

15. Jack McCallum, "2 Michael Jordan." *Sports Illustrated.* Sept. 1994, p. 52.

16. Halberstam, p. 294.

17. Tim Grover, *Relentless: From Good to Great to Unstoppable.* New York: Sribner, 2014, p. 55.

May 7, 1995

1. Miller, p. 27.

2. Austin Murphy, "Hoosier with a Hot Hand." *Sports Illustrated.* January 1986, p. 50.

3. Smith, *Jordan Rules*, p. 198.

4. Fury, p. 59.

5. Alexander Wolff, "That Championship Touch." *Sports Illustrated.* Apr. 1987, p. 36–37.

6. R. Scott Carey, "Hoosier Whiteness and the Indiana Pacers: Racialized Strategic Change and the Politics of Organizational Sensemaking." *Sociological Perspectives on Sport: The Games Outside the Games,* ed. David Karen and Robert Washington, London: Routledge, 2015, p. 370.

7. Thomsen, p. 110.

8. Fury, p. 156.

9. Fury, p. 161.

10. Pluto, p. 135.

11. John Feinstein. *A Season on the Brink.* New York: Macmillan, 1986, p. 63.

12. Fury, p. 271.

13. Fury, p. 272.

14. Bob Berghaus, "Bucks Give Skiles a Ticket Home." *The Milwaukee Journal.* Jun. 22, 1987, p. 56.

15. Jim Slater, "Mounting Losses Are Destroying the Spirit of Indiana..." *UPI.* Jan. 3, 1989. Web.

16. Matthew VanTryon, "Remembering When Everyone in Indiana Hated Reggie Miller for Becoming an Indiana Pacer." *IndyStar.* Jun. 22, 2017. Web.

17. Dan Klores (dir.), *Winning Time: Reggie Miller Vs. the New York Knicks.* ESPN, 2010.

18. Thomas Bonk, "NBA Draft: UCLA's Miller Surprised at Being Picked by Indiana." *Los Angeles Times,* June 23, 1987.

19. VanTryon.

20. Jim Slater, "The Indiana Pacers Improved Their Backcourt Speed and Outside..." *IndyStar.* Jun. 22, 1987. Web.

21. ESPN Stats & Info, "Reggie Miller Was Most Clutch Sharpshooter." *ESPN.* Sept. 7, 2012. Web.

22. Miller, p. 50.

23. Miller, p. 15.

24. Michael Walton, "Do You Remember When Michael Jordan 'Almost' Joined the New York Knicks?" *NBC Sports.* Aug. 28, 2019. Web.

25. Jonathan Abrams, *Boys Among Men. How the Prep-to-Pro Generation Redefined the NBA and Sparked a Basketball Revolution.* New York: Crown Archetype, 2016, p. 82–84.

26. Larry Platt, *Only the Strong Survive,* New York: ReganBooks, 2002, p. 127.

27. Mike Wise, "N.B.A. Playoffs: Do You Believe in the Magic? Indiana Pacers Do." *New York Times.* Jun. 5, 1995, section C, p. 1.

28. Selena Roberts. "The N.B.A. Playoffs; an Era Continues as Jordan Pushes Bulls Past Pacers." *New York Times.* Jun. 1, 1998, section C, p. 1.

29. Shaquille O'Neal. *Shaq Talks Back.* New York: St. Martin's, 2001, p. 234.

30. Marty Burns, "Miller, as in Thriller," *Sports Illustrated.* June 1998, p. 42.

31. O'Neal, p. 243.

32. Chris Broussard, "N.B.A. Finals: Lakers Vs. Pacers; View from Pedestal Makes O'Neal Teary." *New York Times.* Jun. 21, 2000, section D, p. 6.

33. Michael Bradley. "Midwest Swing." *SLAM.* 69, Oct. 2003, p. 118.

34. Conrad Brunner, "Reggie Miller Says 'I Just Believe It's Time.'" *NBA.com,* Feb. 11, 2005. Web.

35. Tony Gervino, "Original Old Shool: The Black Hat." *SLAM,* Oct. 2, 2010. Web.

36. Ira Berkow, "A Garden Finale Starts with a Boo," *New York Times.* Apr. 6, 2005. Web.

37. Gervino.

38. Miller, p. 49.

39. And would remain one pretty much until the 2010–11 season, Blake Griffin's rookie year.

40. Tom Friend, "Pro Basketball; Brown Is Here, There and Now Nowhere." *New York Times,* May 21, 1993, section B, p. 17.

41. Platt, p. 129.

42. Barry Popik, "The Only Man Able to Stop Michael Jordan Was Dean Smith." *Barrypopik.com,* Nov. 25, 2015. Web.

43. Kent Babb, *Not a Game: The Incredible Rise and Unthinkable Fall of Allen Iverson.* New York: Atria Books, 2015, p. 135.

44. Klores.

45. William C. Rhoden, "Sports of the Times; Watching the Knicks at Their Ebb Tide?" *New York Times.* Jun. 3, 1994, section B, p. 15.

46. Jack McCallum, "Hot Hand, Hot Head." *Sports Illustrated.* May, 1993, p. 24.

47. Fury, p. 243.

48. Miller, p. 32.

49. Miller, p. 237.

April 19, 1996

1. Hank Hersch, "Scouting Reports 11–20." *Sports Illustrated.* Nov. 1988, p. 71.

2. Teddy Mitrosilis, "Enjoy These 13 Times the Great Larry Bird Was Just a Ruthless Bastard." *Fox Sports.* Mar. 12, 2015. Web.

3. Jackie MacMullan, "Inside the NBA." *Sports Illustrated.* Mar. 1996, p. 87.

4. Alan Hahn, *The New York Knicks:*

The Complete Illustrated History. Minneapolis: MVP Books, 2012, p. 146.

5. Ken Berger, "The Forgotten Finals." *CBS Sports*. Jun. 2, 2014. Web.

6. Rem Rieder, "O.J. Simpson's Huge Impact on the News Media." *USA Today*. Jun. 17, 2014. Web.

7. Michael Arace, "New Rules Are Radically Changing the NBA." *Los Angeles Times*. Nov. 5, 1994. Web.

8. Grant Hughes, "Does Pace Matter in the NBA?" *Bleacher Report*. Sept. 26, 2014. Web.

9. Johnette Howard. "A True Maverick." *Sports Illustrated Vault*. Oct, 1995. Web.

10. Howard.

11. Phil Taylor, "Agony of D-Feat." *Sports Illustrated*. Dec, 1995, p. 36.

12. David DuPree, "New Twist in NBA: The 3–Point Goal." *The Washington Post*. Oct. 11, 1979. Web.

13. From Wire Reports, "Oakley's Best Lines Not in Box Score." *The Spokesman-Review*. Dec. 3, 1995. Web.

14. Mark Heisler, "If Kidd Is Skipper, the Crew May Go Overboard." *Los Angeles Times*. Feb. 23, 1996. Web.

15. Kevin O'Hanlon. "Perot, McDavid Group Purchase Mavericks." *Associated Press*. May 2, 1996. Web.

16. Johnette Howard, "The Ball's in His Hands." *Sports Illustrated*. Nov, 1996, p. 96.

17. Robert Wilonsky, "One-on-One." *Dallas Observer*. Oct. 23, 1997. Web.

18. Selena Roberts, "Nets Send McCloud to Lakers." *New York Times*. Feb. 21, 1997, section B, p. 11.

19. Rob Mahoney, "The '96 Mavs: The Warriors Before the Warriors." *Sports Illustrated*. Mar. 9, 2017. Web.

20. Jackie MacMullan, "Inside the NBA." *Sports Illustrated*. Mar, 1996, p. 87.

21. David Astramskas, "Dennis Scott—One of the Greatest Shooters Ever." *Ball Is Life*. Sept. 5, 2017. Web.

22. Fury, p. 275.

23. Mahoney, "The '96 Mavs..."

February 8–9, 1997

1. Ethan Sherwood Strauss, "Steve Kerr Q&A: 2015–16 Warriors Vs. 1995–96 Bulls." *ESPN*. Nov. 23, 2015. Web.

2. Bruce Anderson, "Darling of the Desert." *Sports Illustrated*. Dec. 1987, p. 91.

3. Mike Wise, "The Clippers' Barry Hits the High Notes in His Jam Session." *New York Times*. Feb. 11, 1996, section 8, p. 3.

4. Michael Silver, "Straight Shooter." *Sports Illustrated*. Apr. 1997, p. 92.

5. Phil Taylor, "To the Hoop, Hon!" *Sports Illustrated*, Feb. 1997, p. 35.

6. Mike Wise, "Rice Stages His Own Shootout in East's Victory." *New York Times*. Feb. 10, 1997, section C, p. 5.

7. Chris Broussard, "A Stifled Rice Fires Away at Jackson and the Lakers." *New York Times*. Jan. 26, 2001, section D, p. 5.

8. Bill Plaschke, "It's Time for Rice, Jackson to Talk." *Los Angeles Times*. Jun. 13, 2000. Web.

9. O'Neal, p. 239.

10. The exact number was actually 49, as one of the players, Pete Maravich, died during a pick-up game in 1988.

May 26, 2002

1. Dennis Silva II, "Before Lin, There Was Maloney." *Space City Scoop*. 2012. Web.

2. Tim Layden, "A Retrorocket." *Sports Illustrated*. June, 1994, p. 30.

3. Robert Horry, "How to Be a Big Shot." *The Players' Tribune*, Jun. 12, 2015. Web.

4. Mike Wise, "It Must Be June: The Lakers' Horry Comes Alive." *New York Times*, Jun. 11, 2001, section D, p. 5.

5. Wise, "It Must Be..."

6. Tim Cary, "Phil Jackson: 10 of His Worst Insults." *Sportscasting*. Jun. 12, 2015. Web.

7. Horry.

8. Jonathan Abrams, "All the Kings' Men." *Grantland*. May 7, 2014. Web.

9. Horry.

10. Howard Beck, "It's Horry, Yet Again, Who Hits the Big Shot." *New York Times*. Jun. 20, 2005. Web.

11. Howard Beck, "He Who Does Not Hesitate: Horry Is Mister Big Shot." *New York Times*. Jun. 10, 2007. Web.

February 18, 2006

1. Goldsberry, p. 170.

2. Fury, p. 200.

3. Bruce Newman, "Mac Has Been a Real Blast from the Past," *Sports Illustrated*. May 1982, p. 43.

4. Dave Feschuk and Michael Grange, *Steve Nash: The Unlikely Ascent of a Superstar*. Toronto: Vintage Canada, 2013, p. 73.

5. James Herbert, "The Dirk Nowitzki Stories: An Oral History of the Dallas Mavericks Legend." *CBS Sports*. Apr. 9, 2019. Web.

6. In an older retelling of that story the number was 52.

7. Scott Davis, "Charles Barkley Told a Fantastic Story About the First Time He Met an 18-year-old Dirk Nowitzki," *Business Insider*, Feb. 16, 2019. Web.

8. Ian Thomsen, *The Soul of Basketball*, New York: Houghton Mifflin Harcourt, 2018, p. 175–177.

9. Marty Burns, "He Got Game," *Sports Illustrated*, April 1998, p. 39–45.

10. Rick Telander, "Millions from Heaven," *Sports Illustrated*, November 1989, p. 64.

11. Sports People, "Richmond Is Traded for Rights to Owens." *New York Times*, Nov. 2, 1991, p. 34.

12. Jonathan Abrams, "An N.B.A. Move That Crossed the Ocean," *New York Times*, Nov. 17, 2010. Web.

13. Jonathan Abrams, "Arvydas Sabonis' Long, Strange Trip," *Grantland*, Aug. 29, 2011. Web.

14. Ralph Wiley, "Playing Some Big O in Big D," *Sports Illustrated*, Dec. 1985, p. 34.

15. Phil Taylor, "Sonic Soother Sam," *Sports Illustrated*, May, 1993, p. 31.

16. Andrew Sharp, "The NBA's International Takeover: How Sarunas Marčiulionis Opened Pandora's Box." *Sports Illustrated*, Jan. 17, 2018. Web.

17. Jack McCallum, "Simply Marvelous," *Sports Illustrated*, May 2002, p. 41.

18. Feschuk and Grange, p. 73.

19. Cathrin Gilbert, "Dirk Nowitzki's NBA Dream Turns Into a Nightmare." *Spiegel Online*, Jun. 24, 2009. Web.

20. Thomsen, p. 192.

21. Thomsen, p. 85.

22. Thomsen, p. 83.

23. Associated Press, "Dallas Releases Its Maverick, Rodman." *Deseret News*. Mar. 9, 2000. Web.

24. Steve Springer, "Rodman Just Couldn't Stand This Decision." *Los Angeles Times*. Feb. 17, 2000. Web.

25. Cory Stieg, "Ex-NBA Star Dennis Rodman: Mark Cuban 'Had Faith in Me.' *CNBC*. Sept. 12, 2019. Web.

26. Marc Stein, "Ex-Mavs Coach Nelson Wins $6.3M in Arbitration Against Cuban." *ESPN*. Aug. 1, 2008. Web.

27. ESPN.com news services,

"Verbal Deal: Five Years, More Than $65M." *ESPN.* Jul. 2, 2004. Web.

28. Michael Wilbon, "Once a Long Shot, Soviet in 3–Point Contest Aids International NBA." *Washington Post.* Feb. 12, 1989. Web.

June 18, 2013

1. Sam Smith, "How Has Three-point Shooting Changed the Game?" *NBA.com.* Nov. 28, 2018. Web.

2. Nick Jungfer, "Pat Riley Peels Back Curtain On the Wild LeBron Years in Miami." *Basketball Forever.* Apr. 10, 2018. Web.

3. Michael Lewis, "The No-Stats All-Star." *New York Times.* Feb. 13, 2009. Web.

4. Dave McMenamin, "For the Cavaliers, There's a King and There's a Champ." *ESPN.* Dec. 15, 2015. Web.

5. Chris Haynes, "Mike Miller on What Angered LeBron James in Miami: 'LeBron thought [amnestying me] was an unnecessary change.'" *Cleveland.com.* Sept. 30, 2014. Web.

6. Christopher Helman, "The Sordid Deal That Created the Okla. City Thunder." *Forbes.* Jun. 13, 2012. Web.

7. Ray Allen, *From the Outside. My Journey Through Life and the Game I Love.* New York: Dey St., 2018. p. 176–177.

8. Jonathan Abrams, "Ray and Rashard, Reunited." *Grantland.* Jun. 5, 2014. Web.

9. Allen, p. 5.

10. Allen, p. 5.

11. Ben Golliver, "Spurs Fined $250K for Resting Players." *Sports Illustrated.* Nov. 30, 2012. Web.

12. Malcolm Moran, "UConn's Allen Is Worldly and Wise." *New York Times.* Feb. 19, 1996, section C, p. 1.

13. Phil Taylor, "Donyell Marshall." *Sports Illustrated.* Oct. 23, 1995. Web.

14. Harvey Aaraton, "Donyell Marshall, a Holder of the 3–Point Record, Waits for It to Fall." *New York Times.* Feb. 11, 2016. Web.

15. Roland Lazenby, *Showboat: The Life of Kobe Bryant.* London: Orion Books, 2016, p. 411.

16. Paul Flannery, "The Ray Allen–Kobe Feud." *Boston Magazine.* Jun. 2, 2008. Web.

17. Chris Sheridan, "Kobe Objecting to Deng's Inclusion in Bulls-Lakers trade." *ESPN.* Nov. 1, 2007. Web.

18. Thomsen, p. 124.

19. Howard Beck, "For Celtics' Allen, a Moment to Cherish; for the Lakers, a Victory to Savor." *New York Times.* Feb. 10, 2011. Web.

20. Shareef Abdur-Rahim, "The Greatest Draft Class." *The Players' Tribune.* Jun. 22, 2016. Web.

21. Jonathan Abrams, *Boys Among Men*, p. 62.

22. Allen, p. 101.

23. Allen, p. 110–116.

24. L. Jon Wertheim, "Acquired Taste." *Sports Illustrated.* Feb, 2001, p. 53.

25. George Karl, *Furious George. My Forty Years Surviving NBA Divas, Clueless GMs, and Poor Shot Selection.* New York: HarperCollins, 2017. p. 224.

26. Bill Simmons, "The Books of Basketball Lost Pages." *ESPN.* Dec. 15, 2009. Web.

27. Karl, p. 261.

28. Chris Forsberg, "Ray Allen: Years in Boston 'most important time in my life.'" *ESPN.* Sept. 6, 2018. Web.

29. Broderick Turner, "Clippers' Paul Pierce Braces Himself for What Figures to be an Emotional Final Game in Bos-

ton." *Los Angeles Times*. Feb. 4, 2017. Web.

30. Peter May, *Top of the World: The Inside Story of the Boston Celtics' Amazing One-Year Turnaround to Become NBA Champions*. Cambridge: Da Capo Press, 2008, p. 28.

31. Ian Thomsen, "The Old Men of the C's." *Sports Illustrated*. Oct. 2010, p. 83.

32. May, p. 52.

33. Allen, p. 232.

34. Allen, p. 240.

March 8, 2015

1. King, "3-pointer revolutionized Steve Kerr's career."

2. Katie Richcreek, "Steph Curry, LeBron James Were Coincidentally Born at the Same Hospital in Ohio." *Bleacher Report*. May 30, 2015.

3. Karen Crouse, "Stephen Curry Gets Rude Welcome on Warriors." *New York Times*. Nov. 10, 2009. Web.

4. Eric Woodyard. "Utah Jazz's Kyle Korver Still Impacted by of Allen Iverson: 'I really owe a lot to him.'" *Deseret News*. Jan. 27, 2019. Web. Early Influence.

5. Goldsberry, p. 77–79.

6. Connor Letourneau, "Steve Kerr's 'Whirlwind' as Suns GM: A Shaq Trade, a Firing, Many Lessons." *SFGATE*. Mar. 9, 2019. Web.

7. Goldsberry, p. 54.

8. Marc Berman, "Why'd the Knicks Miss Out on Steve Kerr? Jax Was Cheap." *New York Post*. May 16, 2014. Web.

9. Jackie MacMullan, "Rise Above It or Drown: How Elite NBA Athletes Handle Pressure." *ESPN*. May 23, 2019. Web.

10. Goldsberry, p. 46.

11. Goldsberry, p. 49–51.

12. Dan Favale, "Why Kendrick Perkins' Contract Forced OKC Thunder to Trade James Harden." *Bleacher Report*. Oct. 30, 2012. Web.

13. The Cavs' Anthony Bennett, the first pick in the 2013 draft, would eventually top Thabeet's "achievement."

14. Jonathan Abrams, "Clippers Want Griffin, but Little Else in N.B.A. Draft Is Clear." *New York Times*. Jun. 23, 2009. Web.

15. Marina Mangiaracina, "Scott Brooks: Haren Wanted to Play on the Bench." *SB Nation*. Feb. 10, 2016. Web.

16. Zach Lowe, "One Year Later, Draymond Green Has No Regrets." *ESPN*. Jun. 9, 2017. Web.

17. Jared Dubin, "Nearly Every Team Is Playing Like the Rockets. And That's Hurting the Rockets." *FiveThirtyEight*. Dec. 20, 2018. Web.

18. Goldsberry, p. 98–99.

19. Marc J. Spears, "Harden Helped Sell Paul on Rockets." *The Undefeated*. Jun. 29, 2017. Web.

20. Goldsberry, p. 108.

Bibliography

Books and Films

Abrams, Jonathan. *Boys Among Men: How the Prep-to-Pro Generation Redefined the NBA and Sparked a Basketball Revolution.* New York: Crown Archetype, 2016.

Allen, Ray. *From the Outside: My Journey Through Life and the Game I Love.* New York: Dey St., 2018.

Babb, Kent. *Not a Game: The Incredible Rise and Unthinkable Fall of Allen Iverson.* New York: Atria Books, 2015.

Bird, Larry. *Drive: The Story of My Life.* London: Bantam Books, 1989

Feinstein, John. *The Punch: One Night, Two Lives, and the Fight That Changed Basketball Forever.* Boston: Back Bay Books, 2002.

_____. *A Season on the Brink.* New York: Macmillan, 1986.

Feschuk, Dave and Michael Grange, *Steve Nash: The Unlikely Ascent of a Superstar.* Toronto: Vintage Canada, 2013.

Fury, Shawn. *Rise and Fire.* New York: Flatiron Books, 2016.

Goldsberry, Kirk. *Sprawlball.* Boston and New York: Houghton Mifflin Harcourt, 2019.

Grover, Tim. *Relentless: From Good to Great to Unstoppable.* New York: Sribner, 2014.

Hahn, Alan. *The New York Knicks: The Complete Illustrated History.* Minneapolis: MVP Books, 2012

Halberstam, David. *Playing for Keeps: Michael Jordan and the World He Made.* New York: Broadway Books, 1999

Hobson, Howard. *Scientific Basketball.* New York: Prentice-Hall, Inc., 1949.

Hundley, Hot Rod. *You Gotta Love It Baby.* Champaign: Sports Publishing. Inc., 1998.

Johnson, Scott Morrow. *Phog: The Most Influential Man in Basketball.* Lincoln: University of Nebraska Press, 2016.

Karen, David, and Robert Washington, Eds. *Sociological Perspectives on Sport: The Games Outside the Games.* London: Routledge, 2015.

Karl, George. *Furious George: My Forty Years Surviving NBA Divas, Clueless GMs, and Poor Shot Selection.* New York: HarperCollins, 2017.

Klein, Naomi. *No Logo.* Toronto: Vintage Canada, 2000.

Klores, Dan, dir. *Winning Time: Reggie Miller Vs. the New York Knicks.* ESPN Films. Aired March 14, 2010, on ESPN.

Lazenby, Roland. *Showboat: The Life of Kobe Bryant.* London: Orion Books, 2016.

May, Peter. *Top of the World: The Inside Story of the Boston Celtics' Amazing One-Year Turnaround to Become NBA Champions.* Cambridge: Da Capo Press, 2008

Miller, Reggie. *I Love Being the Enemy.* New York: Simon & Schuster, 1995.

Nelson, Murry R. *Abe Saperstein and the American Basketball League, 1960–1963.* Jefferson, NC: McFarland, 2013.

O'Neal. Shaquille. *Shaq Talks Back.* New York: St. Martin's Press, 2001

Pluto, Terry. *Loose Balls: The Short Wild Life of the American Basketball Association.* New York: Simon & Schuster, 1990.

Rosen, Charley. *The Chosen Game: A Jewish Basketball History.* Lincoln and London: University of Nebraska Press, 2017.

Smith, Sam. *The Jordan Rules.* New York: Simon & Schuster, 1992

Thomsen, Ian. *The Soul of Basketball,* New York: Houghton Mifflin Harcourt, 2018

Bibliography

Magazines and Websites

Associated Press ap.org
Ball Is Life ballislife.com
Basketball Forever basketballforever.com
Bleacher Report bleacherreport.com
Boston Globe Media boston.com
Boston Magazine bostonmagazine.com
Business Insider businessinsider.com
Cleveland.com cleveland.com
Dallas Observer dallasobserver.com
Deseret News deseret.com
ESPN espn.com
FiveThirtyEight fivethirtyeight.com
Forbes forbes.com
Fox Sports foxsports.com
Grantland grantland.com
The Guardian theguardian.com
The IndianapolisStar indystar.com
Los Angeles Times latimes.com
The Milwaukee Journal jsonline.com
NBA nba.com

NBC Sports nbcsports.com
New York Post nypost.com
New York Times nytimes.com
The New Yorker newyorker.com
Open Court opencourt-basketball.com
The Players' Tribune theplayerstribune.com
SB Nation sbnation.com
SFGATE sfgate.com
SLAM slamonline.com
Slate slate.com
Space City Scoop spacecityscoop.com
Spiegel Online spiegel.de
The Spokesman-Review spokesman.com
Sports Illustrated si.com
Sportscasting sportscasting.com
Sportslingo sportslingo.com
The Undefeated theundefeated.com
UPI upi.com
The Washington Post washingtonpost.com
Yahoo! Sports sports.yahoo.com

Index

Index

Index

Index

Index

Index

Index

Index